The
Red Sox
and
Philosophy

Popular Culture and Philosophy®
Series Editor: George A. Reisch

For full details of all Popular Culture and Philosophy® books, visit www.opencourtbooks.com.

Popular Culture and Philosophy®

The
Red Sox
and
Philosophy

Green Monster Meditations

Edited by

MICHAEL MACOMBER

OPEN COURT
Chicago and La Salle, Illinois

Volume 48 in the series, Popular Culture and Philosophy®,
edited by George A. Reisch

**To order books from Open Court, call toll-free 1-800-815-2280,
or visit our website at www.opencourtbooks.com.**

Open Court Publishing Company is a division of Carus Publishing
Company.

Printed and bound in the United States of America.

Library of Congress Cataloging-in-Publication Data

The Red Sox and philosophy : green monster meditations / edited
by Michael Macomber.
     p. cm.—(Popular culture and philosophy ; v. 48)
    Includes bibliographical references and index.
    ISBN 978-0-8126-9677-6 (trade paper : alk. paper)
    1. Boston Red Sox (Baseball team) 2. Baseball—Philosophy.
  I. Macomber, Michael, 1976-
    GV875.B62B85 2010
    796.357'640974461—dc22
                              2009048772

Contents

V Views from the Grandstands   215

VI So Good! So Good! So Good!   285

The Royal Rooters, famed early twentieth-century Red Sox fan club.

Courtesy of the Boston Red Sox. Photographer unknown.

Foreword

New England is a unique geographical area. It juts into the Atlantic Ocean daring Mother Nature to unleash its fury. The pine tree covered northern coastline is cold and foreboding. Glacier-strewn rocks, hills, and mountains adorned with majestic forests and swirling rivers, comprise a six-state area that is nationally known by those two words.

For hundreds of years, various sea-faring adventurers from Europe investigated the mysterious and austere shoreline. Finally, in 1620, the Pilgrims landed and miraculously carved out an existence under harsh conditions. I doubt that we can really comprehend what they had to endure to survive that first winter.

Think about the ensuing two hundred and fifty years bringing us to the beginnings of baseball in America: the tenuous relationships with the long-time Native American inhabitants; the toughness to overcome the ravages of terrible diseases such as smallpox; the development of small clusters of roughly-built homes into villages, townships and larger municipalities; the growth beyond simple farming methods to just produce family food into larger farms to supply the growing populace; the ingenuity that took advantage of the many ocean inlets that enabled the building of seaports and dry docks and ships of all sizes and types. It took determination, creativity, and perseverance to forge ahead successfully. Over many years, an image began to develop of the makeup of the New England inhabitants who were arriving from all parts of Europe. Mostly they were stern, god-fearing, tenacious, tillers of the soil, and oceanic adventurers.

The development of the game of baseball in America in the nineteenth century was also not a simple task. There's evidence of various types of "games of ball" being played for several centuries earlier in many parts of the world. However, in the mid-nineteenth century the game, as we now know it, began to emerge. Whether it was in Cooperstown, New York with Abner Doubleday or in New York City with the Knickerbocker Nine, or in other parts of the nation, there was a new sporting event in the making. The Massachusetts Game and Town Ball in Philadelphia all became part of the expansion into a more formalized, national game.

Following the 1875 season, the National Association was replaced with the National League. In 1876 Boston had its first pro team, the Red Caps, and Boston has been part of the major leagues ever since. When a variety of factors led to the formation of the new, renegade American League in 1901, Boston became a two-team major league city and the Boston Americans were a cornerstone. After two years of roster-raiding and acrimonious dealings, the owners of the National League-leading Pittsburgh Pirates and the American League first-place Boston Americans agreed that if their teams were pennant winners they would play a best of nine series to determine a "world championship." New England fans reveled as Boston made a great comeback to win this initial "World Series" in 1903. It was another first for Boston. What other region could weather this unknown initiative?

Ironically, in 1904, Boston again won the American League pennant, this time by beating the New York Highlanders (later to become the Yankees) on the final day of the season. However, the haughty National League-leading New York Giants were concerned the Highlanders might edge Boston and refused to continue the new postseason concept.

The Boston Americans became the Red Sox for the 1908 season and dominated the league by winning pennants and World Series in 1912–15–16–18. The annual optimistic outlook (unusual for this area) came to a crash in the 1920s as club ownership sold or traded away its best players to the Yankees. Until thirty-year-old millionaire Tom Yawkey bought the club in 1933, local fans had little to hope for each baseball season.

New England baseball fans needed a stoic outlook as the Braves and Red Sox suffered through the ignominy of being mostly doormats in their respective leagues in the 1920s and 1930s. Could they have inherited the ability to endure these long periods of adversity from their forefathers who had miraculously survived many years before?

One of my earliest recollections of Boston baseball is listening as a youngster to a broadcast of Game Seven of the 1946 World Series and hearing how Enos Slaughter beat Johnny Pesky's relay throw home in the last of the eighth inning for the series-winning run. Boston fans had waited since 1918 for another World Series and the loss was a huge disappointment. More disappointments followed, however, when the 1948 Red Sox lost a special one-game playoff to Cleveland in Fenway Park that prevented what would've been Boston's only inter-city World Series. Yet the playoff was another first as there had never been an American League one-game, end of season showdown. Naturally it took place in Boston. There was more dismay as the Red Sox again lost the pennant on the final day in 1949 and in the last week in 1950.

An inter-city World Series was my dream as a young boy, and, unfortunately, it never materialized. The Braves' promising rise lasted only a couple of seasons before mediocrity crept in, attendance dropped dramatically and the team surprised the baseball world by packing up and heading to Milwaukee just prior to the 1953 season. The ensuing years were bleak for Boston baseball, and rays of hope were few and far between.

By the mid-1960s the Red Sox were an annual second-division team with not much promise ahead. Or so it seemed. Our endurance and loyalty were really being put to the test. Then the club hired a brash young manager, Dick Williams, who promised the fans that in 1967, "We'll win more than we'll lose." That hadn't happened for eight years, so it wasn't easy to have much faith in such a statement. Our positive beliefs had dwindled drastically!

However, the seeds of success had been planted, and as the season unfolded unusual circumstances arose. The woeful Red Sox were no longer woeful. A nice mixture of skilled young players joined with a handful of competent veterans and a resilient group of Red Sox amazingly went on a mid-season, ten-game winning streak. Suddenly they were at the top of the standings in a daily struggle with several teams for a drive to the American League pennant. It was too good to be true. The daily heroics of Carl Yastrzemski at bat and in the field and the stellar pitching of Jim Lonborg captivated the region, and the fans began to cautiously believe. Then, when Yaz had four hits and Lonborg notched his twenty-second win as the Red Sox beat Minnesota on the final day of the season to win the "Impossible Dream" pennant, impromptu celebrations erupted all over New England!

A few years later, May 30th, 1972 to be exact, I was hired by the Red Sox as assistant director of public relations and statistics and thrust into the maelstrom of Red Sox fervor. Fortunately my local roots aided me immensely in coping with what was to become known as Red Sox Nation.

Despite the fact that from 1967 on the Red Sox won over 3,500 games and had the second-best record in all of Major League Baseball, trailing only their biggest rival, the New York Yankees, there developed an underlying feeling that they were not winners. As the years went by and the Red Sox failed to capture a World Series title (more seventh-game losses in 1975 and 1986), pessimism crept into the fan psyche. Even when the team would be battling for the league lead the attitude was "Don't get too excited, they'll fall apart."

I can't count how many times I was confronted by disgruntled Red Sox fans who would ask, "Why don't we ever win?" My response was always, "What is your definition of winning? If it's to win the World Series you're correct. We haven't won since 1918." I would then point out that we've been in the World Series, we've won the Eastern Division, and we've advanced to the American League Championship round. At least we give you the chance to get frustrated! In some cities you don't have that opportunity since the teams are seldom ever in contention and there's never a hopeful outlook.

It was ironic that when the Red Sox were about to begin their rebirth in 1967, a new support group was formed called the BoSox Booster Club. It's hard to believe nowadays, but the original goal of the club was to help the team sell tickets after attendance had dropped abysmally. The 1966 Red Sox finished ninth in a ten-team league (just ahead of the Yankees, no less). But the influx of young talent from a newly refurbished minor league system and the maturation of some of the talented players on the team began to come together, and the Red Sox had a good second half. It was a little flicker of hope and Boston-area businessmen gladly joined the new Booster Club. A series of luncheons were held during homestands and uniformed personnel from the Red Sox and their opponents attended. Baseball, especially the Red Sox, was promoted and the BoSox Club decided to also honor amateur championship teams from the area. Thanks to the "Impossible Dream" pennant, the BoSox Club took firm root and has maintained a membership of eight hundred or more ever since.

Around the same time another group was formed to the south. There are many transplanted New Englanders who work in New York City and are Red Sox fans. However, they were a quiet minority, reluctant to show their Boston loyalty, during the Yankees' championship reign from the 1920s to the mid 1960s. In 1963 several of them decided the time had come to emerge from the shadows of the perceived Yankees invincibility and form an open allegiance to the Red Sox. The new group called themselves the BLOHARDS, Benevolent and Loyal Order of Honorable and Ancient Red Sox Diehard Sufferers of New York! Luncheons still are held when the Red Sox come to New York and are notable for the passion displayed for the Red Sox and the disdain shown for the Yankees.

So despite the overall lethargy around New England for the hometown team during this time, there were pockets of loyalists who still believed a new day was coming. It took grit and, what those who don't know a New Englander's inner makeup would call unrealistic, optimism.

Finally, in October of 2004, euphoria swept over what's now called Red Sox Nation. The eighty-six year World Series Championship drought ended in storybook fashion! The Red Sox had to overcome adversity in an almost impossible manner while doing something never before accomplished in Major League Baseball history. The Red Sox appeared overwhelmed by the Yankees who won the first three games of the ALCS. An ankle injury to pitching ace Curt Schilling in the first game and the Yankees' dominating 19–8 win in Game Three in Fenway Park brought out all the clichés about the Red Sox fortunes: their inability to defeat the Yankees when it really counted, that they take you to a certain point and then let you down, and on and on. Trailing by a run and facing the great closer Mariano Rivera in the last of the Ninth of Game Four, the Red Sox tied the score on Kevin Millar's walk, pinch runner Dave Roberts's magical stolen base and Bill Mueller's single. When David Ortiz slammed a game-winning home run in the last of the 12th, the Red Sox were alive for another day. Three games later the Red Sox won the American League pennant by thrashing the Yankees in New York with a home run barrage. Another baseball first, coming back from a three-games-to-none deficit to win four straight series games!

Despite facing a formidable St. Louis Cardinals team in the World Series the Red Sox rolled to the championship with four straight wins. Although the games were tense struggles, after the series with the Yankees, the World Series was almost an anti-climatic affair for Red Sox fans who had a newfound faith.

Since then, Red Sox fans approach each season with an outlook that in the end, the team will prevail, not fail. The fear that there's no way we can overcome the Yankees has been replaced by an attitude that we can defeat the Yankees when it counts, but don't ever underestimate them.

Since 2004 Red Sox Nation has grown tremendously and the organization has even developed a fandom that's led by a Red Sox Governor of each state. Faith in the club was further bolstered when just three years later the Red Sox again won the World Series, the first team to have multiple championships in the twenty-first century!

That New England heritage, developed from the amazing inner strength that led to survival under the most difficult of conditions, *had* to be an ingredient in the long, dedicated following of New England baseball fans for their hometown nine.

It is in that spirit that the authors and fellow fans have given you *The Red Sox and Philosophy*. The contributions to this volume embody the passionate nature of Red Sox fans, and at the same time, offer reflective and creative attempts to capture the often tragic, but recently redemptive history of the Boston Red Sox. The chapters that follow reflect the heartache and joy of Red Sox fans by examining many important philosophical issues including faith, morality, and community. The storied history of the Red Sox is examined through the history of ideas from ancient Greece and China, to Medieval and Enlightenment Europe, and contemporary American philosophy.

The authors represented here, and the philosophies they discuss, display the same perseverance and mental toughness that have defined this region and the Boston Red Sox franchise from the beginning. *The Red Sox and Philosophy* is a book by fans for fans! Go Sox!

—DICK BRESCIANI
Vice President and Official Historian of the Boston Red Sox

Acknowledgments

There are many people that deserve my sincerest thanks for helping me put together my very first book. Thanks go to George Reisch who believed in the project from the beginning and offered innumerable hours of advice throughout the process. Thanks, also, to David Ramsay Steele and everyone at Open Court for all of their hard work and without whom this project wouldn't have been possible.

I must also thank the Boston Red Sox for allowing me access and permission to use their photo archives. Special thanks goes to Dick Bresciani for capturing the enthusiasm of the project so well in his wonderful foreword. And, additional thanks go to Debbie Matson, of the Red Sox, for her help in compiling the wonderful photos that appear in this volume.

Thanks go to Bill Nowlin, who caught the spirit of this project early on, offered valuble advice throughout the entire process, and helped me with some much appreciated proofreading. I'd also like to thank MaryCatherine Youmell, whose ability to see the project from start to finish offered a constant sense of support. Without her countless hours of proofreading and advice this project would've had a hard time reaching its end.

And, finally, to my wonderfully imaginative authors, who extended the full force of their rigor and creativity and truly embodied the spirit of the Boston Red Sox, I cannot thank them enough for all of their hard work. Truly, without their thoughtful contributions this book wouldn't exist.

*Dominic DiMaggio (1917–2009), played his entire career with the
Boston Red Sox from 1940 to 1953.*

From Professor Thom's to the "Little Professor"

Red Sox fans are amongst the smartest baseball fans in the world. You need not look any further than your local sports bar or Fenway Park to prove this statement. In a big moment during the game, there's no need for the scoreboard operator to flash a big "Let's go Sox!!" on the giant screen. The fans don't need prompting. When there are two outs and two strikes on the opposing hitter, the crowd is already on its feet, the fans at the Cask 'n' Flagon are already chanting. And, for Sox fans, it's not just a mere understanding of the situation; it's a deeply ingrained feeling of oneness with their team.

I felt something similar to this when I was doing my graduate work in New York City. That's right, New York City, the home of the Yankees. I used to frequent a few Red Sox–friendly establishments. One in particular, Professor Thom's, in New York's East Village, displayed the same mixture of understanding and passion that one finds inside the friendly confines of Fenway Park. Except, it was even more intense. It had to be; after all, we were in hostile territory. There was a heightened sense of urgency watching Sox games in the Yankees' backyard. There was a shared sense of unity; we were all entwined with the fate of the team, for better or worse.

For a philosopher, the melding of intellectual and emotional lives is usually quite tricky. Sox fans, however, display a delicate balance between the knowledge needed to understand the Red Sox and the passion each of us wraps ourselves in as the season unfolds. This isn't just true of Sox fans, but also, the players. Take Dominic DiMaggio for example.

Dominic DiMaggio, one of the finest center fielders who ever played for the Boston Red Sox, died this past year at the age of ninety-two. I can't think of a more appropriate way to begin a book on the philosophy of the Boston Red Sox than to pay tribute to the too often overlooked former center fielder, called the "Little Professor."

Although some say the nickname the Little Professor was given because he wore glasses, it was actually more indicative of his style of playing baseball. In the book *The Teammates* (2003), David Halberstam credits Ted Williams with the ability to identify DiMaggio's intellectual prowess. Williams wasn't only known for his ability to hit the ball, but was able to examine every facet of the game and its players. Williams, Halberstam writes, "judged other players not just by their athletic talent, but by how smart they were about the game. He was acutely aware that Dominic was an uncommonly intelligent player, who used his intelligence to overcome any physical shortcomings" (pp. 19–20). It's entirely fitting to pay tribute to Dominic DiMaggio at the beginning of a book, which looks to examine the Red Sox in a thoughtful and intelligent manner.

So, from the beginnings of an idea at Professor Thom's to the culminating tribute to the Little Professor, I offer you *The Red Sox and Philosophy* and hope that this book works to pull together both the thoughts and feelings of an entire nation of Red Sox fans.

—MICHAEL MACOMBER

Root, Root, Root for the Red Sox

Fans gather outside Fenway Park on Yawkey Way just before game time.
Courtesy of the Boston Red Sox. Photo by Phoebe Sexton.

1

What Binds Us Together

MARCUS GIAMATTI

A noble knight was riding swiftly on the plain,
Clad in mighty armor, and bearing a silver shield
That was deeply dented, marked with the cruel blows
Of many a bloody battle.
His fierce horse champed against curb and bit.
The knight rode easily.
Yet his face was solemn, almost sad.
Faithful and true he was in word and deed,
Fearless, serious and grave;
For this was the Red Cross Knight,
And on a great adventure he was bound.

—Excerpts from *St. George and the Dragon*, by EDMUND SPENSER

Oh, Dear Red Sox fans of today—you blessed people who go forward with the absolute comfort, the innocent glee that it does, it did, and it *can* happen for *you*. How *odd* this is for me to watch. You happy Sox fans, with your can-do *winning* Boston attitude. How rich and strange you seem to me.

Chances are, you know nothing about a particular philosophy of survival. It belongs only to us "Old School" Red Sox fans who grew up amidst the doom, paranoia, and perpetual self-doubt that once seemed to fill all of New England. That was before everything changed. Before the unthinkable, the unimaginable, happened in October of 2004.

Yes, to you, I am a Boston baseball dinosaur. To you, we survivors of the dark, anguished years of misery are the aliens. With furrowed brows and confused looks you "new fans" (as we call

3

you) bristle as I rant and rave, shake and fume with fury, babble, frothing at the mouth, of the Doctrine of the Unfair. I have hang ups, you say. I need help, you pronounce, as you turn and walk away. "You have no idea!" You will hear me cry. Because, truly, you don't. So, forgive me, reader, if I sound antiquated when expounding upon my Red Sox fan methodology, my philosophy, and the tales of survival through which it developed. If it all seems out of date, it's no less true.

Dame Mutability

Alas, I do not possess the noble gift of prose. Or the eloquence, to capture the Moment, in its entire "still-now-and-then-forever-ness." I am an actor, a musician, and merely a crude observer of this crazy thing called life. Of which I realize I know so little, as I stand now on the crest of this knoll called middle age. Thus, I peer back over my shoulder, down life's rise, and I can say with a firm absolute, and confess perhaps most importantly: I am also a base-ball fan. Specifically, a Boston Red Sox fan. My first real memories took root in the late 1960s, "The Impossible Dream," and shortly thereafter, I began to see (and, eventually, understand) that there is a method to this Red Sox fan madness—this addiction, this disease.

First, I had to grasp the concept, that this is what it would mean to have a "passion" for something—something larger than yourself, something huge. And that from this passion (as long as you don't hurl yourself through a window along the way) you can learn awareness and enormous life lessons. If you stick with the team, if you just *believe*. At least, that's what I was told.

Like Dame Mutability. I knew her well. So did my Red Sox fan father, and his father before him. She sat (in those days) amongst the spectators at Fenway Park. Or wherever the Red Sox played. After every heartbreaking Red Sox loss, especially after the Sox would set us up and then blow another postseason game, I would look as a young boy to my father for an explanation. With his eyes cast down, he would shake his head. "Dame Mutability, boy." Then gravely he would explain to me the power of her spell. There was, you see, no escaping it. She would always be there. *Always.*

I imagined her in a wide-brimmed, black hat, a cheap fur coat, donning huge coke-bottle specs. Her countenance wiry and mean as she would always arrive late (but not too late, of course) and disrupt everyone sitting in her row. ("The Dame" is not to be confused with the proverbial "Fat Lady"—that's a different story). I looked for Dame Mutability every time we went to Fenway or watched a game on TV.

"I don't see her Pa," I'd say.

"Oh, she's here. Or will be soon. You'll see."

His eyes were blank, with the ten thousand yard stare—the kind condemned men have as they walk down that green mile to the gallows loft.

There was no point of thinking differently back then—no point in believing that the outcome would somehow be favorable for our Red Sox. Because she *did* show up to cast her spells and possess, through her wicked sorcery, various opposing players over the seasons, like Bucky Dent, Mookie Wilson, and Aaron Boone. And she would even inhabit a few of our own: Calvin Schiraldi and Johnny Pesky. She pushed balls just out of reach, or squeaked them between our infielder's legs or plopped them over walls. Time after time after time. She was pure evil. So, no matter how hard you prayed, no matter how entitled you felt that, "This time we really deserve it . . ." or, "It can't happen again . . ." it always would. She was always there to make sure, to smother our joy, to break your heart. You have no idea.

Coaches and Poets

My Lord, why? I used to ask. How do you make any sense of this? As I grew older and the disappointment continued, the addiction (as well as the affection) deepened, I thought that maybe the answer to that gnawing question would come from the inside, sort of backwards. Let me explain.

When I played the game myself, the coaches would sermonize:

> The game is straightforward. Throw the ball. Hit the ball. Catch the ball. Arrive at the plate every time expecting to get a hit. It's a game of failure. A game of inches. A game with no time. Honor the game, and it will honor you. You succeed by making *adjustments*—constantly, daily. It's your work. It's your religion. The only way to persevere.

Fair enough. Now mix in my being raised by a father who was a scholar, avid Red Sox fan, and baseball poet. I can still hear him wax eloquent of the game's deeper meaning. Deeper lessons. Such as the importance of "home." How, in baseball, one is always leaving home—like Odysseus—to encounter adventures and quests out on the wild seas of the infield. Out there, you will face many struggles—engage in many battles—in your quest to return home. The ultimate goal. This quest is sacred. "Baseball is played in a timeless Garden," he would say, "full of mystery and hope. It is played outside—in the sunshine, under blue skies—in an enclosed, perfect, space."

But neither the wisdom of the coaches nor my father seemed to help me achieve a balance. No conclusive remedy was revealed to aid in my understanding—or overcoming—my attachment to this team. Year after year, there was never any satisfaction or reward. Perhaps, I thought, the answer to the riddle lay in the order, the structure, and the balance that the game gave me each day, each season. Perhaps it cloaked itself inside the appreciation of hope that is baseball. Yes, this seemed nice. Tidy. Sane. Simple.

But again, did it provide solace? A mature approach? An "expectation" adjustment? Strength to rise above the pain, as this Red Sox fan time and again watched his team, got hooked, set up, and inevitably shattered? No, it did not. As if Dame Mutability was controlling my own quest to understand and cope, every answer seemed to fail. There was no peace for me. Every time I thought that I had achieved some balance, some stability, the Red Sox found another way to blow it, to fall apart. Again. And I fell apart with them, every time.

So, I deduced, simplicity was not the answer. (Simplicity always seemed reserved for the Yankees fans amongst us). As George Sand put it: "Simplicity is the most difficult thing to secure in this world; it is the last limit of experience; and the last effort of genius." My conclusion? Something was missing. So I struck out again in search of that "something" that my father and coaches had not told me. And this something was fundamental, I would discover.

My Home Run

This something was the key to it all. Lo, and behold, the clouds parted, the light shone down upon me, and I saw the truth: I was a player—a pawn, of sorts, inside an existential baseball trap. Unfortunately, my epiphany struck after my father had left this world. Unexpectedly. Tragically. Without warning. That connection was snuffed out. But what his absence enabled me to discover, as he left me to wander the cavernous mines alone, was that he knew (but never said) that I had been set up for life. Being born into a Red Sox family, the child of a Boston Red Sox fan, you see, you relinquish choice. You have no say. You cannot switch teams. Jump ship. For me there was no team to switch to! Quit on the Red Sox? Get out of "it" somehow? Sacrilege! This was a duty. This birthright put you on a mission, a lifelong quest to rise above and persevere. And one day, if you followed this path with honor and truth, and if you used the great strength you had acquired from the suffering of this journey, you would see a World Series Championship flag raised high above the Green Monster, in Fenway Park. But you had no choice. That was it.

My father must have known. He must have known that I could take it; that I could withstand the pain and disappointment. And that I would figure out the meaning of being a Red Sox fan. He must have. There was no other explanation.

From this plateau, I could finally see it. To be a true fan of this comic-tragic team—shrouded amongst this beautiful game—takes commitment. Total and complete. It takes faith—faith that one day it *will* pay off. And if for some reason it doesn't, then the journey— the process—is the pay off. Ultimately, it's about the character you would acquire for having endured. The wisdom of Self. That is the real reward. Over the next dozen years or so, this was my path: to remain loyal to the quest. I applied the principles. I stuck with them. I stuck with the team.

The Unthinkable

And then came October 2004. See now your hero, this wandering Knight, as I lay curled up in a ball on my living room floor. Alone with the TV set, and the Red Sox. We were at the brink of elimination, once again, at the hands of the New York Yankees, who were behind the previous season's collapse. You remember '03. Grady and Pedro. We Red Sox fans had recovered, and arrived here, mind you, somehow, to do it all over again. The *journey*, you know.

To be plain, I was a mess: a pathetic shell of a man. Weary, oh so weary. The end was nigh. But for real this time. For as I watched the blank looks of the Fenway Faithful on the screen, knowing that our hopes were about to be dashed again, an odd sense of calm came over me. I was to be free. Finally. I vowed, I *swore*, I would never, *ever*, do this again. I would never again feel this way or put myself in the position to feel this way. I was giving up the quest. I was laying down my sword. I had *had* it. I was never getting on this Red Sox train ever again. I had given it a lifetime of effort, but so what? To hell with honor! Duty! Perseverance! FAITH!!

And then, it happened. Mariano Rivera walked Kevin Millar. Dave Roberts pinch ran, sprinted for second and slid in—safe. Bill Mueller drilled a single to center. And the rest is the stuff made for legends. It all came gloriously together. There I was, spectator to the miracle that rolled on: a sweep of the Yankees (the dragon slayed), then St. Louis, and finally the 2004 World Championship Parade. The pain and desperation vanished. The *journey*, the fight, and the wait—the principles of my method—all suddenly made sense. And I would have had it no other way.

A New Path

The mantle will be passed. The method will live on. Bear witness, as I stand now at the foot of a different mystical path, that of parenthood. I am writing in fact on the eve of my daughter's birth. Our first child, Ophelia, who will be a Red Sox fan. Like me, she will have no choice. Through the magic of satellite TV (yes, reader, I watch every Red Sox game, still, and though the Championship flags of '07 and '04 fly, the quest is renewed each year again!) she will join me, and watch the Olde Towne team from atop this odd planet we will cohabit, in Southern California.

Tinsel Town. Where I landed many years ago due to the entertainment business. The arts. Here I will tutor her in the old Bosox philosophy. I will regale her with tales of '75 and '86. Of "Slaughter's Mad Dash" in '46. The Bloody Sock. And Dame Mutability. For what she can learn of my Red Sox Fan philosophy of old, she can apply to her life in all its aspects (just as my father did, and I still do). I will be an example, a reflection, for her. And maybe if I am lucky she will see how I have incorporated such pearls of Red Sox wisdom into my life as an actor and musician: A one day at a time approach; one game at a time. Every opportunity you have to step up to the plate for an audition, you must expect to get the job. Make adjustments, be in the moment. The relaxation is where the power is. Work on your craft. For it is all you have. Whatever your vocation, your passion, dedicate *heart* and *soul*.

So Daughter, as you go into loyal Red Sox battle (like Joan, clad in tie-dye, a quiver of guitars strapped across your back, your trusty Red Sox cap atop your beautiful head—the first thing I bought you once I heard you were to grace my life): go boldly! Faithfully! Trust the wisdom of your Red Sox ancestors. Trust that whatever you do, it CAN happen, and it will. Despite all the trials and disappointments, take it one season, one game, one pitch at a time. Believe in miracles when you expect them least, and be a vigilant guardian of the sacred game, and this sacred team. Honor baseball: The Universal Language! The one constant, from childhood, to old age. Be true to the *process*. There is nothing to fear, if you follow the principles. If you believe. For the "connection" IS the thing. The whole, beautiful, crazy, mixed up thing.

So, Father, I will continue my work. And you can rest assured that I will be forever diligent, and see to it that your granddaughter, due to her geographic fate here in Tinsel Town, will never become a fan of the Anaheim Angels. Or, God forbid, a follower of the San Diego Padres. What could she possibly learn from that?

As for me, I remain locked in a struggle, to find a way to fit in, archaic human that I am, with this strange movement called "Red Sox Nation." As a walking wounded fan from the days long past, I am still the outsider who wrestles every day with the fact that the anxiety never fully subsides. But now I have the tools and wisdom to catch myself, to right myself. Since, now, I understand that the existential game never ends. And most importantly, I understand that the work of baseball, the work of being a Boston Red Sox fan, is never done.

2

Grady Little, the Impartial Spectator, and My Short Fuse

JOHN McHUGH

Careful Not to Overcook that Hot Pocket, Buddy

If I bumped into Grady Little tomorrow, I'd probably say something. Even now. If I saw Bill Buckner there wouldn't be a problem; I've always just felt bad for that guy. Besides, I was five years old in 1986. I know the whole Buckner story—and the Bucky Dent one—as well as everybody else does. I've heard the catch phrases and seen the clips a million times (that whole thing was Rich Gedman's fault, by the way), and none of it means *that* much to me because I wasn't *really* there. (Nothing makes me sicker than unearned sentimentality.) But I *remember* Grady. He is *my* goat, and things would probably get ugly if I lifted my head to see him standing there, all slack-jawed, waiting to use the microwave at Cumberland Farms.

I'm taking it as a given that I *shouldn't* say anything, or at least not the type of thing I'm thinking of saying. Sure, he made a horrific mistake. The most confident, dominant pitcher in Red Sox history[1] had pointed to the sky in reverence, admitting to God almighty that he was out of gas, and Grady inexplicably marched him back out for the seventh, allowing the once dignified ace to get shelled while the temporarily unhittable Mike Timlin and Alan Embree watched from the bullpen, and he himself watched from the dugout with that same stupid "aw, shucks" look on his face that

---

[1] Sorry, Rodg, . . . I would've said that well before you obliterated your reputation.

11

passes for apt managerial restraint among the many old-time baseball men who blindly cling to sayings like "Let your players play"
and "Go with what got you there." But Grady was canned almost
immediately after this debacle, and the Red Sox won the World
Series the very next season. Compared to the nightmares of '78 and
'86, the wounds of '03 healed quickly, so much so that, when
looked at in the right light, the memory of them can make '04 and
'07 sweeter by contrast. Of course, I'm not perverse enough to suggest that we should *thank* Grady for this. I just don't think that the
man deserves to be publically berated by the likes of me. He certainly doesn't need to be *reminded* that he screwed up. (He'd better not, anyway).

Unfortunately, these reflections alone do little to change how I
actually feel, and they certainly don't assure me that I'd be able to
maintain my composure in that microwave line. But they remind us
how generally important it is to control our emotions. Chances are
I won't see Grady Little tomorrow. Even so, I will have to exhibit
some command over my mood, my desires, and my affective reactions to the world, especially if there's a Red Sox game on tonight.

How to Follow the Red Sox without Losing Your Job, Family, or Sanity

One could make a case that *self-command* is the central virtue for
the Red Sox fan. Most of the other virtues that we typically associate with sports fandom can be boiled down to, or are at least essentially connected with, this one. *Loyalty* and *dedication* presuppose
command over despair, distrust, and even occasional boredom
(another five-hour Dice-K start?). *Optimism* presupposes command
over anger and the sometimes powerful, yet ultimately unproduc-
tive, desire to boo (did Julio Lugo boot *another* routine ground-
ball?). And for baseball fans in particular, being *well-informed*
presupposes command over the arguably instinctual aversion to
numbers and statistics (is WHIP or ERA a better indicator of Jon
Lester's performance?).

Most importantly, self-command prevents fandom from clashing
with what remains of life outside of it. We all have identities distinct from that of "Red Sox fan" that often require us to suppress
our fan-related emotions. Even if Jonathan Papelbon serves A-Rod
a fat 0–2 fastball late in a one-run game, we still have to go to work
tomorrow. Within a few hours of their inception, frustration and

fruitless regret must somehow take a backseat to productivity and performance. The same goes for our exuberance when Mike Lowell hits a walk-off wall-ball double. Joy can quite easily turn into distracting reverie, and we wouldn't want to chew up company time.

The importance of self-command for Red Sox fans extends far past our professional lives. We have other, more significant identities as friends, family members, and human beings that also may not wholly overlap with our identities as Red Sox fans. Fulfilling these other roles requires control over our obsession with the team and with sports in general. When it comes to our jobs, the stakes are clear. We will be fired (or at least be less successful) if we allow our identities as sports fans to impinge upon our identities as merchants, teachers, carpenters, or whatever else. The stakes involved in our other roles aren't so well defined—but are also much higher. In order to lead emotionally balanced lives, we must be able to stop ourselves from ruminating over the wins and losses of the previous evening and from focusing exclusively upon the upcoming game, each to the detriment of life in the present. If we aren't careful, our identities as fans can dominate our other identities and leave us unstable and unhappy (or at least leave us as supposedly mature adults whose bedroom walls are adorned with Dustin Pedroia posters). In short, we have to do more than just pay lip service to the fact that "it's only a game."

Why "Red Sox Nation" Is More than Just a Clever Name

Maybe I'm exaggerating the dangers. But consider what genuinely caring about a team does to us. Many people enjoy athletic competition for aesthetic reasons. They enjoy the beauty and grace with which the athletes move and the intricate strategies behind their decisions. Sports mainly stimulate the intellectual side of these people's natures, in a way that differs very little from the effects of painting, poetry, and other art forms. These people aren't "fans" in the true sense of the word because they take very little *personal* interest in the outcome of the performance. The best sports fans not only appreciate the artistry of their chosen sport, but also take a more personal interest in it.

To push the aesthetic analogy a bit further, their viewing experience is more like that of watching their own or a loved one's play

than one written by a stranger. They don't just *enjoy* the wittiness
of the dialogue, the depth of the character development, the pac-
ing of the plot, and the poignancy of the music. They *take pride* in
these achievements. And they aren't just disappointed when the
performance fails; they feel *ashamed* and *angry*. They may even
hate the people connected with the competing play opening down
the street. For Red Sox fans, Kevin Youkilis's swing and Tim
Wakefield's knuckleball are more than just intrinsically beautiful.
They also somehow belong to, represent, and exist for *us*. We're
clearly more emotionally invested in our team than we are in other
sources of entertainment.

It's rather odd that we can get so riled up from *watching* the
Red Sox, when in fact, we aren't, ourselves, *doing* anything. Those
guys on the screen or past the bleachers certainly don't know us,
and whether they "care" about us in even a minimal sense is always
an open question. Maybe we identify with them in some way.
Maybe when we root for them we're rooting for super-athletic versions of ourselves, dreamed up with overactive imaginations fueled
by memories of childhood glory and disgrace. Or maybe we identify not with the guys on the field but with the people next to us
in the stands. This is partly what Jerry Seinfeld meant when he said
that rooting for a team really just amounts to rooting for laundry.
The jerseys all read "Boston" and thus foster the illusion that those
guys from Southern California to Canada to the Dominican
Republic to Japan to parts unknown somehow *represent us* and
somehow have deeper ties to the city than just its being the place
where they play fifty-percent of their games and cash one-hundred-
percent of their checks.

There's something deeply and unmistakably *tribal* about sports
fandom. I find it hard not to extend my hatred for all things
Yankees to all things New York, as if our[2] battles with the Yankees
say anything about me or about anyone from the city that they supposedly represent. Recently at Fenway Park, I saw a guy in a
Yankees hat get publically reprimanded for singing along with
"Sweet Caroline" because he had no right to sing "our song."
(Inevitably, he was ejected while the drunken Masshole who
started the argument was allowed to stay.) As the friend I was with

---

[2] Think about how puzzlingly often we use *that* pronoun in reference to the
Red Sox.

so astutely observed, one of the coolest guys who ever lived sings "their song," while the not-even-ironically schmaltzy, sequined-shirted Neil Diamond sings "ours." Ugh. Does my commitment to the Red Sox also commit me to claiming *that guy* as "mine"? If so, I may have to rethink this whole thing. . . .

How to Shut Off Caveman Tribal Mode

The fan's emotions are not just strong but primal. So how do we turn them off (or at least quiet them down) when we leave the arena and re-enter civilization? Aristotle suggests that we need vicarious emotional experiences—even painful ones—because we must vent feelings that would otherwise have no safe outlet. If we ultimately go to the ballpark to purge ourselves emotionally by "blowing off some steam," then we should leave it exhausted, and somehow cleansed. But this isn't always true. Trips to Fenway Park are often pleasant but rarely relaxing. We walk out of there with heightened, not exhausted, emotions. Sometimes, the electricity of the Big Moment dangerously showers the streets outside with sparks.

Since it takes too long for these emotions to burn out on their own, productivity, happiness, decency, and peace all demand that we control them somehow. The ancient Stoic philosophers are a natural place to turn for advice on how to prevent our violent, fleeting passions from impinging too heavily upon what we take to be the more stable core of our personalities. Like Aristotle and many other philosophers throughout history, the Stoics took virtuousness to be a matter of maintaining one's overall well-being. Stoic sages like Epictetus, a Greek slave living in the Roman Empire, taught their followers to focus entirely upon that which they could control. Epictetus argues that we can control our own actions upon and reactions to the world, but not necessarily the consequences of our actions or what happens to us. These latter sorts of things aren't worth worrying about not only because they're out of our hands, but also because they're parts of the intrinsically rational fabric of the universe and therefore must be the way they are and not otherwise. Today, when we console ourselves over any kind of loss or disappointment with the thought that it *had* to take place or, better, that it happened "for a reason," we express this basic Stoic idea.

The Stoics argued that exclusive attention to the things over which we exhibit some command will make us impervious to whatever life throws at us. Our tranquility will be untouchable. The problem, however, is that the genuinely Stoic Red Sox fan could no longer be a fan at all. Epictetus himself explicitly advised his followers to avoid going to, or even talking about, gladiatorial contests, horse races, and other athletic competitions. Concern for these undignified matters will leave us too heavily attached to things that are too far outside our control and will thus prove detrimental to our internal well-being. If we can't avoid being taken up with these sorts of affairs (as modern-day Boston residents very well may *not* be able to avoid being at least *somewhat* taken up with the Red Sox), we should take care to be equally unmoved by the agony of defeat and the joy of victory. This is why a "Stoic Red Sox *fan*" appears to be a contradiction. Sports fandom of any kind would be the first thing to go for anyone following the Stoic self-help program. Living and dying by the outcome of a Red Sox game is *precisely* the sort of thing that the Stoics teach us to avoid.

So it looks like the ancient Stoics don't really offer the kind of advice we need. We want to *control*, not extinguish our fan-related emotions. Many of these feelings are perfectly appropriate between the hours of 7:00 and 10:30 on typical summer evenings. It's the time between 10:30 and the next evening that's the issue. The most general lesson we can learn from the Stoics is that our reactions to things change if we look at them from a different perspective. If I can't control it, it shouldn't matter to me, and if I step back from it, I will see that it had to happen in the way that it did and that, on a grand scale, everything will turn out for the best. The Stoics want us to look at things from the perspective of the *universe*. From this point of view, however, *everything*—especially Red Sox games— appears hardly worth worrying about at all.

How to Shut Off Caveman Tribal Mode While Retaining the Ability to Turn It Back On

We can benefit from Stoic teaching while avoiding the sports apathy it implies by finding a more worldly perspective to adopt when we need to calm ourselves down. This is the strategy offered by Adam Smith, the great Scottish economist and moral philosopher whose slightly less scary understanding of self-command can provide us with advice that's more practical. Smith had a less dramatic understanding of the human plight than the Stoics did. He thought that the thing we need most in life is not to be in harmony with the universe, but with each other. In order to achieve this harmony, we must ratchet our emotions down to a level that others can enter into (eventually, endless laughter and bellyaching become annoying to even our closest friends). On Smith's view, when no one else is around, the virtuous individual imagines himself in the presence of another person who serves as a representative of a regular human being. This imaginary person understands that we're only human, so he'll let us know when we've taken things too far, but without necessarily condemning our fan-related feelings as indefensibly irrational.

Now *this* advice looks good in practice as well as in theory. When I see Grady Little at a convenience store, when I have to decide between finishing some work and searching for highlight clips, when I'm in danger of becoming a one-note boor who can only converse about a single subject, when I start to consider naming (not just nick-naming) my kid "Papi" or "Tek," when I start imagining how well that Pedroia poster will match the curtains, when I'm beside myself because the Yankees beat us to another free agent, when I'm distracted with glee because that free-agent busted yet again, when I start counting my fingers to see how many more imaginary rings I need to complete a fist, or when I start calling WEEI often enough to become the recurring "John from Saugus," I should consider my behavior from the perspective of another person and restrain myself accordingly.

Of course, this new imaginary friend can't be just *any* other person. There are certain characteristics he must possess in order for his gaze to shame me into altering my behavior. Since one of the main reasons why we must control our emotions is that our lives are filled with people who do not necessarily care about the Red Sox as much as we do, it's crucial that the person we imagine watching us be impartial with regard to the team.

However, now we risk running into the same problem that arose when we turned to the ancient Stoics. From the perspective of a genuinely impartial human being, the Red Sox will appear almost as insignificant as they do from the perspective of the universe. Perhaps such a person would understand the general aesthetic pleasure we take in the sport. Yet this person likely would not sympathize with our borderline yahooistic allegiance to a particular team. Like the Stoic sage, his advice to us will be to stop caring so much, to detach ourselves from that team and to celebrate the game itself. Again, this advice isn't very helpful. As much as we don't want our identities as Red Sox fans to dominate or overshadow our other ones, we also don't want this identity to disappear. It's still an important component of our overall selves. We just need it to take an appropriate place in our personalities.

We obviously must walk a fine line in dreaming up the ideal imaginary person. This person can't just be an aesthete for athletics, who only hopes that everyone plays well and no one gets hurt. But he also can't be just another Red Sox fan. Therefore, it looks like he must be the fan of some other team. Which one?

Candidates for Conscience

This imaginary person's impartiality must not only prevent him from being intrinsically averse to particular allegiances in general but also from being intrinsically averse to *our* particular allegiance. So we can rule out certain teams right off the bat. Yankees and Red Sox fans probably understand each other better than any other two groups of people on the planet, but their interests are too directly contrary for them ever to be mutually impartial. We normally wouldn't ask someone who wanted us to lose for advice on how to cope with the loss. This also rules out fans of any other team in the American League East or, for that matter, the rest of the American League. We may think that our interests run contrary to those of Seattle Mariners fans only on certain nights, but the Wild Card playoff system perpetually puts us at odds (consider the mini-rivalries that have recently popped up between the who-knows-what-California-city-they-claim-to-be-from-now Angels and the Red Sox or Yankees). Again, the people who inhabit the impartial, third party perspective we need must have no obvious reason to root against us.

Let's try turning to the National League. Our interests only really conflict with those of a National League team in isolated cases. Interleague play doesn't yield any lasting consequences in this regard. Interests clash more strongly in the World Series, but since, at that point, the vast majority of the league is at rest, (almost) any other team's fans' perspective can serve as an impartial one. All things being equal, your average San Diego Padres fan doesn't really care if we beat the Philadelphia Phillies in the World Series.

So the National League is a place to start. However, there's another complication we have yet to consider. We can't just adopt the perspective of a fan with no vested interest in the outcome of the *particular game* we happen to be playing. This is because there's one *permanent* source of conflict between the Red Sox and *every* other team, National League ones included: the annual off-season auction for free agents. Whenever any other team signs an available player, it means that the Red Sox didn't. An additional, more fundamental source of hostility particular to Major League Baseball lurks behind these sorts of conflicts; even with a complex revenue sharing system in place, baseball's lack of a salary cap makes the gap between the haves and the have-nots practically unbridgeable. This gives fans of small market teams a defensible reason to root against the Red Sox almost as zealously as Red Sox fans root against the Yankees. The more the Red Sox succeed, the higher their payroll can climb, and the harder it is for small market teams to compete consistently. The perspective of a Pittsburgh Pirates fan can therefore be just as partial against us as that of a Yankees fan.

This last point adds a wrinkle to the problem we're trying to solve. I have been trying to suggest not only examples in which we must control grief and anger, but also ones in which we must control joy. It's obviously important for us to control our negative emotions. They can make us unhappy and potentially dangerous, or at least unpleasant to be around. As Stoics, addicts, and generally excitable people know, however, extended euphoria can be similarly problematic. As another friend once wisely pointed out, life's highest highs will always be followed by the lowest lows; hence the postgame or postseason hangover with which most of us are all too familiar.

Frequent success can also lead to intolerable gloating. This should be readily apparent to Red Sox fans. The '04 and '07 seasons let us appreciate the meaning of the phrase "embarrassment of riches." No longer can we claim that the Yankees "buy championships"—and not just because it took them nearly a decade to win one after this phrase became fashionable. We won in '04 because we went out and threw the most money at the best available starting pitcher (Curt Schilling) and the best available closer (Keith Foulke). (Think about how ridiculous it is for Larry Lucchino to say that there are "three things money can't buy—love, happiness, and the American League pennant.") Since three-fourths of the league doesn't have that luxury, we must learn how to enjoy ourselves without rubbing it in (at least not too much). Granted, the Red Sox caught up with the Yankees also by building from the inside, via the draft. The cost of signing Scott Boras-represented first-round draft picks aside, this option is open for any team. Nevertheless, a team like the Kansas City Royals could never afford to make the mistakes we have. They simply wouldn't have been able to recover from overpaying for J.D. Drew or from making multiple, costly gaffes at shortstop (see Edgar Renteria and Julio Lugo). This is not to mention all the mistakes the Yankees prevented us from making by nobly making them themselves (see Carl Pavano). We have plenty of reasons, then, to practice some celebratory restraint and plenty of reasons to expect the fans of many, if not most, other teams not to like us.

Red Sox fans can practice self-command by imagining themselves in the presence of someone who understands and generally sympathizes with their allegiance to a particular team but who is emotionally distant enough to help cool them off. A fan of a small market team with a tiny payroll might be able to do the job, but it'd be tough to find a lucid one who doesn't actively hate the Red Sox as a source of "the problem" with Major League Baseball. If I rooted for the Minnesota Twins, for example, I would absolutely despise the Red Sox. To rule out jealousy, it has to be someone who follows a team with at least a moderately sized payroll, and to rule out a more basic form of partiality, this team must have no preexisting rivalry with, or an obvious interested reason to root against, the Red Sox. It can't be a Mets fan. There's too much history there, and despite his likely sharing our hatred of the Yankees, his merely being associated with New York doesn't help. It also can't be a Cardinals fan. That World Series sweep was too recent. Since the Red Sox have a history with so many teams, it seems like this search could go on for days. Who is left?

Fittingly, Conscience Wears a Blue Hat with a Red "C" on It

The best candidate appears to be a Cubs fan. The Cubbies have a huge payroll and a Red Sox-like history, plagued by a long championship drought, terrible fluke disasters (the infamous Steve Bartman foul ball incident), and a made-up curse (the Billy goat). Looking at ourselves through the eyes of a Cubs fan will be effective for toning down both our arrogance and grief, because it will remind us just how bad things used to be. Human nature being what it is, we might expect jealousy of our recent success to prevent a Cubs fan from being impartial towards us. But I think the decades of inherited pain give Cubs and Red Sox fans enough of a shared identity to mitigate any envy-fueled hatred. Of course that's easy for me to say because I'm not a Cubs fan, but the few I have met harbor no ill will towards the Red Sox. They just want to win one themselves.

The benefits of this arrangement would be mutual. Change the Grady Little example to a Steve Bartman one. Despite how arguably excusable his mistake was, a Cubs fan may have a hard time not being a jerk to that guy. He assuredly could not have anticipated the repercussions of getting in Moises Alou's way; he was probably just reacting without thinking at all. On the other hand, you *never* interfere with your own guy when he goes into the stands to make a catch. As a Red Sox fan, I can understand the Cubs fan's inner struggle. I just don't feel it to the extent that he does because, after all, I am not him. I don't root for the Cubs, and my imagination is only so strong. If the Cubs fan can imaginatively adopt my perspective, he'll be able to restrain his anger without unrealistically pretending that it doesn't exist or hopelessly trying to convince himself that it is *completely* without justification.

Big Brother Isn't So Bad as Long as He's Not Only Big, but Also a Brother

If we want to become sincere self-commanders (instead of mere masters of denial), the eyes we imagine watching us must belong to a person who we think *gets it* but *feels it* to a lesser extent. If I see Grady tomorrow, I will imagine a Cubs fan's eyes upon me, judging me, and perhaps also judging himself to the extent that he sees Bartman in Grady and himself in me. The "fanness" of the Cubs fan will allow him to understand my allegiance, while both his "Cubness" and his natural distance from my emotions will allow him to calm me down. If we can learn to see our fanaticism with eyes that are thusly both empathetic and judgmental, we'll learn to properly compartmentalize our love for the team while still follow-ing it religiously.

Still, these notions of "getting," "understanding," and "empathiz-ing" are tricky. As we've seen, it's easy enough to find someone who's impartial to our predicament (99.9999% of people in the world don't care about us or the crap that consumes us). Complications arise, however, when we try to find a figure who can combine this impartiality with an adequate understanding and appreciation of what it's like to be a fan. The question of how to be a virtuous *Red Sox fan*, (which is much different from, though not unrelated to, that of how to be a virtuous *person*) has a highly particularized answer that suggests the existence of a specific "fan conscience" somehow distinct from "conscience proper" or other "consciences" we might have. These other, non-fan-related consciences guide us when we play all the other social and personal roles that constitute our lives. Our inner Cubs fan, then, must be part of an inner *team* that collectively helps us navigate life's complexities.

Red Sox Fandom and Internal Harmony

The idea of a collection of inner voices or consciences may seem surprising, if not troubling. But consider how we actually deliberate. When we're trying to figure out what course of action to take in a particular situation, the inner voice we turn to for advice often changes. Just as we'd never ask someone who doesn't care about sports to show us how to be a virtuous fan, most of us wouldn't ask an imaginary version of our mothers for advice on how to properly handle the bar fight in which we've suddenly found ourselves. Neither of these people has the requisite understanding to be of any help. Mom in particular might get us to think about the wrong kind of thing for that moment, like what we were doing in a bar in the first place. It seems, then, that we have heads full of voices with varying levels of situational expertise. This inner diversity reveals itself when we preface evaluative claims by referring to the standpoint from which we make them: "as your attorney, I advise you to . . ." When we do this, it's as if we call one of these characters forward so we can let the audience know who's about to speak.

Clearly, this notion of internal imaginary voices is metaphorical. We don't *always* deliberate or reflect by consciously turning to a particular, identifiable imaginary person. Yet our tendency to weigh options in terms of the different roles we play naturally suggests an internal conversation between many different figures. We should accept the possibility that we work this way. We often point to the collaboration of as many different perspectives as possible as a model for good group decision-making. Our deliberations as individuals might be similarly democratic in that we each personally encompass different perspectives for each of the different social roles we play and identities we embody. In this way, our lives seem to amount to the internal collaboration of different voices.

The grand mystery in all this is what underlies these identities and voices and thereby makes their collaboration possible. Our choice is either to accept that we're fractured all the way down or assume that there's some pure, but elusive, self hiding back there, pulling the strings and directing the actors to, from, and around our internal stage. But no matter which of these metaphysical alternatives we prefer, the practical problem of living a good life remains that of somehow bringing these internal voices and external roles into concord and harmony. This is why ancient philosophers like the Stoics, and more modern ones like Smith and his immediate predecessors, so strongly emphasize personal integrity, or "self-sameness." These philosophers, Smith especially, were certainly not blind to the fact that we have many different roles to play and that different situations call for different kinds of conduct. The connection they drew between being virtuous and being "self-same" wasn't meant to imply that we act exactly the same in all situations but that we figure out a way to combine these different aspects of our personalities into a harmonious system instead of a cacophonous mess.

The particular problem we've struggled with here is that of ensuring that the Red Sox fan element of ourselves fits appropriately into our self-systems. We don't want this aspect of our personalities to impinge upon other, more important ones, but we also don't want to kick it out of the system entirely. Again, it matters little in practice whether we think of the self as one thing that wears different hats or as a constantly evolving system of many different elements. What does matter is that we recognize the need to achieve, if not unity, then internal harmony between these many diverse components. Hopefully, this exercise of reflection upon what it takes to be a self-commanding Red Sox fan will help us keep at least one of these parts of ourselves in line.[3]

---

[3] Thanks to Albee Tecci, Fast Eddie McCourt, Dan Paglia, and Whitney Johnson.

3

The True Red Sox Fan

COREY McCALL

You've no doubt seen them at various sporting events, perhaps even at Fenway: the loud, boisterous fans who drink too much beer and bellow silly things at the opposing team. Or maybe you're more familiar with another type of fan: the quiet, dignified, and dedicated fan who comes out to watch her team without fail. Indeed, the second type of fan is regularly recognized by teams for long years of service. The first type, not so much. But which type of fan is the true fan? More specifically: is there a true type of *Red Sox* fan, and, if so, is it the sort of fan who regularly sits in the beer-soaked bleachers yelling "Yankees Suck!" regardless of whether the Red Sox are actually playing the Yankees? Or is the true Red Sox fan "Big Pappy," one-hundred-year-old Arthur Giddon who recently fulfilled his childhood dream of becoming a batboy for the Red Sox. Certainly the first type of fan is more prevalent, but fans like Arthur Giddon earn our automatic praise and respect. Why? And what (if anything) sets Red Sox fans apart from fans of other teams?

I'll come back to Arthur Giddon toward the end of the chapter. Before that, I need to figure out what constitutes a true Red Sox fan and why this identification with the Red Sox is so important to this type of fan.

Today's Red Sox Fan: Not Just a Glum, Beer-Swilling Bleacher Creature

The cliché is well known by now: the long-suffering Red Sox fan whose team hadn't won a World Series since 1918. They had won

in 1912, in a titanic victory against the New York Giants the year
the *Titanic* sank; in 1915 and 1916; and then with Babe Ruth leading the way in 1918. After Harry Frazee sold Ruth's contract to the
Yankees for a song (or, more accurately, to finance his Broadway
flop *No, No, Nanette*), there was nothing but the Curse of the
Bambino, a curse that seemed more real as the years wore on. Yet
there was dignity in this suffering. Flinty New Englanders wore
their suffering as a badge of honor, and always bore it with a stiff
upper lip. Suffering went with the territory—if you were unlucky
enough to be a Red Sox fan, then *of course* you suffered.

Since 2004 all of this has changed. In 2004 (and again in 2007),
the suffering came to an end, to be replaced first with a sense of
euphoria at the championships and the teams that had won them.
Subsequently, however, new feelings could be sensed among some
of these formerly long-suffering fans, ones that were less expected.
Among longtime fans, one could sense both a feeling of nostalgia
for those long years without a World Series Championship and a
feeling of resentment of those new fans who had recently jumped
on the Red Sox bandwagon. The relevant philosophical question
can be found here in terms of these feelings of nostalgia and
resentment. What, after all, makes for a true Red Sox fan? What
makes the fans of today, these latecomers, somehow less worthy
fans than those long-suffering fans?

It doesn't take long to find examples of these sentiments on the
various Red Sox fan message boards, but one can also easily find
examples in the various fan accounts written after the Red Sox
World Series win in '04.

In "Red Sox Fans—Turning into What They Loathe," a blog post
that appeared on the eve of the 2007 World Series, the author wonders whether the price for overcoming the Curse and winning the
2004 World Series was that his beloved team of scrappy underdogs
was fated to become what its members and its fans most despised:
another version of the Yankees. As the blogger explains:

> With the Yankees now vanquished and leaderless, and their principal
> owner's [George Steinbrenner's] faculties in question, the Red Sox can
> no longer be portrayed with much sympathy. The sentimental under-
> pinnings on which the Red Sox Nation was created owed everything
> to that team in the Bronx. The Red Sox can be underdogs only in rela-
> tion to the Yankees. (www.streethop.com/sports/90251-red-sox-fans-
> turning-into-what-they-loathe.html)

This story is as old as the Biblical tale of David and Goliath. The tragic edge comes when one asks what becomes of David once he has slain Goliath. Is he destined to become another Goliath? Are the Red Sox, now that the Yankees are objects of pity rather than fear, destined to replace baseball's Goliath and become New England's version of the hated Bronx Bombers? The fear here is real, but it's a version of the resentment felt by long-standing fans to the team's newfound success. Success can lead to both resentment and contempt as the Red Sox trade one accursed state for another.

The specific resentment cited by the author of this post is that the team has become, like the hated Yankees, little more than a mercenary outfit, buying the services of the highest bidder. The author points out the discrepancy in payroll numbers between their 2007 ALCS opponent, the Cleveland Indians, and the Red Sox themselves, and points out that the Yankees and Red Sox respective payrolls are much closer than those of the Red Sox and Indians. While there are certainly differences in the amounts of their respective payrolls, from the point of view of Indians' fans, the differences look pretty insignificant. The Indians take on the role of David opposite the Red Sox Goliath. The author concludes his post by pointing out that if you had once been a fan of the Red Sox in part because of the payroll sins of the Yankees, aren't you then obliged to now root for the Indians? Oh, the tragic shame of it all.

A closely related idea is present here as well, and it's the idea of authenticity, which represents the idea that rooting for a club that's bought somehow makes you inauthentic. You're rooting for a fake team, and this makes you somehow fake as well. Your identity is less than genuine, for a true fan would root for a team that was made up of "Dirt Dogs" like Trot Nixon and Brian Daubach. Consider what Stephen King writes about Daubach and other members of the 2004 team at the beginning of his book with Stewart O'Nan called *Faithful: Two Diehard Boston Red Sox Fans Chronicle the Historic 2004 Season* (2004):

> Dauber was a real old-time Red Sox player. Like he was born to play for the Red Sox. Millar is that way, and Varitek, of course. And you know, Pedro Martinez wasn't born a Red Sox guy, but he has become one. He finished his becoming in the seventh game of the ALCS last year [2003], don't you think? . . . Man, I root for the Dauber . . . but I don't give him a dog's chance [of making the team]. (p. 6)

These players had to work for everything, they weren't handed anything on a silver platter. They didn't have the innate ability of a player like Alex Rodriguez, they were blue-collar players, and they were genuine. And as a fan if you could associate yourself with them, why then you would be genuine as well: a true fan. But notice that this idea of truth isn't the usual one, it isn't like when we say that it's true that "2+2=4." We're not talking factual truth here. We're referring to the idea of truth as authenticity.

Authenticity, or Why Sox Fans Felt Great when 'Tek Bashed A-Rod in the Face

I'm sure we all remember the scene in '04: a long, hot July—for some reason late summer always usually seems longer if you're a Red Sox fan. The team had been playing okay baseball, but it seemed the team was wilting in the summer sun and a long August would soon be replaced by an even longer offseason of second-guessing and regret. The Sox trailed the Yankees by nine and a half games in late July (sound familiar?), and they'd just come off a brutal 8–7 loss the night before. The Sox were down 3–0 in the third inning and Bronson Arroyo plunks A-Rod. A-Rod stops on his way to first and gets a mouthful of catcher's mitt from the captain. Benches clear, and the moment was largely seen as a turning point. The Sox won the game on a Bill Mueller homer, and everybody knows what happened next. When we look back on that epic season, this was one of the games that showed us all that the Red Sox could do it, that this was, just maybe, a team with enough heart to accomplish amazing feats. We all want our teams to have heart: it makes us feel good to root for a team that is true, an authentic team that won't wilt under pressure. This seems obvious, but it's actually philosophically pretty interesting.

This idea of authenticity is an old one. Scholars tell us it's a defining idea of the modern age, which they agree begins sometime between the sixteenth and eighteenth centuries. One of the key characteristics of this period is that people begin to rely upon their own individual reason instead of some external authority and this ideal of individual authority became one of the key features of an intellectual and social movement that came to be known as the Enlightenment. Immanuel Kant, one of the key representatives of this movement, famously wrote that a basic feature of this age was that people were slowly coming to rely on their own reason as their sole authority. In a 1784 essay for a Berlin newspaper that had asked well-known thinkers what the term "Enlightenment" means, Kant writes, "the motto of enlightenment is therefore *Sapere aude!* Have courage to use your own understanding" (*Kant: Political Writings*, Cambridge University Press, 1991, p. 54)

While it may not appear obvious, the idea of authenticity is closely related to Kant's formulation of the significance of the enlightened individual and, by extension, the Enlightenment. For Kant, what distinguishes us from other living beings is that we have the ability to reason and to think for ourselves. In short, we need to be autonomous. This means that we can't rely upon any external authorities to tell us what to think (Kant isn't advocating anarchy here. We can certainly rely on authorities to tell us what to *do*, but not what to say, think, or write). Nobody tells you who to root for, and it's this choice that can become a significant one in determining who you are. Authenticity is about the choices we make and how they impact our lives. In order to understand what our lives mean, we have to authorize them ourselves; we can't depend upon our religious, social, or moral values in order to do so. It is solely through the use of our own reason that we will make our lives meaningful.

Immanuel Kant likely wasn't thinking about sports fans in Königsberg, and he certainly couldn't have been thinking about Red Sox fans when he was writing at the end of the eighteenth century, but he remains important for our story of the true Red Sox fan. His writing is representative of the move from a medieval to a modern worldview in Europe, one that increasingly centers on the individual as the locus of meaning. This idea that each individual needs to use her reason or some other feature of her personality to make a meaningful life influences many dimensions of our lives today, from the various incarnations of the self-help movement in figures such as Oprah and Dr. Phil, to Romantic literature and Existentialist philosophy and to, yes, the idea of the true Red Sox fan. As the philosopher Charles Guignon writes at the beginning of his recent book on authenticity, "the ideal of authenticity is a project of becoming the person you are" (*On Being Authentic*, 2004, p. 3).

The key here is that the individual's identity is the most important thing, and it's this identity that becomes the basis for a meaningful life. While other affiliations might be important (political or religious affiliations, for example), these identifications help the individual determine who she is, and not the other way around.

Individual identity comes first, before any of these other affiliations. The primacy of individual identity becomes one of the defining traits of modernity.

The key difference between Kant and the various figures that
followed him in seeing the individual as the author of her own
identity is that Kant focuses almost exclusively on the role that reason plays in the formation of identity. Later figures in philosophy,
literature, and popular psychology will tend to focus on emotional
factors or social and political factors in addition to the faculty of
reason, while others will disregard the role of reason altogether.
This last option prevails in literary and artistic movements during
this period, beginning with Romanticism. Romantic poets such as
William Wordsworth emphasize the role that feeling plays in the
formation of the self, and believe that reason is a pale substitute for
the depths of the self revealed through one's emotional life.

Looking back on Varitek's encounter with A-Rod on that warm
summer day in July of 2004, it's now plain that what happened was
that the identity of the team crystallized in that moment. Here was
Varitek showing A-Rod and the rest of the Yankees that the Red Sox
wouldn't just roll over and play dead. We all wanted to be like
Varitek, stuffing it to the overpaid, pampered Yankees and showing them who's boss. But maybe some fans also saw a little of
themselves in Varitek: who they were, or at least who they wanted
to be. If we think about it, our identification with Varitek and that
Red Sox team can tell us a little about who we are.

The Authentic Red Sox Fan, or The Importance
of Turning off NESN and Finding Something
Else to Do

Surely no one takes this game so seriously as to derive meaning
from it in the same way that the Romantic poets did from feeling
and nature or Kant did from reason and autonomy? While there
may be an analogy between these Romantic poets with their sin-
cerity and Enlightenment philosophers with their reason, that's all
it is, an analogy, right?

Anyone who believes this really doesn't know too many Red
Sox fans—or many true fans. Sure, there are plenty of casual fans,
and there are some annoying fans, but Red Sox Nation has more
than its share of dedicated fans who derive a sense of meaning
from their identity with the Olde Towne Team. Think back to "Big

Pappy" and his dream of serving as a batboy for the Red Sox. For true Red Sox fans like one-hundred-year-old Arthur Giddon, his individual identity is tied up with rooting for the Sox. His story isn't unique, either. There are countless stories of fans, both heralded and unheralded, who derive meaning and a sense of identity from the Red Sox.

This sense of fandom has its dark side as well. People who live for the Red Sox may have a problem. Stephen King describes the problem in terms of an addiction, and he describes his feelings as a fan as a substitute for other types of addictive behavior. Red Sox fans can become addicted to their team, in the same way that one can be addicted to alcohol or drugs. Trust Stephen King to focus on the dark side of fandom, but he has a point: couldn't someone become so into the Red Sox that they lose themselves, and this identification with the team, far from helping an individual form her own identity, instead causes her to lose it?

This fan who identifies with the team at the expense of everything else becomes the opposite of the authentic individual described above; she becomes the antithesis of the true fan. This is what makes authenticity so interesting. Certainly, there are those fans who lose themselves in their team, whether it be the Red Sox or another team. We tend to not think too highly of such people: they've lost themselves in their team, and they've become in a sense losers themselves. They live for the Red Sox, and would probably die for them as well. They become one of a mass of other people who mindlessly root for the Sox, come what may, "my team, right or wrong." Or consider the fans you find furiously demanding the head of manager Terry Francona on various fan message boards for a decision they find objectionable, without considering how he manages the team and the success his teams have achieved. These uncritical attitudes aren't really very far from those mindless fans who sit in the bleachers swilling beer and yelling obscenities. In each case, fans have deluded themselves into thinking that they are true fans because they yell louder than the others, because they don't question the moves of their team or its players, or they question team personnel based on a single event.

Maybe going back to Kant would help clarify what I mean. Recall that for Kant, it was our capacity to reason that marked us and set us apart from the mindless beings that populated our world. It was only if we used our reason that we could make the move from an unreflective and unenlightened life toward an enlightened one and thereby construct a meaningful identity for ourselves. Of course our feelings are an important dimension of our selves, but they do not define us in the same way that reason does, at least according to Kant. This doesn't mean that the authentic fan must be coldly analytical and think about her team rather than feel for it. Instead the authentic fan is the *critical* fan who thinks about the moves that the team is making, how the team is playing, and how management constructs the team while she feels for every blown save and come from behind victory. The critical fan doesn't lose sight of the bigger picture—she doesn't let a single decision made in a game determine what she thinks of a player or coach. In addition to feeling the euphoria of victory and the pain of defeat, the true fan knows how to evaluate and think about her team so that she doesn't let these feelings for the team overwhelm her. She doesn't identify with the team to such a degree that she loses her identity. It becomes a part of her identity, maybe even the most important part, but not the *only* part. It's when the sole dimension of one's identity is her identity as a fan that one can begin to worry about fandom becoming fanaticism and the fan as an addict.

This is the case with anything: if we pursue it to the exclusion of everything else, then we have by definition become fanatical about it. A line has been crossed, and we're no longer using this particular endeavor or this practice as an ingredient to define ourselves. Rather, we have become defined by the activity to such a degree that it can in fact become unhealthy.

Arthur Giddon, on the other hand, gives us a great example of the critical, or authentic Red Sox fan. He gave up his job as a batboy so that he could attend Harvard Law School and practice law in Hartford until his retirement in 1985. Now his wife reports that the Red Sox are "the best vitamin for him," but only because the team helped him to define who he was, rather than letting himself be defined by the team (*Boston Globe*, April 24th, 2009). This is what authenticity as originally conceived by Enlightenment thinkers is all about: choosing to define yourself by your circumstances rather than letting your circumstances define you. In other words, determining your fate. It's a subtle distinction, but let's see if one final recent characterization of the Red Sox and the team's fans helps to sort this out.

In a column written for the *Boston Globe* on August 28th, 2005 ("The Tragedy of '04"), Scott Stossel wonders whether Red Sox

Nation might have been better off not winning the World Series the year before. In uttering this heretical thought, Stossel wonders whether the fans lost something important when the team shrugged off its burdensome history first by defeating the Yankees in epic fashion and then dispatching the Cardinals in four games to win the World Series. According to Stossel, there's something tragic in the fate of the long-suffering Red Sox fan, and this sense of doom was lost as soon as the World Series was won. I'm not denying this loss of the tragic dimension in the authentic Red Sox fan, but perhaps we can think about the loss of a sense of doom this way: in losing a sense of accursed fate, fans are left to themselves, to decide for themselves whether and how the Red Sox will continue to impact their lives. Fans have been freed of the burden of fate, but this freedom brings with it the burden of decision—and with it the question of reason and problem of authenticity itself. Just as Kant wrote during the eighteenth century, it's up to us to critically choose what we will be and how we will let our experiences define us. Each of us can be a true Red Sox fan, should we choose to do so.

The Art of Losing

DAVID ROOCHNIK

> The art of losing isn't hard to master;
> so many things seem filled with the intent
> to be lost that their loss is no disaster.
>
> —ELIZABETH BISHOP

October 3rd, 1998

Another dark day. They scored two, and so, yet again, we lost. Emotions flood in, and the result is a deep throbbing: the familiar throb of loss.

We look at the winners. Smiles blister their faces as they slap and hug and gleefully shake each other. They are celebrating, oblivious to our pain. A few moments after their victory, they collect themselves, and congratulate us, the defeated, for playing well. "Good game, good game, good game," they tell us, as they extend their hands to perform the mechanical ritual of sportsmanship. In some tiny way, we're grateful for their kind words, but we know there's nothing substantial behind them. They're consumed by their victory, and we have disappeared from their radar screens.

On the morning of Saturday, October 3rd, the Fireflies, my daughter's fourth-grade soccer team, were defeated by the Mercuries, 2–0. In the early evening, the Boston Red Sox, my local baseball team, were defeated by the Cleveland Indians, 2 1 and eliminated from the playoffs. The day was long and framed by loss. By its end, I was depleted and didn't even have the energy for grief. We had lost twice, simple as that.

But losing is never simple, and that's where this story begins.

Losing is a vastly more complicated experience than winning. Victory captures the victors, makes them feel as if they, for the moment, are on top of the world. Winners, having won, are glad just to be where they are. If they're good sports, they won't taunt the defeated, but the feeling of victory is so captivating, that regardless of how dignified the winners might be, they can muster no real sympathy for the losers. Sympathy means "feeling with," and the feeling of victory is just too strong, too good, to leave anything left for the vanquished. Victory is of the moment, and the moment demands celebration and affirmation. Victory, gratifying so powerfully, renders past and future irrelevant. Like sugar, it's a taste so sweet that it obliterates all others. The game is over and life feels rich.

But the pain of losing includes sympathy for the victor, for what makes defeat so painful is just the awareness that the other has won. It hurts to lose because it feels so good to win. The essence of loss is contrast. We lost, victory is what we don't have, and what we don't have makes us who we are: losers. Loss is complicated because it includes both itself and what is not itself. And while it's true that, just like losing, winning requires a contrast, victors don't celebrate just because they're not losers; they celebrate because they've won. Victors relish being who they are; losers feel the pain of who they are not.

It's into this strange, negative space, that the art of losing enters. Its first appearance is through the imagination. Winners, so taken by the reality of their achievement, are not sparked to imagine a world that never was. But losers are. *If only* Sarah had remembered that a midfielder must also play defense; *if only* Allie hadn't stopped to tie her shoe; *if only* Mo Vaughn hadn't hit into a double play; *if only* the past were not exactly what it in fact was. The images generated by the *if only,* by the might-have-been-but-was-not, are so vivid to a loser that they can almost satisfy.

October 4th, 1998

It's 2:00 A.M. and I'm thinking about the softball game in which I played fifteen years ago. There I was at the plate, batting in the bottom of the seventh with two men out. We were one run down, but had runners on second and third. The outfielders were playing shallow, and so were just begging me to blast one over their heads.

But, for reasons I am unable to fathom, I, a dead pull hitter, swung at an outside pitch. By clumsily trying to go to the opposite field, I popped it up to the third baseman for an easy out. For weeks afterward I replayed the pitch. I saw myself exercising some discipline and checking my swing, waiting for the next pitch. I saw myself sending it to the fence, and I noted with satisfaction that the outfielders simply turned their heads and didn't even bother to run after it. My teammates easily scored and we won the game. I felt the easy stride in my legs as I, who had no need to stretch the hit into a double, made it to first at a comfortable jog. I felt the hard pats of friends as they congratulated me by pounding my shoulders. I carried myself with dignity.

None of this happened. But, alone at night, the images are still so vivid that I can easily call them back. For years after that game in 1983 I often fell asleep watching the ball roll confidently towards the warning track. And I'm trying to do the same thing on this miserable night as well.

This, then, is the first lesson that the art of losing teaches: the past is no prison, for we are creatures of the imagination who can transform it. The imagination, not our bats or our baseball gloves, not the statistics engraved in the won/lost column, is our greatest resource. For it has the power to negate. Losing is negative: it feels terrible. And so the loser must invoke the imagination in order to negate what is negative. The ball, rolling to the fence, was a positive image designed to defuse the pain of losing. When cultivated properly, when working hard, the imagination—*if only, if only, if only*—promises freedom.

Of course, the loser realizes that this is but fantasy. The facts are too powerful to deny: I popped the ball up. I was the one with head slumped, walking back to the dugout. I lost, they didn't. All I had was a dream. But the dream was so compelling, so enticingly superior to reality, that I'm reminded that reality isn't all it's cracked up to be. The art of losing thus reminds us all that we live suspended somewhere between two worlds: image and fact, dream and waking, *if only* and was. In losing we realize that this precarious in-between, and not stable ground, is our true home.

There is another way in which losing activates us. The pain of loss is so intense that, once it relents a bit, the loser must summon the intellect to construct defenses against it returning again. One way to do this is to declare that the game was not so important after all.

"It was only a game," says the loser. Losing isn't so bad because the game itself wasn't such a big deal. Saturday, October 3rd, was just a single day in a long season, and a great season it was. So, there you have it: losing to the Cleveland Indians wasn't as terrible as it initially felt. The great Red Sox shortstop, Nomar Garciaparra, seemed to be saying something like this when the game ended. Instead of retreating to the clubhouse, he spent minutes waving gratefully to the fans, reminding them what a good year it had been, and what hopes there were for the future.

"It was only a game." After all, Darryl Strawberry and Joe Torre of the Yankees were diagnosed with cancer. Now that's something truly serious.

"It was only a game. It wasn't real life."

But losers who are honest know the lies all too well. The refrain of "only a game" is a rationalization, a way to defuse the hurt. We diminish the importance of the game only because we were on the losing side.

Or do we? Maybe we're right. Maybe games actually aren't that important. Maybe it was only a game.

No, that's the way losers talk. Even in the face of deadly illness, victory still means something. It is, after all, what we're playing for.

Losers, experts at rationalizing, are forced to become reflective. For they must wonder when they are lying to themselves, and when they're telling the truth. Does beating the Indians, or the Mercuries, really matter, or not? Losers are never sure. And this is what makes losing an art that *is* "hard to master." Losing makes us wonder what, if anything, really matters. It makes us into philosophers. Victors are not driven to become reflective, for they are overwhelmed by the immediate surge of good feeling that comes with victory. They're filled with the gladness of having won and have no need for anything else. They have no need to think.

All of the greatest athletes have suffered intense defeats at some points in their career. One of the greatest TV commercials ever made expressed just this point. Michael Jordan, the winner of winners, is shooting foul shots, while his voice-over recounts all of his failures. The missed shots, the failure to make the high-school varsity team, the years of frustration on a losing team. Failure, the commercial implies, is what makes success possible.

Before I moved to Boston, I lived in Iowa, where I rooted for the Chicago Cubs, the greatest losers in history. But I feel even more at home as a Red Sox fan than I did with the Cubs. For the

Red Sox are haunted by loss in an unparalleled way. There is a depth to the losing here, a deep awareness of its inevitability. Boston fans are called the "Red Sox Nation," and the title tells another story about what the art of losing can teach. Losing forces the loser to look desperately for meaning. And, after having been driven inward, the next move is outward. For the greatest consolation comes from sharing doom. The losers' search for meaning can create a community like no other force. The only reason we have communities is because we need each other and in the face of loss, this we surely do.

Notice that there is no New York Yankees nation. There's just New York, the biggest, wealthiest city on earth. To be a Yankees fan is to demand the best and lay claim to the riches of the world. But it's also to indulge in the greatest of all self-delusions, the one that says there really is some way to avoid losing. This just isn't true. In the end we all lose . . . first our strength, then our health, then our lives. Yankees fans can't understand this the way we do. They treat loss as an insult, rather than the life-lesson it is. For this reason, there is no more vacuous and ignorant soul in American sports than George Steinbrenner. By contrast, a citizen of Red Sox Nation has faced loss too many times, and in too many absurdly unfair ways, and so has thought about it again and again. We've imagined victory, and wondered about defeat. And so we are more reflective, better able to face up to the losses inevitably heading our way. A citizen of Red Sox Nation knows it's not a matter of "if we lose," it's only a matter of "when." And this attitude towards life is right. It makes us more open, more able to sympathize, more alert to the sufferings of others, and to the riddles of human existence.

Of course, everything above is said by a loser. I can hear George Steinbrenner in the background: "Sour grapes, you weak-kneed, loss-loving coward, sour grapes!"

George is right. The story of the sour grapes is about the fox who desires what looks to him to be delicious fruit. When he's not able to get what he wants, he decides it's not so good after all. This is what losers do. They have to in order to survive the pain of defeat. But we who have mastered the art of losing are too smart not to realize when we're playing the sour grapes game. And yet we can't stop playing it. And so we're forced to ask ourselves: are the grapes really sour or are they sweet as can be?

For losers, you see, life is full of such questions. And this is the final lesson the art of losing teaches: life is questionable. The

Yankees will tell you that it's great, pure and simple, to win and be rich. But of course they're wrong.

May 20th, 1999

The Red Sox, in first place, have just beaten the Yankees twice in a row. The image of victory is sweet, so why not dream? Pedro Martinez mowing them down; John Valentin getting hot when the weather does; Juan Pena and Brian Rose, two rookies, continuing their spellbinding pitching; Bret Saberhagen off the DL; the ever wonderful Nomar, hands twitching, smacking the ball all over Fenway; Flash Gordon, closer extraordinaire; Mike Stanley hitting home runs. Why not take it all the way? Why not want it all?

The Red Sox are haunted by the passage of the seasons. It's only spring and an entire lifetime of summer will have to be endured. And when the weather cools in September, the willies creep in. At the end of every passing day, every passing week, stand the specters of Bill Buckner and Bucky Dent. Unlike George Steinbrenner, citizens of Red Sox Nation understand William Shakespeare's Macbeth perfectly: "To-morrow, and to-morrow, and to-morrow / Creeps in this petty pace from day to day / To the last syllable of recorded time." The last syllable will be loss. The flow of autumn time will eventually swallow all our springtime achievements. There may be infinite hope, but not for us. We, so well schooled in the art of losing, know who we are. And yet we will always continue to play.

October 17th, 2003

The grief is unimaginable. After the game I fell almost immediately asleep. But I woke up just an hour later with a piercing pain in my chest. Real pain, not the superficial kind that signals mere discomfort or disappointment. The magnitude of the ill-fated decision is unfathomable. The bullpen had been nearly perfect throughout the playoffs. Pedro had put in seven good innings. Time for a change. When he was still at the mound in the bottom of the eighth I told my wife that surely he'd stay in only until he gave up a hit or walk. Only if he could mow down six would Grady Little, the aptly named Red Sox manager, leave him in. But that's not the way the game was played. Jeter hit him and then Williams. Lefties coming up, and so Embree was the no-brainer. But Pedro, a man of deadly pride, refused to budge, and Grady capitulated to a force greater than his own. Then the ferocious Rivera took over, Wakefield's knuckleballs were too high, and doom, doom, doom, in the 11th inning. No rationalizing today. Just mourning.

The next day the entire town is engulfed by grief and feels funereal. I have trouble speaking to my students and I force them, most of whom don't come from Boston, to acknowledge the gravity of the moment. I call for a moment of silence before class. The Red Sox fans in the room understand why this loss hurt so terribly, why the Curse, triggered by selling the Bambino eighty-five years ago, is alive and real and tearing our hearts to shreds. Losing to the Yankees in such a confoundingly unnecessary way.

Even if the blame for losing the series can't fairly be placed on Grady Little's shoulders, on that one decision alone, the Red Sox management made the correct, and probably the only decision that they could've made: they fired him. Had he returned, the Curse would have returned with him.

October 16th, 2004

We lose the third game in a row to the Yankees, this time by the unthinkable score of 19–8. This defeat is not a result of the Curse, for it is not strange or undeserved, as it was exactly a year ago when Grady left Pedro on the mound. This time we just get whipped. I'm demoralized and sad, and my body feels heavy, but the pain is not sharp. I have distanced myself from the loss.

I have a new colleague in my department who recently arrived from Germany. "Manfred" is his first name, but in honor of the great Ramirez I call him "Manny." He's good-natured, and so doesn't seem to mind. I attempt to explain to him the cultural underpinnings of Red Sox Nation. First, it's a certainty that we will lose this series. No team in baseball history has recovered from a 3–0 deficit. Second, losing is an art, well understood by the literary and philosophical traditions we represent to our students. "Think Greek tragedy," I tell him. Every spring the Athenians entered the theater of Dionysus in order to witness the catastrophic fall of Oedipus the King or Agamemnon, Ajax, or Hippolytus, or Pentheus. Somehow the collective witnessing of the hero's catastrophe is cathartic and forges deep bonds that keep the community whole. I tell "Manny" to think of this as he watches the crowds pour into Fenway Park, which is close to our campus. I tell him to appreciate and even to try to participate in the depth of our suffering and the civic therapy that results from it.

I tell my German colleague that he should re-read Socrates's speech in Plato's *Symposium,* for there he will find the doctrine of Eros, of human love and striving. To love, Plato tells us, is to love some object, some X. Eros, in other words, is intentional. Furthermore, to love X is to lack X. Without the lack, without the powerful presence of absence in our lives, we'd have nothing to go after; we'd be inert. To cite what for Plato is the best example: the philosopher knows that he is not wise, and so he loves wisdom and spends his life seeking it. Were he ever to attain wisdom, his activity, his very life, would come to an end. Lacking what we love makes us into who we are. And citizens of Red Sox Nation, who have lacked a World Series victory for eighty-six years, understand this well.

October 17th, 2004

In the history of baseball, twenty of the twenty-five teams that went into Game Four of a seven-game series with a 3–0 advantage won that one too. But the Red Sox defy the odds, even though we were behind 4–3 in the ninth inning. We managed to tie it, and then Big Papi smacked a two-run homer in the 12th inning. There's no doubt that this team of "idiots," as they like to call themselves, has a big heart. "Big deal," I tell myself. We're down 3–1 and, to repeat the mantra, no team in baseball history had rallied from a 3–0 deficit and won a seven-game series.

October 18th, 2004

Dan Shaughnessy of *The Boston Globe,* long-time and devoted chronicler of all things Red Sox, wrote the following on this day:

> In perhaps the most thrilling and torturous postseason game in 104 years of Red Sox baseball, the Sox last night beat the Yankees, 5–4, when the mythic Ortiz singled home Johnny Damon from second base in the bottom of the 14th at 10:59 P.M. It was the longest game in League Championship Series history (5 hours 49 minutes) and came less than 23 hours after the same Ortiz cracked a walk-off homer to win Game 4 at 1:22 yesterday morning.

Hope is rising in the Nation, and so I fear the inevitable pain. I'm reminded of Nick Hornby's *Fever Pitch*, his wonderful autobiography of being a fan of his beloved football team, Arsenal. Unlike me, Hornby has a fearless heart. He never relents, never closes his eyes, does not fear the pain of defeat, even when defeat seems overwhelmingly likely. I remember the grief of 2003—those damned Yankees!—too well, and so I did not watch this game. When I read about the victory, I feel ashamed.

October 21st, 2004

It's back-to-school night and, dutiful parent that I am, I'm sitting in my daughter's Chemistry classroom. The teacher is earnestly explaining the curriculum when the principal's voice comes over the loudspeaker. "Damon hit a grand slam in the second inning! We're way ahead and Lowe is mowing them down!" The entire building shakes with giddiness as parents, like their children on normal school days, rush out of the building when the final bell sounds, head for their cars, and race home to watch the rest. It's a sweeping, miraculous victory. Joy erupts.

October 28th, 2004

We sweep the St. Louis Cardinals. How could it possibly be otherwise? What a wonderful crew! David Ortiz, author of magnificent home run finales; Pedro Martinez, undaunted even though the Yankees consistently beat him; heroic Curt Schilling of the bloody sock; Derek Lowe resurrected from the dead and pitching superbly; Manny-being-Manny and pounding the ball with that beautiful swing from the right side of the plate; Terry Francona, an intelligent dignified, baseball lifer; Kevin Millar, the self-styled idiot who occasionally hits the ball hard and keeps the locker room loose; old reliable Bill Mueller at third base, with a stunningly high batting average to boot; rock-solid Jason Varitek, who punched A-Rod's lights out and ignited a nation; Trot Nixon, who hit that 0–2 pitch for a huge double; heart-throb Johnny Damon, great speed and an occasional, perfectly timed grand slam; closer supreme Keith Foulke, who tossed the ball underhanded to first base to seal the first World Series title in eighty-six years; who broke the curse, who made us normal.

October 28th, 2007

I'm visiting a friend who lives in a glorious house in the hills of Berkeley, California. The weather is perfect and through her huge windows we have a spectacular view of the San Francisco Bay, the Golden Gate Bridge, and Alcatraz. I realize that California has one cultural advantage over the Northeast: a night game doesn't start at night. Instead, we turn on the TV around 6:00 P.M. We grill some steaks and drink the fabulous wine that we just purchased in a vineyard fifty miles north of here. And as we eat we watch the Red Sox mow down the Rockies and conclude another four-game sweep of a World Series. Jonathan Papelbon, visibly drained from the long season, reaches deep into himself and comes up with just barely enough heat to get the last out. The feeling of victory is altogether pleasant, sweet, gratifying and, dare I say it, a tad familiar. We're living the life of luxury here in the hills and life is good.

April 6th, 2009

Opening Day. The game against the Tampa Bay Rays begins in a few hours. I cannot, of course, attend. The tickets are far too expensive, but I plan to follow the game on the Internet. Even though it's chilly and cloudy outside, with rain predicted for later in the day, it's the resurrection of baseball, of real spring, of life. As usual, the Yankees have spent hundreds of millions of dollars to re-arm themselves, and they'll have Mark Teixeira, C.C. Sabathia, and A.J. Burnett in their dugout. Tampa Bay, who whipped us in the ALCS last year, has a young, powerful pitching staff, terrific defense, and a good dose of hitting and so will also present serious competition. But we're not without hope. We solidified the bullpen and have a long list of starting pitchers: John Smoltz and Brad Penny in addition to old favorites Josh Beckett, Daisuke Matzusaka, and the geezer himself, Tim Wakefield. Our hitting will be good, but might not be good enough. Jason Bay is a first-rate ballplayer but is no Manny Ramirez. Jason Varitek is slowing down and can't hit from the left side any more. That J.D. Drew won't play more than ninety games is a safe bet. Jacoby Ellsbury might do good work in center, but he faltered at the plate last year. We're a good team, but it seems unlikely to me that we're the best. But you never know.

Opening Day is always a thrill. But it doesn't have the crackle of previous years. To christen the season, *The Boston Globe* prints Dan Shaughnessy's article on the front page. He informs us that the

TV ratings for Red Sox games dropped twenty percent last year. The ratings for the pregame show were down by a full third. He wonders whether it's because the team has become bland. Ramirez, Millar, and Damon are gone. We've become a team of hard-playing, no-complaining professionals now, and we're certain to win a lot of games. But in the process, we may have become boring. Shaughnessy interviews Theo Epstein, general manager of the Red Sox, for his article, who replies to this charge. "I think when you have twenty-five guys working hard, playing selflessly with a common goal, it's anything but boring," says the franchise architect. "I find it meaningful and invigorating when that happens."

Neither Shaughnessy nor Epstein considers another explanation for the decline in ratings. The Red Sox have become normal. We're better than almost everybody else, but with the exception of the Chicago Cubs, we now do what everyone else does: we win some and we lose some. We won it in 2004 and 2007, and lost it to Tampa Bay last year. We're no longer plagued by the Curse, and this is good. But it means that we're also no longer as well schooled in the art of losing. As a result, the paradoxical lure of the Red Sox, and perhaps the glue that held the Nation together, is now gone. We're on the verge of forgetting all those lessons that only the art of losing can teach. We've tasted the sweet nectar of victory and lost ourselves in joyous celebration of being world champions twice in this decade alone. And so this year we're less wary and worried, but also less thoughtful and sympathetic to others. Our dreams have been fulfilled in reality and so perhaps our imaginations will fall asleep. I fear that, mega-budget team that we now are, we've become more like the Yankees.

Of course, and I can't say this strongly enough, IT'S GOOD TO WIN! That's why we play the game, and if winning isn't the goal then there's no reason to take the field in the first place. And if the goal has been achieved, as it has been here in Boston, then this must be cause for celebration. But never forget those dark and haunted days before October 2004. We were special then. Never forget the strange sensation of being cursed, being tainted, that was with us for so long. Those were painful times. But there was dignity in those defeats and a sense of purpose, no matter how thwarted we inevitably were. We understood ourselves back then. Maybe the ratings of Red Sox broadcasts have declined because we no longer quite recognize ourselves. Maybe when the Curse ended something weirdly valuable was lost as well.

Typical Red Sox Fans

ANDY WASIF

Depending on which language you are speaking, the term "*typical* Red Sox fan" has two totally different connotations. If you're speaking Yankee, it means "a fan who constantly whines about something he knows nothing about."

Yet, if you use a Fenway dialect, the meaning is more positive—a typical Red Sox fan is the type of fan that's intelligent about not only the Red Sox, but other teams as well; practices exceptional ballpark etiquette like when to start the wave and when to let it die; is always fearful of the "other shoe" that can drop at anytime; and leaves no opportunity to berate the Yankees unfulfilled.

Looking closer, though, a clarification of part of the term is needed. "Typical" based on what, a comparison to other fans? Impossible, for Red Sox fans are nothing like other fans. Or are we referring to a representative sampling as matched up against other Red Sox fans? Well, even then it's a broad term and is tricky to explain.

If you look at the composition of a Red Sox fanatic's brain, they're unique only to their own kind, yet in a uniform manner. The brain contains centers that shape the collective personality. In one case, they have overly pronounced *emotional centers* which make it ultrasensitive to the slightest divergence from the status quo.

Take, for instance, the example of the radio talk show host who speaks of the team's recent win streak and the return of Dustin Pedroia to the team from witnessing the birth of his first child:

> RADIO TALK SHOW HOST: Beckett's turned it up a notch, Youk is hitting .400 in August, Pedroia's back . . .
>
> TYPICAL RED SOX FAN: OH NO! What's wrong with Pedroia's back?! [*He sticks his head in the oven*]

Then there's the *perception center*, which controls how an event is perceived. First of all, a Red Sox fan's perception

47

center is noticeably smaller than his emotional center. This presents a "confused" perception much of the time, which is the basis of the majority of issues they find themselves experiencing.

In essence, Red Sox fans possess more *pinhole vision* than other fans would. Look at it as you would a spectrum. Whereas, there are seven colors, a Red Sox fan only sees one—red. Use this as a reference point when considering how a Red Sox fan reads the daily newspaper. (Or, for those of you who have never read a newspaper, let's say "how a Red Sox fan views the Internet.") When the headline reads:

- Snow Storm Paralyzes City for a Week,
  —the Red Sox fan sees
  Papelbon Out for Season

- Seventy Percent Chance of Rain for Fireworks Celebration on Hatch Shell,
  —the Red Sox fan sees
  Sox not given much of a chance versus Yankees

- Killer Swans Descend Upon Public Gardens; Mayor Issues Curfew,
  —the Red Sox fan sees
  Ortiz Leaves Eight Runners in Scoring Position; Manager Considers Benching Him

Yet even in these standard deviations, there are different variances in the actions taken revealing several subsets of the typical Red Sox lover.

For one, there are the *pink hats*. A pink hat believes that all games end with the reality dating show "Sox Appeal," wonders why the crowd constantly boos Youk (they're saying, "Yooooooouuuuuuuk!"), and doesn't necessarily wear those pink hats. However, whatever they do wear, it's creaseless.

A more passionate breed, the *Dirt Dog* may be the most selfless, true-blue fans in all of Red Sox Nation. They will keep track of the outs for everyone around them—"Okay, two away! We need one more, people."—they know the right chant and when to start it, they'll wear the same clothing, right down to their skivvies, during a winning streak and burn their entire wardrobes during any losing streak exceeding three games, and they won't let you celebrate *before* the late-night talk show hosts start having Red Sox on as guests.

I, myself, am of the *Ostrich* variety of Red Sox fan. My kind disappears during tense game moments. Don't let that fool you. We are among the most loyal of Red Sox fans. We're doing it for the good of the team; for we believe good things won't happen if we're there to see it. Anecdotal evidence has proven this to be true in the three no-hitters Tim Wakefield has taken into the late innings that I've ruined by tuning in just in time to witness one of the next two batters get a hit. Our motto is "it hasn't happened if you don't watch it happen."

So though not all Red Sox fans are alike in every regard, there are generalities that indicate them as such. In a nutshell, a typical Red Sox fan sets every alarm in his house to 7:05 P.M., owns at least one shirt that says something bad about Derek Jeter, has a pet or family member named after a current or former player, can name every player on the roster, yet can't remember his sister-in-law's husband's name, pulls a hamstring when one of the players does, and experiences anxiety, shortness of breath, the shakes, dry mouth, dry heaves, ringing in the ears, rapid heartbeat, palpitations, vomiting, blurred vision, uncontrollable sobbing, depression, euphoria, anger, love, vertigo, pride, dismay, ennui and, in rare cases, paralysis, all during the singing of the National Anthem.

In short, being a *typical* Red Sox fan is anything but typical.

Curse Reversed

*Bill Buckner is greeted by cheering fans during Opening Day
festivities on April 8th, 2008.*

Courtesy of the Boston Red Sox. Photo by Cindy Loo.

5

Billy Buck Had No Moral Luck

BRYAN PILKINGTON

Up 3 games to 2 in the 1986 World Series, playing the Mets in Shea Stadium . . . Calvin Schiraldi got the first two outs in the bottom of the 10th inning, to put the Red Sox one out away from victory, but then Gary Carter and Kevin Mitchell singled. Schiraldi threw two strikes past Ray Knight, but he fought it off and hit a broken-bat single to score Carter. Bob Stanley replaced Schiraldi, and after getting two strikes on Mookie Wilson the Red Sox were one strike away again. Wilson fouled off two pitches and then Stanley's next pitch got away from catcher Rich Gedman. Mitchell scored from third and Knight moved up to second. After fouling off two more pitches, Wilson squibbed a funky roller toward Bill Buckner at first. When Buckner misjudged the hop and let the ball bounce through his legs, Knight scored from second to win the game, and the Mets went on to win Game 7 and the Series. (Reason #86)

This is how David Green describes the moment, which he believes, "probably defines the Red Sox as much as any other single event in their history" (*101 Reasons to Love the Red Sox and 10 Reasons to Hate the Yankees*, 2005). Whether this is the most defining moment, I can't say, but Buckner's error is undoubtedly the most infamous play in Boston Red Sox history. All baseball fans remember or have heard of the slow rolling ground ball that Red Sox first baseman Bill Buckner could not field in Game Six of the 1986 World Series against the New York Mets. New York went on to win Game Seven, giving the Mets their second World Series Championship and adding more credence to the Curse of the Bambino. A curse isn't a particularly satisfying target for blame, so many turned to the veteran All-Star affectionately known as "Billy Buck" to relieve their anguish.

53

Not until the 2008 season did Red Sox Nation appear to forgive Buckner, giving him a standing ovation after he threw out the first pitch on Opening Day at Fenway Park.

Since '86, the cruel treatment Buckner received was only made worse by his becoming the icon of sports blunders. But is this fair? Is it even right to blame Buckner for the Red Sox loss in that game? In the World Series that year? By reflecting on the concept of moral luck and applying it to Buckner's unfortunate situation, I think we can better understand what we should and shouldn't blame him for.

The concept of moral luck is most notably addressed by the philosophers Bernard Williams and Thomas Nagel.[1] Following the eighteenth-century philosopher Immanuel Kant, many people have thought that moral worth cannot be subject to luck or chance. This is a very natural thought for us to have. If something seems to be outside of someone's control, we often do not praise or blame the person for that thing.[2] As Williams describes it, ". . . what is not in the domain of the self is not in its control, and so is subject to luck" (p. 20). We can think of moral luck as applying to situations in which a person performs or fails to perform an action, and external factors affect the situation. Because these factors are outside the control of the person, these situations challenge our views regarding the praise and blame of that individual. We struggle with whether we should praise or blame a person solely for the action, or for the action and its consequences. When Mike Lowell hits a home run in the top of the ninth to put the Sox up 3–2, do we praise him only for his home run or also for winning the game? I think that by reflecting on cases of moral luck and our opinions about these types of situations, we can better understand what we can hold Buckner accountable for.

Not all Red Sox fans blame Buckner for losing the 1986 World Series or even Game Six. But for those loyal fans who didn't fault Buckner, there were just as many baseball fans and members of the media that did blame him and that leads one to believe this issue

---

[1] Bernard Williams, "Moral Luck," in *Moral Luck: Philosophical Papers 1973–1980* (2002), pp. 20–39; Thomas Nagel, "Moral Luck," in *Moral Luck*, edited by Daniel Statman (1993), pp. 57–72.

[2] With the obvious exception of Carlton Fisk's willing the ball fair in the 12th inning of Game Six of the 1975 World Series. There's no concrete evidence that the ball was under his control but, as it flirted with foul territory, everyone suspects he had some special power over the ball and willed it fair.

hasn't been settled. Let's think clearly about the situation that arose in the 10th inning of Game Six and look at some insights from philosophy that should help to resolve this question of blame.

Moral Luck and Accountability: Lucky Lester?

When we ordinarily say that someone is lucky, we're suggesting that something occurred which was out of that person's control and it turned out well for that person. Suppose that in preparing for a game against the New York Yankees, Jon Lester is studying the tendencies of their hitters. Lester forgets to study the last page and so misses reviewing the tendencies of Hideki Matsui, Jorge Posada, Alex Rodriguez, Nick Swisher, and Mark Teixeira. Lester realizes this just before the game starts. However, he has no time to review the tendencies for these batters because in a desperate attempt to finally win a game against the Red Sox, Joe Girardi has mixed up his batting order and Lester sees that Matsui is leading off, followed by Posada, A-Rod, Swisher in the clean up spot, and Teixeira, batting fifth. The Yankees batters proceed to hit five solo home runs off of Lester and Terry Francona has no choice but to pull Lester in the first inning. Lester is unlucky. If he would've looked at the last page of his Yankees Batter Tendency Sheet, he would've had no trouble with the batters, but he forgot to flip over the sheet and the result was devastating. After the game, Josh Beckett tells Jason Varitek what happened and they agree, "Lester was unlucky."

However, luck is symmetrical. Suppose that after a late night on the town, A-Rod sleeps through his alarm and doesn't make it to the ballpark on time (nor do four of his friends, Hideki, Jorge, Nick, and Mark, to whom he had promised to give rides to the game that day). In this case, Lester doesn't need to know how to pitch to these batters because they don't show up. Having studied the tendencies of the other Yankees batters so well, Lester pitches a flawless game and picks up a no-hitter. After the game, Josh Beckett tells Jason Varitek what happened and they agree, "Lester was lucky."

These situations are cases of moral luck because something outside of Lester's control greatly affected how (and for what) he is evaluated. If those Yankees batters don't show up to the game, Lester throws a no-no. If they show up, he gets shelled and fails to record an out. Evaluating the consequences of Lester's action and evaluating the action itself yields disproportionate results. This is characteristic of moral luck cases, at least the most challenging ones, but it isn't a necessary requirement for a situation to be characterized as a case of moral luck. Lester's failure to flip over the Yankees Tendency Sheet doesn't seem like a very big deal, and when the first five batters fail to show up, it proves meaningless. However, when those batters do show up, Lester's failure turns out to be a very big deal. The consequences are great in the second instance, but Lester's failure to turn over the sheet is the same action in both cases. The disproportionality complicates our views on these types of cases. How could we blame Lester more if those Yankees show up? He does the same thing in both cases; he doesn't turn over the sheet.

Fenway Franks and The Negligent Driver

To further clarify the concept of moral luck, let's look at a case often discussed by philosophers: the negligent driver. The details of the case vary, but the insight remains the same. Suppose Ricky is driving his truck down Yawkey Way to deliver a shipment of Fenway Franks for the game that afternoon. He's obeying the speed limit and the road signs. Ricky is generally a good truck driver. He's conscientious of others on the road and has never gotten in an accident. Today, while driving to Fenway, Ricky sees a child step out in front of his truck. He jams on the brakes, but he can't stop in time and he runs over the child. He feels terrible about what has happened and blames himself for it. In attempting to console Ricky, his good friend, Cal, tells him there's nothing he could've done. However, Ricky confesses that he did not check his brakes that month. Ricky is usually quite diligent about maintaining his vehicle, which includes a monthly brake check, but the Red Sox had a long homestand this month and that meant that a lot of franks needed to get to Fenway. When Ricky and Cal checked, the brakes were worn dangerously low, and worse, it was obvious that if Ricky had checked his brakes, he would've seen this, gotten them fixed, and been able to stop in time to avoid the child.

Ricky is morally unlucky. He killed a child because he didn't perform his weekly brake check. Like Lester, Ricky failed to do something, which led to a bad consequence, but his situation was influenced by something external, that is, something outside of his control. As Nagel notes, "there is a morally significant difference between reckless driving and manslaughter. But whether a reckless driver hits a pedestrian depends on the presence of the pedestrian at the point where he recklessly passes a red light" (p. 58). There's something outside the driver's control, which affects the situation, namely, the pedestrian walking in the street. Yet this external influence does play a role in how we evaluate the situation. If we run a red light, we may wind up with a ticket. If we run a red light and kill a pedestrian, we'll have taken a life and probably do some serious jail time. In evaluating cases such as those of Lester and Ricky, we should focus on some key questions, which highlight the difference between blameworthiness in normal cases and in cases of moral luck.

The Frank Consequences of Too Many Hot Dogs and Not Preparing for a Game

What can we blame someone for? In many cases the answer to this question is easy. Because Lester forgets to flip over the sheet, Matsui launches a ball over the Green Monster and Francona blames Lester for poor pitch selection. Consideration of moral luck suggests that there're actually two things for which we might blame Lester. Initially we may be tempted to think that when (A) Francona blames Lester for throwing the wrong pitch and when (B) Francona blames Lester for not reading the rest of the Yankees Tendency Sheet, Francona is blaming Lester for the same thing. They appear the same because what Francona wants is for Lester to throw the most appropriate pitches for the situation (given the batter, the count, the score, and the inning), and that can only happen when Lester knows the correct pitch to throw. Francona may blame Lester for (A) his poor pitch selection and for (B) not reading the rest of the sheet as if they were the same thing, but they aren't. Recall the version of this case where the first five Yankees batters don't show up for the game and Lester pitches a gem. In this situation, Francona can blame Lester for not reading the rest of the sheet, but he can't blame him for his bad pitch selection because in this version he throws no bad pitches. The challenge in thinking about these moral luck cases is whether to blame Lester and Ricky for their initial, less serious failures, or to also blame them for the consequences of those failures even though the consequences are due in part to external factors and out of their control.

Therefore, we focus on a second question: Since we can either blame someone for their action, or for their action and the consequences of that action, what should we do? The problem we have with blaming someone for the consequences of their action is the challenge of moral luck situations. We'd be blaming people for something outside of their control and we usually require a person to be in control before we hold them accountable. Ricky has control over checking his brakes, but he doesn't have control (at least not in the same way) over hitting the child. Ricky did not want to hit the child. When he saw her, he slammed on his brakes, but because he hadn't checked them (something he did have control over), he killed the child. This illustrates why cases of moral luck complicate questions, which are more straightforward in other cases. If someone must be in control to be responsible for an action and Ricky isn't, then it follows that he isn't responsible for killing the child, but only for not checking his brakes. (If Ricky had performed the required brake maintenance, but unbeknownst to him, Cal cut the brake lines, we would not blame Ricky for not being able to stop in time to avoid the child.)

This isn't how we normally evaluate these types of situations, and to do so may be to fall into a trap that Nagel warns us about. It's important not to place too much emphasis on control and not to give too much weight to external factors. For if we do this, we're in danger of not being able to hold anyone responsible for anything. Nagel writes:

> If the condition of control is consistently applied, it threatens to erode most of the moral assessments we find it natural to make. The things for which people are morally judged are determined in more ways than we at first realize by what is beyond their control...Ultimately, nothing or almost nothing about what a person does seems to be under his control. (p. 58)

If we take control too seriously, we may not be able to blame Ricky or Lester in either case, or for anything, for that matter. What can we do? Williams suggests that one's awareness that one has "done the harmful thing" comes from one's thought that the occurrence of the bad thing is a consequence of one's action and that "the cost of its happening can in the circumstances fairly be allocated to one's account" (p. 28). Nagel makes a similar point in differentiating a driver who's negligent (as Ricky was) and one who wasn't:

> The driver, if he is entirely without fault, will feel terrible about his role in the event, but will not have to reproach himself. . . . However, if the

driver was guilty of even a minor degree of negligence...then if that
negligence contributes to the death of the child, he will not merely feel
terrible. He will blame himself for the death. (p. 61)

The latter is a case of moral luck, as Nagel notes, because the driver "would have to blame himself only slightly for the negligence
itself if no situation arose which required him to brake suddenly
and violently to avoid hitting a child. Yet the negligence is the same
in both cases, and the driver has no control over whether a child
will run into his path" (p. 61).

This similarity makes evaluating moral luck cases so challenging. We feel bad for Ricky, just as we feel bad for Lester when he
gets shelled. However, if we're to remain honest with ourselves, we
must not blame the situation instead of the person. In the beginning of this chapter, I wrote that a curse isn't a particularly satisfying target for blame, and neither is a set of circumstances. As we
have seen, if we give too much weight to external influences,
there'll be nothing for which we can praise or blame anyone.
Moving on, if we consider how Lester and Ricky evaluate their own
situations, we'll have another reason why the person who performs
the action is the appropriate target of blame: considerations of
"agent-regret."

Agent-Regret: Feeling for Ricky and Lester

Williams defines agent-regret, writing: "In this general sense of
regret, what are regretted are states of affairs, and they can be
regretted, in principle, by anyone who knows of them. But there
is a particularly important species of regret, which I shall call
'agent-regret,' which a person can feel only towards his past
actions" (p. 27). Agent-regret is a type of regret that can only be
applied to the person who performs the action, or the "agent." We
may regret that Babe Ruth was traded to the Yankees on
December 26th, 1919, but only Harry Frazee can feel the "agent-
regret" that Williams discusses. It wasn't an accident that Frazee
sold Ruth, so one might object to applying agent-regret to the
cases of Ricky and Jon Lester. However, as Williams notes, ". . .
even at deeply accidental or non-voluntary levels of agency, sentiments of agent-regret are different from regret in general, such as
might be felt by a spectator, and are acknowledged in our practice
as being different" (p.28).

The fans, other players, and the manager don't blame themselves for Lester's mistake; nor does Cal blame himself for Ricky's mistake. Only if Cal or Francona thought he could've (and should've) done something to affect Ricky or Lester would this type of regret even make sense, and in this sense it's the regret of an agent, of a person who performed an action. The very fact that we feel for Lester and Ricky illustrates that there's something special about them and their relation to what has happened. As Williams writes in discussing his case of the driver, "We feel sorry for the driver, but that sentiment co-exists with, indeed presupposes, that there is something special about his relation to this happening" (p. 28). Ricky and Lester performed the actions. Ricky neglected his brakes and ran over the child. Jon Lester failed to prepare for the game and gave up five home runs in the first inning. They didn't want to do those things, but they did.

However, even understanding this, we still have the most challenging problem of moral luck lingering: Can we hold a person responsible for external circumstances? It feels wrong to blame Ricky for killing the child because if the child hadn't stepped into the street at exactly that moment, he wouldn't have killed her. Holding Ricky responsible for the child's death seems to amount to "holding [him] responsible for the contributions of fate as well as for [his] own— provided [he has] made some contribution to begin with" (Nagel, p. 63). If Ricky failed to check his brakes, but no child jumped out, then we wouldn't blame him for killing a child. Why? Because he didn't kill a child. We can't blame Ricky for something that never happened. Still, Ricky performs the same action in both instances.

Reasonable Expectations: Come On! You Should've Had That!

By using the phrase "reasonable expectation," I intend to focus our attention on certain standards, which we generally seem to apply to persons in certain circumstances. Consider the aforementioned cases of Jon Lester and Ricky the Truck Driver. Both failed to perform an action which resulted in more serious consequences and the notion of reasonable expectation may help explain if it is or is not appropriate to blame them.

If Lester was reading through the Yankees Tendency Sheet, but the copy he was handed had no back page because someone, mistakenly, hadn't copied it for him, we might not hold Lester responsible for not knowing how to pitch to the first five Yankees batters. Further, if he had reason to believe that those five sluggers would-n't be playing in the upcoming game, say, for example, he heard from someone that they were nursing injuries and saving strength for later in the season, he might not expect their names to be on the sheet. In this version of the case, we might not reasonably expect Lester to know how to pitch to those five batters if they show up to the stadium. This version of the Lester case seems very different from a version where Francona hands Lester a good copy of the sheet and instructs him to pay special attention to Matsui, Posada, Rodriguez, Swisher, and Teixeira, saying, "All five are hit-ting quite well and you'll have to select your pitches carefully to get past them." In this version, we should reasonably expect Lester to know how to pitch to these batters.

These two versions are at either end of the spectrum of rea-sonable expectation. Many cases of moral luck will fall in between. Consider versions of the case where Lester is given a good copy of the sheet, but no special mention is made of the five batters, or a similar version except for the fact that he hears a rumor about those five batters not playing. How are we to deal with these cases? The notion of reasonable expectation should help us, but we'll have to rely on our opinions about what's reasonable in order to under-stand what's reasonable for us to expect. Though some of us may disagree on what counts as reasonably expectable, there'll be par-adigmatic cases that we agree on and consideration of reasonable expectation should help clarify why we disagree on less clear cases.

The actions of others is one consideration, which may serve as a barometer for reasonable expectation. For example, if every other pitcher on the Red Sox staff would've been ready to pitch to those batters in Lester's position, this suggests that preparation for them is something, which is reasonable to expect. On the flip side, if we polled a large number of people unfamiliar with baseball and they all said they would've done what Lester did, this wouldn't inform us about our reasonable expectation of Lester and what it should be. Reasonable expectation allows us to take into account the spe-cific details of a situation. Lester is a professional and experienced pitcher. It wouldn't be right to compare Lester to any person, just as it wouldn't be right to compare Ricky to someone who wasn't familiar with trucks and their brakes. What we can expect others to do in similar situations isn't always an accurate predictor of whether something is reasonably expectable, but it can serve as a loose guide for what we can reasonably expect.

If we consider again the case of Ricky, we may be able to understand it better given our new insight into reasonable expectation. It seems reasonable to expect that if a truck driver doesn't check his brakes, his brakes will wear down, and he'll be unable to stop quickly if he needs too. It's also reasonable to expect that a professional truck driver would be aware of this. Therefore, we should blame Ricky because it's reasonable to expect him to check the brakes and to know that he would endanger the lives of others by driving with worn brakes. If Cal had cut the brake lines, we wouldn't reasonably expect Ricky to have anticipated this, so here we should blame Cal and not Ricky.

Billy Buck and Moral Luck

Having reflected on the concept of moral luck, what can we say about Bill Buckner's error? Putting aside the issue of whether this type of action can appropriately be called moral, Bill Buckner's error is indeed a case of moral luck. If Buckner performs the same actions and the ball isn't hit to him or takes a funny bounce into his glove, instead of through his legs, the Red Sox do not lose Game Six. Recall that it's characteristic of moral luck cases that the action performed originally elicits different evaluations due to the disproportionality of consequences and the action performed. In the Bill Buckner case, the action performed is Buckner failing to get his glove down, and thus failing to field the ground ball. The disproportionate results are that the Red Sox lose Game Six and go on to lose the World Series. If we attempt to evaluate Buckner's error in isolation from the circumstances, it doesn't seem like a very big deal. This is a mistake that many major league players have made over the years. However, given that this occurred in extra innings of a World Series game, it was a huge deal.

Should we blame Buckner for the error? For the error and its consequences? For neither? Let's focus on three features from our reflection on moral luck in evaluating Buckner's case: the role negligence plays (from Nagel), the notion of agent-regret (from Williams), and the notion of reasonable expectation.

From our consideration of agent-regret, I think it's clear that this applies just as well in the actual case of Bill Buckner's error as it does in the fictional cases of Ricky the Truck Driver and Jon Lester.

Though many people regret what happened, only Bill Buckner can feel agent-regret. He's the person who failed to get his glove down and catch the ball. Bob Stanley may feel as though he could've thrown a different pitch, a pitch which would've yielded an easier ground ball or, even better, a third strike. Stanley contributed to the play, but he didn't make the error. To get a ground ball to the first baseman is probably the next best thing to a strike out. Considerations of agent-regret support holding Buckner accountable for the error.

Second, recall our above reflection on negligence. Nagel correctly points out that the minor negligence involved in the driver not checking his brakes is the only thing that he blames himself for unless his negligence contributes to the death of the child. Buckner is negligent and doesn't get his glove down. If the Red Sox are up by ten runs in the game and they go on to win the game and the World Series in the next inning, Buckner only blames himself for the negligence of not getting down for the ground ball. If the stakes are much lower and this is a regular season game without any serious playoff implications, Buckner would blame himself for the negligence and for losing the game (since his negligence contributed directly to this); however, the ramifications wouldn't be as serious. In light of these other cases, it seems appropriate to blame Buckner for the error, which cost the Red Sox the game in the actual case.

Finally, consider our above reflection on reasonable expectation. Though this type of consideration less readily gives us concrete answers because it relies on our opinions about a situation, I believe it's the key to evaluating cases of moral luck correctly. Is it reasonable to expect Bill Buckner to cleanly field the ground ball in question? The answer is yes. It must be taken into account that the play was ruled an error by the official scorer. Official scorers can make mistakes and there are plays, which could be ruled either way. Suppose a hard line drive is hit toward Dustin Pedroia, who does all he can to knock it down, but double clutches on the throw to get a better grip on the ball. The runner steps on first just before Kevin Youkilis catches the ball. Is this an error because of the hesitation or a hit? This depends on whether it's reasonable to expect Pedroia to have made that play. I doubt official scorers explicitly use the notion of reasonable expectation when ruling on plays, but it isn't hard to believe that an implicit understanding of it works in the background.

In questionable cases, the ruling may not have much weight. However, Buckner's error is not one of those cases. The ball hit to Buckner should've been fielded. The official scorer reasonably expected Buckner to field the ball and ruled it an error because he let it go through his legs. Also, I think we're tempted, as we are in cases of moral luck to blame the circumstances (or a curse) and not Buckner because we feel bad for the situation he was in. Two reasons often cited to excuse Buckner are: a. Red Sox manager Jerry McNamara often replaced Buckner late in games with a stronger defensive player, and b. Buckner, though a seasoned veteran and All-Star, had bad knees. Are these good enough excuses?

No. I believe that to use these excuses is to make the mistake Nagel warns us about and focus too much on control and external influences. McNamara may have wanted to keep Buckner on the field for the seemingly assured Red Sox victory. Buckner's bad knees may have made it harder for him to get his glove down and field the ball. However, to blame the circumstances and not the person is a mistake. We can reasonably expect a seasoned veteran, such as Bill Buckner, to know how to field such a ball and to make the play. If Buckner was unable to do this he could have asked McNamara for a substitute. By playing in that inning he assumes the responsibilities of one who can make certain plays, and it's therefore reasonable to expect him to make that play. If a screaming line drive had been hit just past Buckner's outstretched arm, this might not be the case. Some might say things like, "If he had only gotten a better jump on the ball" or "If Dave Stapleton was playing, he might have made that play," but that would be an entirely different situation. A screaming line drive down the first base line might not be a play that we reasonably expect many first basemen to make. If it's a play, which some spectacular defensive first baseman could make, we still might not hold Buckner accountable for failing to make such a play. The level of reasonable expectation shouldn't be too high, but the expectation of a veteran to make a play on a routine ground ball isn't very high at all.

If Only . . .

Considerations of moral luck and reasonable expectation favor blaming Bill Buckner for the error. Though the case isn't as strong, they also favor blaming him for the loss of Game Six. If Buckner had made that play, a play which he can be reasonably expected to make, then Ray Knight doesn't score and the Mets are down 3–2 in the Series, going into the 11th inning with Rice, Evans, and Gedman coming to bat. To look at Buckner's circumstances and fail to blame him is to put too much emphasis on those external circumstances. It's inappropriate to blame someone else for the loss of the game, such as Stanley for not striking out Wilson or for not throwing a pitch which resulted in a routine ground ball to another player, or Stanley and Rich Gedman for the wild pitch that allowed Kevin Mitchell to score from third. It can be done, but the cases that can be made are not as strong. Anyone who makes a case that someone other than Buckner should be blamed for the Game Six loss must contend with a challenging piece of evidence: the game was not lost until Buckner committed the error.

Though it's appropriate to hold Buckner accountable for the Red Sox loss in Game Six of the 1986 World Series, he surely did not deserve the ridicule and vilification he has received throughout the years. Reflection on situations where consequences of an action are outside someone's control have shown us the challenge of these types of situations and recommend empathy. We can empathize with Buckner, just as we can with many people in cases of moral luck, coming up with numerous "If only . . ." lines. We can see ourselves making minor mistakes, which lead to grave consequences. But it would be a mistake to blame anyone else for the loss of Game Six and an even worse mistake to blame someone else for his error.

As for blaming Buckner for the loss of the World Series, this is going too far. As many people have noted, there was another game played. What's more important, even if Buckner had made the play and sent the game into the 11th inning, there's no guarantee that the Red Sox would have won Game Six. Avoiding a loss isn't the same thing as ensuring a win.[3]

[3] I would like to thank Ana Pilkington, Bryan G. Pilkington, and Thomas Mulherin for comments on earlier drafts, and Ed Sewell, Mark Sewell, and Marty Scwell for helping me understand the rich history of the Red Sox. I would especially like to thank Jennifer Sewell for her many comments and corrections to earlier drafts.

6

Blursed!

ERIN E. FLYNN

Sometime after September 2001, I noticed an increase in the use of extraordinary, even supernatural "explanations" of sporting events. Since the awful events of September 11th exposed us to brutal forces of history and to the fragility and the contingency of our national life, perhaps we were encouraged to seek out explanations that exceeded the ordinary and the natural. Such explanations might help to convince us that our suffering (the serious, devastating suffering of war and the much less serious but still real disappointments of sport) has meaning over and above the exposure to the brute contingent facts that cause them. Whatever the reason, I noticed an increased use of such explanations. I began hearing a lot more about baseball curses.

Curses: An Introduction

Naturally I had heard of the Curse of the Bambino, though usually invoked as a way of heaping ridicule on Harry Frazee, the Red Sox owner who sold Babe Ruth to the Yankees to bankroll his Broadway productions. But suddenly people seemed to be asking the question in earnest! Do you think the Red Sox are cursed? I soon learned about other curses. I was startled to find that a fair number of people seemed to think that curses *explained* the failures of the Red Sox and the Chicago Cubs, to name the two most famous cases.

How are we to understand and assess this appeal to curses? It's important to note that for a curse to explain these failures, it must be more than just the sum of all the ordinary, mundane things that cause events on a baseball field to unfold as they do. For if people meant "curse" in that sense, then all they meant was that these mundane things had in one way or another gone against us for all those years. There would've been nothing remarkable or enlightening about that claim. It would have been all too obvious.

By "curse," then, we must mean something over and above these ordinary, mundane causes, perhaps something that directs or alters them, ensuring that they produce a particular result. For example, the curse might somehow have ensured that in 1949 Jerry Coleman's flare would fall just out of the reach of Al Zarilla's glove, or that in 1967 Bob Gibson would grow from a mere Hall of Fame pitcher to an unbeatable epic hero, or that in 1975 Carlton Fisk's fly ball would stay fair so that our hopes might be lifted before the Big Red Machine demolished them, or that in 1986 (I leave it to the reader to insert whatever ridiculously improbable event here), or that in 2003 Grady Little would err on the side of loyalty to disastrous effect.

But is there any sense in saying that a curse explained the Red Sox failures? Could we locate such an operating force over and above the many ordinary causes that culminated in year after heartbreaking year? Or might purposes other than explanation nevertheless justify the description of the Red Sox as in fact cursed?

Two Arguments for the Curse Go Down Swinging

Many of us, I think, would hit our heads incredulously whenever we heard people claim that the Red Sox were cursed. The arguments for the accursedness of the Red Sox always tended to be so bad, and often were exemplary fallacies. For instance, defenders often committed what philosophers call the *post hoc ergo propter hoc* fallacy. Like lawyers, philosophers have long been in the habit of naming things in Latin. In this case the meaning is "after that, therefore because of that." Since so much Red Sox losing (and really bad, heartbreaking losing, alongside so much Yankees winning) came *after* the Red Sox sold the Babe (or after Ruth allegedly uttered the curse, or after whatever other event is said to have occurred), all that losing happened *because* the Red Sox sold him.

Though this argument isn't strong, it is interesting. Why is it supposed to prove that the Red Sox were *cursed?* Presumably because the selling of the Babe had an *unnatural* impact on the fortunes of the Red Sox. There would be nothing miraculous about the selling of the Babe explaining why the Red Sox lost in 1920. Invoking a curse then would've been pointless. Perhaps, given the Babe's stature, there would be nothing miraculous about his sale explaining why the Red Sox lost throughout the '20s. But the sale would eventually be too causally distant to account in any ordinary way for the Red Sox losing. This is what gives the argument the appearance of strength. Eventually it seems clear that *if* the sale of the Babe had enough impact to explain the Red Sox losing in 1946, 1967, 1975, 1986 (all in the World Series, each time in seven games), not to mention 1949 and 2003 (in two particularly galling denials of the American League pennant at the hands of the Yankees), *then* that impact must be of an unnatural or extraordinary kind: a curse.

Of course, putting the matter this way highlights exactly what the argument lacks: any evidence that the sale *is* still having an impact on the fate of the Red Sox. The losing is *post hoc*; it happened after the sale. But this doesn't establish that it happened *propter hoc*, because of the sale. Put simply, the argument swings and misses.

Had you explained this to someone who believes in the curse, you may have heard the following comeback. But *you* can't explain why the Red Sox have lost for so long (and so heartbreakingly, and so often to those vile Yankees). You can't show that they're *not* cursed. They must be cursed! There's no other explanation! This argument commits what philosophers call a fallacious *appeal to ignorance*. It says that since we don't know the ordinary causes for the extent of the Red Sox losing, we don't know they *aren't* cursed. So they must be cursed!

As you can probably see, this is a very bad argument. Our failure to show that the curse hypothesis is false isn't evidence in favor of its truth. Even if it's true that there's no natural explanation for the miserable history of the Red Sox (and I think it's true—a complicated history such as that probably has no explanation, properly speaking), this yields *no evidence at all* for a supernatural explanation. It simply shows that we don't know. Once again, a swing and a miss.

I think these two arguments lean on something important, which seems to count as evidence in favor of the curse: that we can't explain certain features of our world by ordinary means. Perhaps appealing to a curse isn't, despite appearances, an attempt to identify a special cause in our world. Perhaps it's also not an attempt to explain an otherwise bewildering feature of our world. Maybe it's just a name for what we can't explain. This would be an agnostic, intellectually respectable use of "curse." But we go too far if we speak as though we understand that there's an unnatural or extraordinary agency causing things to happen in our world, and act as though an appeal to that agency explains some features of our world. That's the point at which many of us will object. To appeal to a curse *explains nothing*; it's rather an invocation that shows up at the *end* of our ability to explain.

So I've never been very impressed by the arguments for the existence of a curse. They seemed usually to boil down to a species (or a hybrid) of the above two argument styles, often lathered with a number of odd coincidences that seem to bolster the *propter hoc* claim, but which in fact beg the central question: that the coincidence is at all causally related to the losing.

I therefore had little patience with the notion that the Red Sox were cursed. I even considered the belief to be a crutch. We suffered as a result of the Red Sox failures. It's not nice to suffer as a result of things you don't understand and can't control. People believed in a curse because they wanted to think they understood the cause of and hence the reason for their suffering. Whether or not they actually understood or explained anything by believing in a curse was beside the point. They could tell themselves they did, and this was a salve.

But these *were* my reactions against the claim that the Red Sox were cursed. Ironically, what started to change my mind was the Red Sox winning it all, and the particular way they won it all. I don't mean that their ultimate triumph was so perfect that it must have been orchestrated. I sincerely hope it wasn't at all orchestrated by anything or anyone. Nor do I point to odd coincidences that seem to indicate the lifting of a curse. I mean something else.

The Curious Case of "Grue"

To see why I started to change my mind, travel with me back in time to October 2003, back to Game Seven of the ALCS, which has just ended in yet another Yankees victory over the Red Sox. Suppose, after Aaron F***ing Boone hit the Wakefield knuckler out to left, you turn to me and say:

"That settles it; they're cursed."

"You think so?" I ask numbly.

"I do," you reply. "A curse is the only plausible explanation for what we just saw, for what we've been seeing since 1920."

Now if I can overcome my sad exhaustion and engage in the argument, I should reply that a curse is no explanation at all. If you mean to describe the Red Sox or explain their failure, I should say, it's not even clear that the statement "the Red Sox are cursed" is meaningful, much less true. Instead, such a statement expresses our bewilderment, our helplessness, our anguish, and our frustration in the face of yet another impossible defeat. But it most certainly does not explain or describe what just happened. I *should* say that. But I'm in a weird mood. Even though I feel sad and exhausted, I've fallen more deeply in love with that 2003 Red Sox team than with any other. They played reckless and fun baseball, and were the perfect counterpoint to the stiff, joyless Yankees. I cried when Boone hit that home run, but they were tears of exhaustion and even a little joy. The Sox fought harder that series than I'd ever seen them fight. It was the opposite of '86. There was no fold, no tightness, no choke. Maybe there was a bad decision by Grady, but I don't even care about that. Let Pedro face one batter too many? I'll take that bad decision any day of the week. So instead of what I should say, I say instead:

"How do you know they're not blursed?"

"Blursed!?" you blurt out. "What is 'blursed'? 'Blursed' is non-sense!"

This is how it begins.

Before I explain what blursed is, I need to explain another odd word, a famously funny color name. So let's go back another twelve or so hours. Imagine that we're members of the Red Sox grounds crew, sitting around Fenway the afternoon of the day Boone has his fifteen minutes. I ask you:

"What color do you think the blades of Fenway grass are?"

"What color?" you reply. "You nuts? They're green."

"Yeah," I say, "but *all* of them?"

This gives you pause. "*All* of them?"

"Sure," I say. "Is there a law or something that all blades of Fenway grass are green, just like all emeralds are green?"

So you go out in front of the Monster, where Manny, and Jim Rice, and Yaz, and the Kid used to play. You comb left field. And wouldn't you know it? Not a *single* non-green blade of Fenway grass! So you conclude: yes, *all* of them.

Then I ask something a little weird. Like I said, I'm in a weird mood.

"How do you know that all Fenway grass is green? How do you know it's not grue?"

"Grue!?" you shout at me. "What the hell is 'grue'? Grue is not a color, my friend."

So I explain. "Grue" is a color-name invented by the American philosopher Nelson Goodman. An object is grue, Goodman tells us, if and only if it is observed before a particular time (say October 17th, 2004) and is green, or is not observed before that time and is blue.

"That is so stupid!" you say. "What is green if we observe it before October 17th, 2004, but blue if we don't?"

"Anything that's grue," I reply.

"But I observed all those blades of grass," you say.

"Before October 17th, 2004, and they're green," I say.

"But *all* the blades are green," you insist.

"All the blades *you've inspected* are green," I remind you.

"So what, are they going to change color? What's so special about October 17th, 2004?"

"I don't know," I say. "Maybe something amazing and totally unexpected will happen then. And anyway, lots of things change color."

"But," you say, getting a little tired of this now, "why do you think this grass will?"

"I don't," I say. "But why do you think it will stay the same? And anyway, I'm not telling you it *will* change color. I'm just telling you what makes an object grue. If the Fenway blades you have not observed prior to October 17th, 2004 are blue rather than green, then Fenway grass is actually grue, not green."

"And what about after October 17th, 2004? What color do they have to be then?"

"Well, if you observed them before that date, which we'll call *The Steal*, then I assume they'll be green. But if you did not observe them before *The Steal*, then they'll be blue."

"Wait. Why do you want to call that date *The Steal?*"

"Because I'm tired of calling it October 17th, 2004."

"Well, what if they start to grow right after *The Steal?*" you ask.

"Blue," I say.

"But that's crazy!" you protest. "From where we are now, we can't tell whether the Fenway grass is grue or green!"

"That's just the point," I say.

We're now closing in on the lesson of "grue." Grue categorizes objects in an admittedly weird way, a way relative to our observations and to a specific point in time. Some objects (namely those that were observed before *The Steal*) that remain green will count as grue. Other objects (namely those that were not observed before *The Steal*) that remain blue will also count as grue. Finally, some objects that change color at *The Steal* may also count as grue.

Now I agree that it makes little sense to suggest that the grass is grue. I'm not sure it makes any sense to call anything grue! Yet there is a meaningful difference between the statements "all blades are green" and "all blades are grue," since in one case all blades not examined before *The Steal* will be predicted to be green and in the other case they will be predicted to be blue. But the trouble is this. *All* the evidence you used to declare that the blades of Fenway grass are green works *just as well* for the claim that all the blades of Fenway grass are grue. No matter how many blades of grass we observe, there can never be more evidence for the generalization you draw than for the generalization I draw! How can that be?

This is Goodman's "new riddle" of induction. We make generalizations about things (like describing grass as green, or Red Sox fans as bitter and pessimistic) based on a finite number of observations. But no matter how much evidence we pile up, the evidence itself (all those green blades, all those pessimistic fans) can't tell us whether the general description we give (*Fenway grass* is green, as opposed to *this* blade is green *now* and this *other* blade is also green now) is really the right description (Fenway grass is *green*, as opposed to Fenway grass is *grue*). So the evidence *itself* does not show us that "Fenway grass is green" is a more accurate description than "Fenway grass is grue." And yet it is deadly obvious that "Fenway grass is green" *is* a better description than "Fenway grass is grue." Goodman's riddle is why? If it's not the evidence (the number of cases) that shows this, then what does?

There have been many attempted answers to this question, but a lot of philosophers think that part of the answer must be that the evidence the world presents to us doesn't dictate what descriptions (or theories) we use to describe the world. In other words, the evidence *underdetermines* our descriptions (or theories) of the world. We deal with underdetermination all the time. For instance, no matter how much evidence Theo Epstein compiles on a given free agent, from statistics to the testimony of his experienced scouts, there will remain some guesswork in his prediction that the player will improve the team. That's why our arguments at the bar about whether the signing was a good idea can go on and on, encouraging us to buy more drinks, making the bartender happy, as long as we're not too obnoxious about it. The problem isn't that "it's all subjective." The problem is that the evidence, which may be perfectly objective, isn't enough logically to determine a particular judgment, even if the GM has *all* the available evidence.

What's radical about Goodman's riddle is that it seems to show that the evidence isn't enough even in apparently obvious and objective cases like "Fenway grass is green," as opposed to "Fenway grass is grue." So what makes these cases seem obvious, if not the evidence itself? Goodman concludes that some descriptions are better than others because they are deeply entrenched, because they have long served certain practical or theoretical purposes. This ultimately led Goodman to think that there's little sense in trying to achieve a neutral description of *the* world. The very idea depends on the world giving us enough evidence to determine the proper description of it. But the lesson of grue is that even in our most basic generalizations about the world, factors other than the evidence must influence what counts as a *proper* description. Because those factors can be as varied as our practical and theoretical aims, Goodman advised that we speak of there being multiple worlds that we make according to our various systems of description.

The Curiouser Case of "Blursed"

Now if we apply Goodman's lessons directly to the case of the Red Sox and their "curse," what should we conclude? We might say that my earlier dismissals were far too hasty. If the evidence underdetermines what terms and theories we use to describe the world, then maybe I was wrong to complain that the evidence could not confirm the curse. Maybe there are some other practical purposes to which the description "cursed" might well be put. Maybe. But let's not rush to that conclusion. After all, there are good reasons for choosing "green" over "grue," even if the evidence, *strictly speaking*, is not among them. Furthermore, both "Fenway grass is green" and "Fenway grass is grue" are at least supported by evidence. It's not at all clear that "the Red Sox are cursed" was ever supported by any evidence. And even if there were purposes to which "the Red Sox are cursed" might have been put, I don't think *explanation* is one of them. As I said above, this statement expressed a lot of things, but I doubt it identified a cause or an explanation. I don't think, for instance, there were many good explanatory reasons for choosing "cursed" over "poorly managed" or "unlucky" or just "not cursed."

But this isn't the way I want to apply Goodman's lessons to the case of the Red Sox. Instead, I want to turn Goodman's riddle around. I want to say that "cursed" was never the best description of the Red Sox not because the evidence didn't support it, but because there was a better description, a description that ends up looking weirdly like "grue." This startling fact opened my eyes to *both* the value of calling the Red Sox cursed *and* the wrongness of calling them cursed! I hereby maintain that the Red Sox are and always have been *blursed*.

A team is blursed if and only if it's observed before *The Steal* and is cursed *and* it's observed after *The Steal* and is blessed. A team isn't blursed if it's cursed *and then* blessed. When I say that the object observed after *The Steal* is blessed, I mean not that a curse has lifted or that a blessing has been given, but that the object is recognized as having been blessed all along *even though* and indeed *because* it had been cursed.

Recall that we're arguing about whether "the Red Sox are cursed" is the best explanation for the travails of the Sox from roughly 1920 to October 2003, just after Wakefield's knuckleball happened to run into Boone's bat. I have asked why you think the evidence in October 2003 favors the inference that the Sox are cursed over the inference that they are blursed. You are annoyed by my nonsense. But I persist. I think the evidence in 2003 no more favors the conclusion that the Sox are cursed than that they are blursed. I am willing, for the sake of argument, to accept that "the Red Sox are cursed" is a possible explanation, of some sort, of the Red Sox woes. My objection, in a nutshell, is that if the same evidence gets you to the conclusion that the Red Sox are blursed, then you should stop insisting that they are cursed.

Now I assume that if in 2003 you were susceptible to the suggestion that the Red Sox were cursed you wouldn't have been impressed by my invocation of a blursed Sox. Indeed, you may even have argued that, while the evidence alone doesn't entail cursed over blursed, other factors rule cursed in while ruling blursed out as a relevant kind in our system of descriptions.

But what other factors are those? Does a curse have more explanatory power than a blurse? Neither seems to have any explanatory power in the sense of identifying a relevant *cause* of the Red Sox woes, at least not a cause that we can investigate by any ordinary means. Does it allow us to predict or control the fate of the Red Sox any better? It doesn't seem to offer us any control at all. It also doesn't seem to offer us any predictive power, since we don't know how the curse operates or when it might be lifted.

What about the expressive factors I mentioned above? Does calling the Sox "cursed" express our bewilderment, helplessness, anguish, and frustration in the face of a world impervious to what we care about? Yes, I think it does. But is that all we want a description to express? What about our hope, our resilience, our joy, our enthusiasm? "The Red Sox are cursed" does a very poor job of expressing these. Instead it forces us to explain such virtues as deficiencies of some sort, as irrational responses to a world set to deny us.

So it's not clear to me that the factors in favor of "cursed" as a relevant kind really would have outweighed the factors in favor of "blursed." Even back then "cursed" would've had no greater explanatory or predictive power, and only a limited expressive power. More importantly, it turned out the Red Sox *were* blursed rather than cursed. *The very observed properties* that had apparently made the Red Sox cursed prior to *The Steal* are now properties that make the Red Sox blessed. Indeed, to be more precise, the curse proved to be a blessing after *The Steal*.

The Sox Were Always Blursed, Just Ask Jim Rice

The first thing to bear in mind about a blurse is that the occurrence of *The Steal* doesn't lift a curse, nor is it the result of a curse having been lifted. In the case of the Sox, this means that the victory in 2004 only is what it is because of what had been called the curse, namely the extended suffering of Red Sox Nation.

If you're a Red Sox fan of a certain age, you have a personal story of that suffering. My story centers on 1986, the summer I turned fifteen and was most susceptible to depression by sport. That the Red Sox might compete for a World Series was in that summer unbelievable to me. I had no memory of the '75 Series and only a dim sense of what Bucky F***ing Dent's cheating home run meant. In the years I had been a Sox fan, they had been decent but never a serious contender. Suddenly they were playing for a pennant. The way they beat the Angels, after falling behind 3–1, fueled by a furious Game Five comeback that included home runs in the ninth by Don Baylor and Dave Henderson, defied explanation. I was on Cloud Nine.

And then came the Mets. The Mets, you will recall, were a juggernaut. They'd won 108 games. They were loaded and seemed on the verge of dynasty. The Red Sox had no chance. Yet there I was, alone in my basement, watching the 10th inning of Game Six in utter disbelief. Henderson had just homered *again*? An insurance run in the form of Wade Boggs driven home by Marty Barrett? This didn't happen. Two batters up in the bottom of the 10th and two outs. A two-run lead with two outs and no one on in the bottom of the 10th? This didn't happen. And as you know, it *didn't* happen. Instead, the (second) most ghastly choke in the history of sport happened. You know the details. Don't forget how much blame there is to go around. A lot fell apart before that last dribbler.

That night defined me as a fan. I was then and there inducted into a legion of suffering and obsession. Had the Red Sox won in '86, I might have stopped caring so much. Do any of us really think that the Yankees fans who were in their early teens from '96 to '00 can ever get too down about the Yankees? Their life as fans has been defined by the blithe expectation that the Yankees will soon rise again to assume the mantle of dominance.

This gets me to my point about blursed. If the victory in 2004 was simply the lifting of a curse, then we should say that we would trade it for a victory in '86. After all, that's eighteen fewer years of curse. But the thing is, you wouldn't trade it. I wouldn't trade it for all five of the Yankees' recent Series wins. I wouldn't trade it for all twenty-seven of their wins, for that matter. The reason is that we experienced something that no Yankees fan will ever experience.

We experienced a bliss that can only be born of impossible disappointment. The Yankees' collapse in 2004 makes the Red Sox choke in '86 look like an honest mistake. Every single event that allegedly showed the Sox to be cursed took on an utterly new light in 2004. The curse turned out to be a blessing, a necessary condition of the impossible joy that dawned with Roberts's steal of second, overwhelmed us in the rout in Game Seven and culminated in the sweep of the Cardinals in the World Series.

This is why I say the Red Sox curse was not lifted. They turned out never to have been cursed. But neither should we simply say that they were always blessed. Only the most blindly faithful fan would call the '86 team blessed. And anyway, if you call that team blessed, then you miss the whole point of what I'm calling the blessing of the team in 2004, which is that the "curse" really was reversed, in the sense of redeemed, shown to be something that previously it could not have been.

Without 1986, no 2004. I don't mean that a different series of events would have unfolded had the Red Sox closed out the Mets in '86. That might be true, but it's uninteresting. I mean that even if the Sox had fallen behind the Yankees 0–3 and had still come back to win in that improbable way, the 2004 comeback would not have been the same event. For one thing, it wouldn't have been the Red Sox, guilty of the most notorious choke in World Series history, who came back on the Yankees. It would have been some other Red Sox. It's an odd thing about historical events and figures. They can never be defined in isolation from other historical events and figures.

The event of 2004 couldn't have been what it was without reference to these other events. The team responsible for the worst championship collapse pulled off the greatest comeback in the history of sports playoffs. What afflicted those Red Sox teams contributed to the comeback, but not in the sense of fueling or hindering it. It's doubtful that the affliction exerted any sort of causal influence at all. It didn't slow Dave Roberts down nor did it speed him up. It contributed to the comeback by helping to make the comeback the event that it was, not by helping to ensure that the comeback itself happened.

Hence no team could've done precisely what the Red Sox did in 2004. We experienced something that no other fans could've experienced. The event was sweet in a way and to a degree that no Yankees championship could've been sweet. When the White

Sox, who'd been without a World Series championship for *longer* than the Red Sox, won the following year, no one suggested that they did what the Red Sox did. Nor should anyone argue that a Cubs victory in the near future would duplicate the feat. One reason for this is that neither the White Sox nor the Cubs have the history of near misses and devastating failures the Red Sox have. And neither has a nemesis like the Yankees, by far the most successful franchise in baseball, at whose hands the Red Sox suffered so much.

Some may nevertheless want to say that the Red Sox weren't cursed, blessed, or blursed. What I have been describing as a blursing they will say is better described just in terms of the suffering and elation of the fans. There's no need to talk either of blessings or curses. The only misgiving I have about this resistance stems from the fact that, as I've said, in 2004 I became thankful for 1986, something I wouldn't have thought possible. And for the first time I appreciated the value of calling the Red Sox cursed—not because it explained the losses, or even because it expressed my earlier frustrations, but rather because it heightened my pleasure. The suffering itself took on an entirely new significance. It suddenly had a purpose for me, a gift that made possible the singular bliss we felt as the Yankees crumbled and the Red Sox ascended. What else, after all, could a blessing be?

The End of a Curse

My case is, I admit, largely aesthetic. The world is more beautiful and pleasurable with a blursed Red Sox in it. (At least for everyone except Yankees fans.) My point about the Red Sox and their blurse is that in one sense our talk about curses was always a dicey affair. When the very property you think you have evidence for (in this case accursedness) turns out to be something like its opposite, you should doubt whether your description had any evidence going for it in the first place. Yet if we accept Goodman's lesson, support by the evidence is not, and in fact cannot be, the only criterion according to which we describe our world. "Blursed" helps us see that people were always barking up the wrong tree when they searched for evidence that the Red Sox were in fact cursed.

We are also better off denying the idea that a curse names a force behind the failures of our teams, and certainly better off letting go of the notion that naming the curse adds to our control over our fate or our team's fate. In other words, we shouldn't treat such descriptions as *explanations* of the failures of the Red Sox, since again the abblursedness of the Red Sox reverses that explanation. And we should definitely not use them as aids in *predicting* what will happen to our ballclubs. But this is primarily because of the pragmatic limits of using these descriptions in these ways. They won't work for those purposes.

You may take this as the negative objective of this essay: to dissuade us from calling teams cursed, on the grounds that they might just as well be blursed. But my second, positive objective has been to suggest that "blursed" in fact renders the Red Sox more rightly than "cursed." This forces me to the paradoxical conclusion that "blursed" helps us locate the value of calling teams cursed (since an appeal to accursedness is part of the appeal to abblursedness), even though we usually misplace that value. I have argued for an aesthetic rightness to that description, in the sense of rendering the world in a way that accents its beauty and its pleasure by sensitizing us to its pains.

The odd description "blursed" makes this pretty clear. Once defined, it obviously does not explain *why* the Red Sox lost in 1986. It also clearly provides no means for predicting when the Red Sox would win, since you have no way in advance for accurately fixing the time of *The Steal*. But a blursed object, at least in the domain of sport, does reveal something about the beauty of the object and the pleasures it might bring, at least to some of us. And the property isn't for that reason unreal. This abblursedness is part of what the Red Sox are. No one writing their history could write it well without taking into account their abblursedness, even if the author didn't call it by that name.

To sum up, I think it's wrong to say that the Red Sox were cursed. But the wrongness doesn't flow from the fact that it's *false* that they were cursed. The falsity of "the Red Sox were cursed" is beside the point. It's wrong because to call them cursed doesn't render them rightly. It's to fixate on frustrations and disappointments and coincidences that only tell part of the story. To call them cursed was in many respects always an empirically irresponsible thing to do. But worse still, it was an aesthetically irresponsible thing to do. For in the end, saying that the Bambino cursed the Red Sox got the Red Sox *wrong*.

7

Tragedy and Fisk

JAMES F. PONTUSO

When a colleague of mine discovered that I was headed to spring training over break, he asked me to bring back a Red Sox cap for his son. The boy had become a Wade Boggs fan in those days when the Sox third baseman hardly ever seemed to make an out. "Sure," I said, "but if he becomes a Sox fan, you are condemning the youngster to a life of tragedy."

Although my colleague looked at me a bit askance, I didn't mean to suggest that the young man would disappoint his parents or face horrible obstacles and ultimately fail (in fact, he's been a success doing socially important work). Rather, I meant that as a Red Sox fan, he would comprehend tragedy not just as a literary genre, but as an experience of existence.

Martin Heidegger and the "Thrownness" of Contemporary Life

It was the loss of the modern world's relationship to tragedy that inspired the greatest—or at least the most written-about—philosopher of the twentieth century: Martin Heidegger. Heidegger maintains that the development of science and technology makes it possible to understand, manipulate, organize, and master the material world. We have turned the planet into what he calls "standing reserve," ready to be bent to our will whenever the need arises and a new technology is conceived to satisfy that yearning. The extraordinary success of the scientific-technological project creates the impression that humans are fully capable of conquering chance and of becoming the lords of Being, or existence. Heidegger scholars distinguish Being (capital B) from the beings, or the things of the world. Being is prior to the beings or things, for no-thing can exist without first Being. But, Heidegger warned, no matter how much we master the material world to gratify our desires, we cannot fully solve the mystery of existence. There will always be part of life beyond our control: bad luck, old age, the loss of loved ones and, of course, our own ultimate demise, just to mention the most obvious examples of our tragic fate. For Red Sox fans tragedy always seemed to be meted out by teams from New York as they were in the 1978 one-game playoff against the Yankees and in 1986 in the World Series by the Mets.

The conquest of the material world has affected human psychology. According to Heidegger, the very technology that's supposed to make life easier actually becomes our master. What was once a luxury quickly becomes a necessity, as any lost driver without a cell phone or GPS knows. Who can wash their clothes without a washing machine? It's no longer possible to enjoy television when the remote has vanished. We are dependent on technology, and rather than making life easier, technology has made our lives more complicated. It once was respectable to answer a letter several weeks after receiving it, but an email requires a response within a few hours. Why does everyone have to text a picture of Sox games on their cell phones instead of just enjoying the game at Fenway?

My aunt kept box scores of games she listened to on the radio for my father who worked after school. Somehow those box scores taken of games in 1927 between the Yankees and Red Sox capture more about what in Heideggerian terms would be called an "authentic" experience of the Murderers Row Yankees club than do all the latest technological inventions including the Internet and instant replay.

Technological inventions have made us so busy with daily tasks that we have little or no time to wonder about the meaning and purpose of all the things we do. We are mired in what Heidegger calls "everydayness," a cutesy term for never having a moment for ourselves. Of course, people in every age have been caught up in the activities of daily living, but the pace of life has quickened along with the speed and convenience of new inventions.

People in past eras were rooted in their cultural beliefs, committed to family, community, nation, and religion. Their beliefs gave significance to their activities exactly because they accepted them as truths. We live in a more skeptical time. The same principle on which modern science is based—believe only what you can prove—has undermined attachment to God, country and, indeed, any non-physical concept of morality or truth. For us, the ultimate meaning of life is an impenetrable mystery, a mystery that becomes more apparent as we live longer, more prosperous lives. Today, even religiously oriented people understand that faith is a choice and that an alternative truth exists—a mechanical but meaningless existence. An awareness of the possibility of a meaningless existence is the source of our anxiety. As Heidegger puts it, we have lost our home.

Ironically, Heidegger maintains, our anxiety over the loss of meaning drives us even further into the arms of the technology of power. We attempt to master our fate by living longer, more prosperous lives. We seek out new ways to conquer nature in an attempt to control our destiny. To build ever more advanced gadgets we depend on large corporations, government-financed university research faculties, both of which are controlled and administered by bulky bureaucracies. These distant anonymous entities rob more and more of our individual choices. Devices meant to improve our lives instead make us frantic and dependent. Technology quickens the pace of daily living, thrusting us further into the soulless activities of everydayness. Too caught up in tasks to ponder the deeper meaning of life, we deny our vulnerability and mortality and keep our sense of tragedy at bay (now often with the help of prescription drugs). Heidegger claims that "Everything functions, and the functioning drives us further and further to more functioning, and technology tears people away and uproots them from the earth more and more" (*Der Spiegel*, September 23rd, 1966).

Is it possible to recapture the authentic feeling of belonging that people of the past experienced? Heidegger doubts it; we just cannot make it home. The principles that inspired past cultures were relevant only for their time, and that time has passed. Is there any escape from the mindless everydayness and the purposeless angst? Heidegger responded that we should wait for a new revelation of Being, adding cryptically, "Only a god can save us."

So what does Heidegger have to do with the Red Sox? After all, Heidegger was a crusty, America-hating German professor who flirted with becoming a Nazi. Although he introduced the concept of being "thrown," what he meant had less to do with a fastball than with being cast into a meaningless existence. Yet Heidegger's ideas do explain something about the state of Red Sox Nation.

Heidegger's Everydayness and Pinky Higgins Teams

Every Red Sox fan—well, at least baby boomers like me—knows that Red Sox history, like Julius Caesar's Gaul, is divided into three parts. The pre-1967 Sox of our childhood were clubs of staggering mediocrity. They weren't really teams as much as groups of players interested like their role model Ted Williams—one of the greatest hitters who ever lived—primarily in individual achievement. The best thing to be said about manager Pinky Higgins's never-changing line-up was that grade schoolers could learn both the skill of memorization and art of statistics without too much effort. Red Sox fans were rooted in Heidegger-Higgins "everydayness."

What broke the monotony of the 1950s and early 1960s Sox were the team's occasionally colorful players. Jimmy Piersall, who played for the Sox from 1950 until 1958, led the way. He really was crazy, or at least he was portrayed so by Tony Perkins, whose performance as Piersall in the movie *Fear Strikes Out* was eerily similar to his characterization of Norman Bates in Alfred Hitchcock's classic film *Psycho*.

Dick Stuart, "Dr. Strangeglove," hit 75 home runs and drove in 232 runs in the two years (1963–64) he was with the Sox. His 43 errors at first base don't tell the whole story. His lack of fielding acumen was legendary. He had the range of the Pesky Pole (the right field foul pole at Fenway Park). He knew he was liable to blow fielding chances, so he often stood immobile, hoping to avoid the wrath of the official scorekeeper, as the ball flew by him on its way to right field. Stuart was my neighbor. Occasionally he hunted squirrels with a pellet gun in the woods behind our houses. The squirrels seemed thankful that his aim was more like his fielding than his hitting ability.

These oddities barely relieved the tedium of being a Sox fan; they were mere distractions from the everydayness of owner Tom Yawkey's mid-century teams. Of course the Red Sox hadn't always been so bad. Once they were world champions—in the days when Theodore Roosevelt, William Howard Taft, and Woodrow Wilson were president. But by the 1950s, hardly anyone remembered Tris Speaker or Babe Ruth actually wearing red socks. The baby boomers' parents, "the greatest generation," lured their children into the Red Sox Nation with tales of extraordinary players and superb Boston clubs. Ted Williams hit .406 in 1941, the last major leaguer to top .400. The 1942 team finished 93–59 before the players were called off to World War II. When Williams, Dom DiMaggio, Johnny Pesky, and Bobby Doerr returned from military service in 1946, the Sox won 104 and lost only 50. It was Pesky's infamous "hesitation" on a relay throw from the outfield that allowed Enos Slaughter to score the winning run in the St. Louis Cardinals' victory in the '46 World Series.

Although the post–World War II Red Sox did well, attaining a winning percentage of over .600 four times, the club never quite lived up to expectations and fell apart in 1952 when fiery Lou Boudreau became manager and traded away or alienated the core of the team.

We baby boomers heard about great Boston teams, but in our formative years we never saw one. From 1950 to 1966, the Sox finished no higher than third place—in the last seven of those years they were a sub .500 team. Things went from bad to worse just as the Age of Aquarius was about to dawn and define my generation. In the three-year stretch from 1964 to 1966, the club lost 280 games—100 in the particularly dispiriting year of 1965 alone. Fans were so disgruntled that only 1,247 showed up at Fenway Park on September 16, 1965 to watch Dave Morehead pitch a no-hitter. Such lack of interest is astonishing for a franchise that today boasts more than 500 consecutive sell-outs to rabid fans who often outnumber the home-team rooters in ballparks along the East Coast.

I have some personal experience with an empty Fenway Park. Once I attended a day game with my best friend, and we decided to see who could sit in the most seats. I surrendered at 2,500. My wiry and energetic friend kept going, totaling 6,000 different seats. During the whole experiment, he never had to excuse himself or ask another patron to move.

Why the Red Sox Gave Us High Anxiety

Then the Impossible Dream came in 1967. It was a revolutionary event, not quite as globally significant as what the French pulled off in 1789, but of more interest to New Englanders. So profound was the shift in public sentiment during the magical season that even girls my age followed the team, something that had never happened before. Sox fans discovered that the Red Sox could hit in the clutch, make key fielding plays at critical moments and actually work as a team to win decisive games. Carl Yastrzemski won a Triple Crown (hitting .326 with 44 home runs and 121 RBIs), and Jim Lonborg went 22–9. The '67 Sox won the division by one game over Detroit and Minnesota. At the time Sox fans thought that the 1967 season was a new revelation of Being, but it turned out we were naively mistaken. First we needed to be reminded of how tragic life could be.

The World Series was enthralling, tantalizing, and, of course, ultimately disappointing. St. Louis Cardinals pitcher Bob Gibson was invincible. Sox fans had a sensation similar to that of the ancient Trojans as they peered over the walls to witness combat between their soldiers and the god-like Achilles.

What happened during the next generation was a string of astonishing, agonizing, gut-wrenching, and humiliating near-misses, ones that reminded Sox fans of Heidegger's insight—we're thrown into a mysterious existence that we cannot fully control. Many trees have been sacrificed and much ink spilled detailing the dreadful turns suffered by Sox clubs, but few authors have noted that these reversals of fortune have made Red Sox fans more cognizant of an authentic relationship with Being. Other clubs have had their misfortunes, but none came so close, so many times, only to experience tragic loss. Even the hapless Cubs have only flirted with success two or three times before being beaten. But the Red Sox—well, it's hard to count. What follows is a brief excursion into the dark history of the Sox tragic period from which all Boston fans believed there would be—to paraphrase Heidegger's Existentialist follower Jean-Paul Sartre—no exit.

After 1967 Sox teams were good; they usually played better than .500 baseball and finished the season in first or second place seventeen times. The closer they got, the more they tempted their fans to believe. Beantown's team, we let ourselves think, could taste a portion of the success of our bitter rivals, the New York Yankees, with their thirty-nine pennants and twenty-six world championships. But just as we were poised on the precipice of triumph, fate betrayed us. It became embarrassing to be a Sox supporter. The team was the butt of jokes and snide comments about chokes and late season swoons.

In 1972 the Sox lost the pennant to the Detroit Tigers by half a game. They might have won it if Louis Aparicio, who had led the league in stolen bases nine times in his career, had not fallen down—twice—rounding third base on what should have been an inside-the-park home run by Yastrzemski. Aparicio never scored, and the Tigers won the game and the pennant.

The Sox collapsed again in 1974. After leading the Baltimore Orioles by eight games on August 30th, they faded in September and lost the pennant to the Orioles by the same eight games. After the debacle, Leigh Montville of the *Boston Globe* wrote, "The Red Sox Fan, of course, is mostly mad at himself. He finds he was tricked again by those beguiling storm-door and aluminum-siding salesmen from Lansdowne Street" (Dan Shaughnessy, *The Curse of the Bambino*, 2004).

In 1975 the Sox again made it to the World Series, led by a team that fielded Carlton Fisk, Yastrzemski, Dwight Evans, Cecil Cooper, Rick Burleson, and the "Gold Dust Twins," Jim Rice, and 1975 Rookie of the Year and Most Valuable Player Fred Lynn. The Sox had to play in the Series without their powerful rookie, Rice, who missed the entire postseason after Tigers pitcher Vern Ruhle broke his left hand with a pitch during a meaningless game in the last week of the regular season. It was an exciting Series, reviving popular interest in baseball which had suffered from the big shadow of the National Football League. The Series was actually decided on a controversial call when umpire Larry Barnett ruled that Ed Armbrister had not interfered with Fisk when the Boston catcher attempted to field his errant bunt and throw out a runner at second base. Fisk's throw went into center field; the Reds scored and took the victory in Game Three.

Game Six of the Series is considered one of the most exiting sporting events ever played. Every baseball fan has seen the video of Fisk's joyous moment of triumph as he wills his fly ball fair for a walk-off, game-winning home run. But Sox fans who see the replay know that although we won the battle, we lost the war. The baseball gods directed Joe Morgan's lazy single into the outfield and gave the Cincinnati Reds a come-from-behind victory in the seventh and deciding game. Sox fans' expectations soared in spite of the defeat. But even though the young team was loaded with talent, as always, it failed to deliver.

In 1978 the Sox enjoyed a commanding fourteen and a half game lead in July, but then came the inevitable late-season collapse, culminating in the "Boston Massacre," a four-game sweep by the Yankees at Fenway Park. The team rallied in late September, finishing the season with 99 wins and tying the Yankees for the division lead. But, Sox hopes were crushed again in a playoff game when a pop-fly-home-run off former-Yankees pitcher Mike Torrez by the light-hitting Bucky "Bleeping" Dent, as he came to be known around Boston, gave the Yankees the lead and the pennant.

To add insult to injury, in 1980 Red Sox management let one of the most endearing and professional ballplayers in club history, New England native Carlton Fisk, slip through its fingers without getting even a draft pick in return. Fisk went on to play thirteen more seasons for the Chicago White Sox.

By 1986 it was clear that the Red Sox were cursed—although the book actually proclaiming "the curse" did not appear until 1990. The Sox had won the pennant after an improbable victory in the ALCS over the California Angels. Down three games to one, and behind 5-2 in the ninth inning, the Sox pulled ahead with home runs by Don Baylor and Dave Henderson, the last when the team was one strike away from elimination. The Sox easily took two back at Fenway and headed into the World Series with momentum.

Boston beat New York's other team, the Mets, in the first two games at Shea Stadium, then lost two at Fenway. But they took the third game at home and returned to New York confident that their ace, Roger Clemens (that year, 24–4, and winner of both the Cy Young and Most Valuable Player awards) would end Boston's championship drought. He pitched well, but after developing a blister on his pitching hand, he was relieved in the eighth by Calvin Schiraldi, a pitcher with talent but without the psychological make-up of a big-game player. The Mets tied the game to send it into extra innings. But the Sox scored two in the top of the 10th, again on a Henderson clutch home run.

When Schiraldi got the first two batters to fly out, my brother-in-law called from California to celebrate the victory. I reminded him of the existential truth that life can change in a split second and that no Sox victory is secure until the final out. Then, as if on cue, the mystery and misery of Being became apparent again to Sox fans. With two outs in the last of the 10th, and leading the Mets 5–3, the Sox reliever allowed three straight singles bringing the tally to 5–4. Bob Stanley entered the game and promptly threw a wild pitch to tie the score. Mookie Wilson then hit a slow ground ball, which, to the horror of Sox fans, the hobbled Billy Buckner couldn't han-dle. The Mets won that game and—as all Red Sox fans, expressing the fullness of Heideggerian angst, knew in their heart would happen—the seventh game and the Series.

Like many Sox fans, I swore this was the end. I was as fully alienated from my team as Heideggerian existentialists are from life in general. The love-relationship was finally over. From now on, I would root for another team, or perhaps give up watching baseball altogether. Like an addict, I took the pledge to keep away from things that evoked my dependence. But, the high-tech age brought the ignominy of my and other Sox fans' collective frustration back to life in what seemed to be never-ending re-runs of the baseball gliding through Sox first baseman Buckner's legs.

Yet the mania couldn't be tamed. The Sox were too good a team, making the ALCS in 1988 and 1990. Even better—or perhaps worse—in 1998 the Sox traded for one of the most dominant pitchers in baseball history, Pedro Martinez. In seven years with Boston, Martinez won 117 games while only losing 37, a winning percentage of .760. Then in 2001 the Sox bought the services of Manny Ramirez, one of the greatest hitters in the game. With homegrown super-shortstop Nomar Garciaparra, the Bosox again raised our hopes, which, of course, they eventually dashed.

The Sox were good, but finished second to the Yankees during the regular season for eight consecutive years beginning in 1998. They were beaten by the Yanks in the ALCS in 1999 and again in 2003, the latter when manager Grady Little left a tiring Martinez in the game too long. Aaron Boone, a hitter with slightly more pop in his bat than Bucky "Bleeping" Dent, administered the *coup de grace* with an 11th-inning home run.

The Yankees defeated us again. They were seemingly unbeatable the most successful franchise in the history of sport. They were talented, disciplined, well groomed, and successful. Their legendary teams boasted great hitting, good fielding, and unbeatable pitching. They embodied Heidegger's "technology of power"—part of the modern project's effort to entirely command human fate. When they couldn't develop players in their minor league system, they went out and bought the best through free agency. Like their owner, George Steinbrenner, they were cocky and self-assured. If they weren't really an *evil* empire, as Sox owner Larry Lucchino labeled them, they were certainly, to paraphrase Heidegger, the lords of baseball's Being.

On the other hand, we Sox fans were like Oedipus, who, at the pinnacle of his power and success, found that life had thrown him a nasty curve. Sox fans came to believe that existence wasn't fair and that there were no happy endings. Our highest hopes and most intense faith would inevitably be shattered by ghastly failure. Many Sox fans, including the master of the horror genre, Stephen King, adopted an expedient similar to that of the chastened Oedipus: at key moments in important games they turned off the television or radio in hopes of blinding themselves to the inevitable devastation (Stephen King and Stewart O'Nan, *Faithful: Two Diehard Red Sox Fans Chronicle the Historic 2004 Season*). Sox fans were anxiety-ridden, bitter, and envious. For them, every silver lining gave way to a dark cloud. Sox fans came to have a fatalistic view of existence, a perspective similar to followers of Heidegger, who in the words of Madan Sarup, saw life as "uniformly hollow, sterile, flat, 'one-dimensional', empty of human possibilities" (*An Introductory Guide to Post-Structuralism and Postmodernism*, University of Georgia Press, 1989, p. 105).

Safe at Home and Language as the House of Being

Why then were Sox fans so faithful? One reason is charming Fenway Park, the oldest ballpark in baseball. There's a sense of astonishment as you enter the field from busy, urban, and quite ugly Kenmore Square. Suddenly everything is green; the grass, the roof, and of course the Green Monster almost hurt your eyes. Fenway is beautiful in the same way as an old, oddly shaped, unique, and well-used Victorian house. It's quirky, too, with its turn-of-the-century restrooms, steel columns supporting the roof but blocking the view, and seats installed when the average man weighed about 145 lbs. (it is now closer to 190 lbs). But even the eccentricities make the park attractive. Yankee Stadium is the home of champions, but it is cold, efficient, and heartless. It may have been the house that Ruth built, but it was also ruthlessly proficient at jamming in paying customers. While many of the new retro-classic ballparks built after Camden Yards in Baltimore (1992) seek to capture some of the charm of Fenway, Wrigley Field, and other "Jewel Box" parks, the new Yankee Stadium (2009) seems even more sterile than the old.

Fenway, on the other hand, gives people a sense of continuity. In the ever-more-hectic technological age, Fenway conjures images of more innocent times when fathers went to church and then spent all day with their sons at Sunday doubleheaders. It's a place where one can imagine people dressing up to go to a game or where whole families could afford to enjoy a day together in the bleachers. Baseball was played at Fenway before nuclear weapons were invented, before Adolf Hitler and Joseph Stalin murdered millions, before the trench warfare of World War I turned the bright hopes for the twentieth century into despair. If time hasn't stood still at Fenway, it has slowed to a pace where it is easy to sense a connection with the past. Fenway is the real-life "field of dreams," as the movie of that name indicates by featuring it prominently in the story. In an age that Heidegger called homeless, Fenway feels— if only for the few hours of a home game—a lot like home.

The Red Sox became a "nation" because so many people went to Boston and its environs to attend one of its many (more than sixty) institutions of higher learning. One of the rites of passage for out-of-town students was to catch a game at Fenway. For many, it was love at first sight. When those students went off to live and work in other parts of country, they took their Sox addiction with them.

All those colleges and universities brought to Boston a great many educators with literary and communications skills. Like their students, Fenway enchanted many of them into cheering for the Sox. (This reality was first brought home to me in October of 1986, when my college campus in Southside Virginia was suddenly awash in faculty sporting Red Sox caps.) Literary people are trained in analyzing books and applying textual principles to practical life. It was inevitable that the literati would compare the Sox reversals of fortune to Greek tragedy and would explain the Bosox woes in terms borrowed from tragedy.

Literary analysis cannot change the score of ballgames, but it does influence how we interpret those results. As Heidegger explains, there are two parts to our understanding of reality: the "being present" of what happens and the "making present" of how we comprehend those events. Language is the "house of Being," because human beings have a unique compulsion and ability to seek explanations for experiences. The literary account of the Red Sox as a tragically fated club deepened the sense of anxiety, foreboding, and challenge facing both the team and its fans. It also made the fate of a baseball team more interesting and important than a mere sporting event. The Red Sox became a symbol for our highest hopes and deepest fears and failures. The Red Sox became a "nation" because their dilemmas transcended entertainment and spoke to the fragility of existence.

Only an Ortiz Can Save Us: Heidegger's Revelation of Being

"'Tis the portion of man assigned to him by the eternal allotment of Providence that every good he enjoys, shall be alloyed with ills," says Alexander Hamilton (*The Papers of Alexander Hamilton*, Columbia University Press, 1961–1979). Thankfully, the reverse is also true, for it's in contrast with immense sorrow that we experience great joy. Everything changed in 2004. Sox general manager Theo Epstein persuaded a known big-game pitcher, Curt Schilling, to join the club. But it was the cheerful smile, Ruth-like physique, extraordinary powers of concentration under pressure, and clutch hits in key situations of David Ortiz that overcame the vaunted foe. The Sox staged an incredible and exciting comeback in the ALCS—the only team to win a series after being behind 3–0—against their bitter rivals, the New York Yankees. After mowing through the St. Louis Cardinals in the first three games of the World Series, on the evening of October 27th, 2004—fittingly after a total eclipse of the moon—they won the World Series against Enos Slaughter's old team with Johnny Pesky looking on attired in his Sox uniform.

The curse was gone: the Sox won their first championship in eighty-six years, existential angst disappeared, and the glow of wondrous joy lasted for months. The depth of feeling for the Red Sox can be seen in the books written after their championship season including: Nick Carfardo, *100 Things Red Sox Fans Should Know Before They Die* (Triumph, 2008); Bill Simmons, *Now I Can Die in Peace* (ESPN, 2005); and, most revealing, Leigh Montville, *Why Not Us?* (Public Affairs, 2004), a book primarily made up of a long string of emails about how lost loved ones would have rejoiced in the Bosox triumph.

The celebration in honor of the championship season was the largest crowd ever assembled in Boston, and the parade might have attracted more than the estimated one million fans had not the weather been cold, rainy, and miserable. There's a pennant from that celebration resting on the headstone of my uncle, the most knowledgeable baseball man I have ever known. He was born in 1919 and died in 2003.

Heidegger also explained that our understanding of Being is linked to time—what we believe is inexorably connected to our historical experience—our milieu. Sox fans are aware of this, too, for we no longer care about Haywood Sullivan, the Curse of the Bambino, or Mike Torrez. After winning the World Series again in 2007, Billy Buckner received a warm welcome at Fenway as the team celebrated its championship on Opening Day of the 2008 season. After two World Series victories, there was nothing tragic about losing the pennant in 2008 to the fresh and determined Rays. In 2009 the often moody Nomar Garciaparra was given a hero's welcome when he returned home to Fenway, despite wearing an Oakland A's uniform. Hardly any Sox fans booed David Ortiz in 2009 despite suffering the worst slump of his career (although many were disappointed that their beloved Big Papi was involved with performance-enhancing drugs). The anguish over losing is gone.

Red Sox fans have thus experienced all three states of Being as Heidegger's penetrating philosophy presents them: There was the "everydayness" of mediocre teams—which were, like most of our lives, quite ordinary. Then there was the sense of tragedy that is an intrinsic element of our existence. Red Sox failures taught us that dealing with sadness, loss, and finally our own mortality—is the most challenging and important phenomena of existence. Finally, there was a sense of wonder and thrill of finally succeeding—what Heidegger calls a revelation of Being. The Yankees have the best winning percentage in the history of *baseball,* and they have twenty-six championships. But the Red Sox have exhibited the deeper meaning of *life.*

8

Forgiveness, Virtue, and Red Sox Nation

RORY E. KRAFT, JR.

Non-baseball fans, or perhaps even worse, non-Red Sox fans, never seem to quite understand the devotion and dedication that baseball, and particularly Red Sox baseball, demands of its followers. We have to, and I mean *have to*, know what's going on with the players, the management, the park, the weather, the concessions, the parking, the public transportation, and—of course—those who happen to be competing against "our boys."

And perhaps it's only Boston fans who can understand that it's important that the local Catholic diocese give dispensation to eat Fenway Franks on Opening Day if it happens to be on a Friday during Lent. Baseball, after all, is an important part of our lives. We understand the calendar in five seasons: Spring Training, Before the Break, After the Break, Playoffs, and Hot Stove time. And for far too long, the Playoff and Hot Stove seasons consisted of heartbreak, suffering, and the oft repeated "wait until next year."

In the midst of all of this heartbreak we are faced with a few central questions of human nature. Which actions and people are forgivable? Who can we support despite flaws in playing or flaws in character? What does it mean to really forgive a ballplayer? Does forgiveness really matter? Why do the umps so rarely call the infield fly rule when they can? (Okay, so I don't handle the last one, but it is a good question.)

Buckner!

In the movie *Fever Pitch*, in a moment that wasn't lost on any Red Sox fan, when explaining the many travails of rooting for the Red

Sox all Ben (Jimmy Fallon's character) is able to say is "Buckner!" This, of course, refers to the painful moment during Game Six of the 1986 World Series when, in the bottom of the 10th inning, Mookie Wilson of the New York Mets hit a grounder through Red Sox first baseman Bill Buckner's legs which allowed Ray Knight to score, winning the game, and forcing a Game Seven—which the Red Sox also lost. Buckner, despite hitting an impressive 102 RBIs in 1986 and being the league leader in at-bats-per-strike-out (at 25.160) quickly became the scapegoat for the downfall of the season, the team, and Red Sox Nation. A joke shortly afterward focused on the apparent simplicity of the routine ground ball:

> "Did you hear that Buckner tried to commit suicide?"
> "Really?"
> "Yeah, he jumped in front of a bus but it went right between his legs."

This gallows humor points to both the routineness and, perhaps more importantly, the stakes of the error. Someone who committed an error this grave ought to see death as the only acceptable form of remorse.

Vin Scully's call—"little roller up the first. Behind the bag! It gets through Buckner! Here comes Knight and the Mets win it!"—is burned in our memory. The emphasis here is on it getting by *Buckner*. We blame Buckner for the error and not manager John McNamara's decision not to pull Buckner for Dave Stapleton—a common move given Buckner's bad ankles. Because of this, Buckner's error now stands apart and is not placed within the context of Buckner's many years of excellent ball playing.

Perhaps the best explanation of the impact of that moment comes from Peter Gammons:

> And when the ball went through Bill Buckner's legs, 41 years of Red Sox baseball flashed in front of my eyes. In that one moment, Johnny Pesky held the ball, Joe McCarthy lifted Ellis Kinder in Yankee Stadium, Luis Aparicio fell down rounding third, Bill Lee delivered his Leephus pitch to Tony Perez, Darrell Johnson hit for Jim Willoughby, Don Zimmer chose Bobby Sprowl over Luis Tiant and Bucky (Bleeping) Dent hit the home run. ("Living and Dying with the Woe Sox," in *The Red Sox Reader*, 1991, pp. 281–82)

Buckner's error represents the way that we come to see people as an extension of their actions. This understanding isn't unusual and has been a component of virtue ethics since the days of the ancient Greek philosopher Aristotle. Virtue ethics is an approach to understanding the moral status of a person or action in the context of personal character rather than ethical rules or based upon the outcome of an action. In Aristotle's view we should evaluate individuals based upon the actions that they take. But where most systems of ethics focus on the individual actions, Aristotle demands of us that we look at the cumulative impact of a lifetime of actions.

For Aristotle the evaluation of one's life is based upon the extent to which one can be said to have reached the state of *eudaimonia,* which can be translated as happiness or fulfillment. We reach this state by living life "in conformity with excellence" (*Nicomachean Ethics*, 1098a). But this conformity with excellence needs to occur "'in a complete life' for one swallow does not make a summer, nor does one day; and so too one day, or a short time, does not make a man blessed and happy" (1098a). Thus, John Valentin's unassisted triple play (July 8th, 1994) while an excellent action, doesn't by itself display that Valentin was an excellent ballplayer. In order to make the later claim we would need to consider that he's the only player to pair an unassisted triple play with hitting for the cycle (June 6th, 1996), lifetime hits of 1093, a serviceable batting average of .279, and an impressive .968 fielding percentage. Thus the individual action (the triple play) is best seen in the context of a lifetime of good to excellent playing on both offense and defense.

For Aristotle we become "just by doing just acts, temperate by doing temperate acts, brave by doing brave acts" (1103a–b). This fits in well with baseball's use of spring training. By repeatedly doing the same actions over and over a player comes to understand the proper way to do things, and eventually the right actions become habitual and need no thinking. Further, we lose our ability to be excellent by either doing an action to excess or insufficiently doing so (1104a). This is easy enough to consider in how one plays the Green Monster. A player can play too shallow and allow balls to drop behind him, or play too deep and not be able to field the ball as it caroms back onto the field. The virtuous mean is somewhere between the extremes, yet varies from player to player and team to team. (Various changes over the years from the leveling of Duffy's Cliff to the addition of the Monster Seats have also changed the way that the fielder ought to "play the Monster.") Further, simply aver-aging the positions mathematically in order to determine the right position would be as foolish as to average the dietary needs of David "Big Papi" Ortiz and a high school baseball player (1106b). The virtuous mean isn't just the middle point or average of the extremes, but is different for each person and in each situation. All this discussion about lifetime achievement returns us again to the question of Buckner. Why is it that his error (and no one will mis-take *the* error with one of the other 145 errors in his twenty-two-year career) cannot be taken in the context of his larger career? After all he has a lifetime batting average of .289, with 2,715 hits, 1,208 RBIs, and 174 home runs. On the fielding side he has a .991 field-ing percentage over 18,647.1 innings. These are impressive numbers to say the least. But then there is *the* error.

Perhaps the best understanding of the importance of Buckner's error is the acknowledgement that there are some invirtuous actions that do not have degrees of badness. While we can under-stand someone who is slightly cowardly, or perhaps somewhat too foolhardy or rash (1108b), we cannot understand degrees of "adul-tery, theft, murder" (1107a) since they are bad by definition. One cannot be slightly adulterous or murder "just a little." These actions by definition are bad, and by taking them a person is doing a lot of damage to his overall *eudemonia*. Similarly, Buckner's error goes beyond a routine error. This is an error that cost a game and a World Series. This error isn't just any error; it's *the* error and as such is perhaps unforgivable.

Wake's Mistake

In contrast to Buckner, Tim Wakefield's bad pitches are cast aside as par for the course for a knuckleballer. I was in the stands in Detroit in August 2004 when Wakefield allowed six home runs— and still got the win. In a stadium that had as many Red Sox fans in attendance as Tigers fans it was noticeable that there were no calls to pull him early. Of course this was helped by the Tigers' pitching allowing Boston to get fourteen hits and timely home runs by Kevin Youkilis and Big Papi.

If Buckner's defining moment was the blown grounder, the moment that could've defined Wakefield's career, but didn't, came in Game Seven of the 2003 ALCS. After winning Game One and Game Four of the series, Wakefield came in as a reliever and pitched a scoreless 10th inning, only to see his accomplishments fade away with a single pitch to Aaron Boone in the bottom of the 11th. Boone's home run won the game, and the series, for the Yankees and sent the Red Sox back home to wait until next year.

However, unlike Buckner who was widely vilified for his error, Wakefield was greeted by cheering fans in his first start the next year. In an apparent reversal of the lack of attention paid to McNamara's role in the Buckner affair, the heat for the loss was put squarely on the shoulders of manager Grady Little. Little's contract wasn't renewed for the next season, and the Red Sox went on to win the World Series in 2004 under Terry Francona. Wakefield pitched in three games in the 2004 ALCS, getting the win in Game Five. When we look at Wakefield we have to ask, why is he a hero and not Buckner?

If we return to Aristotle for guidance we must first begin by thinking about the three possible types of bad actions: mistakes, misadventures, and acts of injustice (1135b). It seems like we can easily dismiss the final category for both Buckner and Wakefield. No sane person would claim that either had knowingly and willfully selected to take an action that would result in a loss. A misadventure occurs when the outcome is contrary to reasonable expectation. If a first baseman has fielded thousands of ground balls that always acted in a similar fashion, it's easy enough to assume that the ball, the glove, and the ballplayer will continue to do as they have always done. Failing to do so is a misadventure. By contrast, a mistake occurs when the action is not contrary to reasonable expectation, but due to ignorance a result followed other than what he thought likely. These seem to be close, and indeed they are, but in the case of mistakes it's the ignorance on the part of the (let's just say) pitcher who allows the batter to get a hit. The pitcher knew that this pitch was going to cross the plate at such and such an angle and height, but was ignorant of the exact moment the batter would swing or if he would go outside his usual hitting zone.

Remember that Wakefield had just struck out the side in the prior inning, and had won two previous games in the series. He had not often faced Boone, and Boone was hitless against Wakefield in the series. When Wakefield releases the ball he has an expectation—a mistaken expectation—of the outcome of the pitch because of his ignorance of Boone changing his batting plan. Rather than taking the first pitch in order to get a read on

Wakefield, Boone decides to swing at the first pitch. Boone told ESPN: "All I wanted was to get on base, to get contact" (Rick Wisenberg, "39: Aaron Boone's Home Run Crushes Red Sox"). This simple change in plan—one which Wakefield was ignorant of and could not expect—led to Boone's home run and the loss.

In comparing this with Buckner's error we see that Buckner played the ball as he thought he ought to—indeed as anyone thought he ought to—but the outcome was different. Buckner's misadventure isn't the same as Wakefield's mistake. Yet, both can be classified as involuntary actions. Neither Buckner nor Wakefield entered the game, the play, or even that moment with the will and knowledge to do what was going to occur. Further, while Aristotle holds that not all involuntary actions are forgivable, both of these actions appear to have occurred "not only in ignorance but also from ignorance" and as such ought to be forgiven (1136a).

As mentioned above, Wakefield was immediately forgiven by all. This may in part be because of the inherent nature of pitching uncertainty, or because as a knuckleball pitcher he's known to be erratic. This is shown in his high number of both batters hit and passed balls. This results in some really odd statistics, like the above-mentioned game against the Tigers when he gave up six home runs and still got the win. In a more rare accomplishment, Wakefield is one of a few pitchers who have struck out four batters in a single inning—a feat he accomplished in the ninth inning of the August 6th, 1999 game against the Kansas City Royals because of a passed ball. Red Sox Nation rallied behind Wakefield because of his career of oddness and selfless playing. In essence, his mistake was forgiven because we believed in his character. As one of the oldest active pitchers in baseball, we see in Wake a determined player who gives his all, sacrifices his own starting positions for the good of the team, and through the unpredictable nature of his pitching confounds and confuses opposing teams.

We Always Forgave Ted Williams

When it comes to storied Red Sox players there are few in the same category as Ted Williams. Whether we call him The Kid, Teddy Ballgame, The Splendid Splinter, or simply the Best Player Ever, Williams is certainly among the greatest in Red Sox history. His remarkable accomplishments become even greater when we take into account that he twice interrupted his baseball career to fly fighter planes for the Marine Corps. The first instance of which occurred after his historic 1941 season when he hit .406, with 37 home runs and 120 RBIs. He served in the military at the peak of his baseball career. His accomplishments on the field would continue until his retirement in 1960, and despite being one of the greatest hitters ever he hit only .200 in the 1946 World Series (his only World Series appearance) against the St. Louis Cardinals. His excellence on the field also corresponds with methods that Aristotle recommended. As Aristotle claimed, "all who are not maimed as regards excellence may win it by a certain kind of study and care" (1099b). Williams famously studied the science of hitting (and named his own book as such), believing that it was not luck but hard work that made him as great as he was.

Yet for all his prowess on the field, Williams had an uneasy relationship with the Boston fans and press. He's perhaps just as famous for not tipping his hat to the fans (including in his last appearance, and final home run, in 1960) and refusing to talk to the "knights of the pressbox" as he is for his athletic achievements He gained a lot of respect from fans by tipping a borrowed hat to the fans on Ted Williams Day (May 12th, 1991), and stated:

> I'm especially thankful, though, to have a chance . . . so they can never write ever again that I never tipped my hat to the crowd . . . because today . . . I tip my hat to *a-a-a-l-l* the people in New England, without question the greatest sports fans on earth. (Quoted in Ed Linn's *Hitter*, 1993, p. 368)

This tip of the hat was the first time he had ever recognized the Red Sox fans. Some of this respect was taken back by his appearance during the 1999 All-Star Game at Fenway where he wore not a Red Sox cap, but a hat advertising his son John Henry's Internet business. But he again waved a hat to the fans.

When we look at the fans' acceptance of Williams as a great Red Sox player, we see that it's not getting along with the media or recognizing the fans that's important but rather good work on the field and, as we found out after his retirement, good work through the Jimmy Fund and other charities off the field. We love Ted because he was a good ballplayer who had a weakness. A weakness we could overlook. Even if that weakness was dealing with the fans. But as Aristotle says, we do "not look for precision in all things alike, but in each class of things such precision as accords with the subject-matter, and so much as is appropriate to the inquiry" (1098a). Thus, we look at Williams as a complete ballplayer, not just as the guy who refused to recognize the fans, or someone who had 113 fielding errors and 709 strikeouts. In Williams, and in Wakefield, we see the whole picture. Players who give their all on the field, can fail, and are able to do much good off the field as well. We forgive Ted; we forgive Timmy.

Can Manny be Manny?

When it comes to controversial figures in Red Sox uniform in recent memory, few surpass Manny Ramirez. Ramirez, known as an exceptional hitter, shortly after signing with the Red Sox hit a home run listed officially at 501 feet—one short of Williams's record of 502 feet. His offensive dominance continued for much of his tenure with the Red Sox, though his defensive play left much to be desired. The fans' attitude was that given his otherwise good play, we should just allow "Manny to be Manny." But openness toward all sloppy play, or indeed toward less than stellar play, wasn't excusable for all Red Sox players. Mark Bellhorn routinely dealt with hearing that "Pokey [Reese] woulda had that!" when he failed to make plays both routine and extraordinary. Something about Manny—his quirky behavior, his fun loving attitude, was endearing. Until it wasn't.

Following years of trade demands, missed games, refusals to play, and memorable fights with other Red Sox players (a June 5th, 2008 fight between Ramirez and Youkilis is the most prominent of them), the Red Sox were finally able to trade Ramirez to another team. Almost immediately after going to the Dodgers the tide had turned. Manny was sloppy, lazy, and no one seemed to like him. Except that we had. We loved Manny being Manny. But when it went too far, we could no longer forgive him.

If we look at his play we see someone who—while streaky— was an excellent hitter but a sub-par fielder. In his seven-plus seasons with the Red Sox, he committed 28 officially scored errors—the vast majority of which (20) were fielding rather than throwing errors. His odd practice of disappearing into the Green Monster during pitching changes raised eyebrows, and prompted suggestions by those who were less enamored of him that in his "Manny being Manny" moments he was playing with less than total effort. His well known laid back behavior, a central part of his appeal to many, also meant that he went onto the field with water bottles in his back pocket, and perhaps didn't always reach quite as far for a fly ball. By being long standing attributes, we clearly see that these are elements of his character, but since they received so much attention, we have to think that on some level continuing to engage in these behaviors was voluntary. For Aristotle the wrong actions when taken voluntarily are acts of injustice and are ones that are blameworthy.

Some of Manny's behavior—such as his frequent calls to be traded—is surely done after deliberation. Others, such as his fight with Youkilis, appear to be based upon the passions of the moment. Aristotle believed that when one acts with knowledge but not after deliberation it's an act of injustice, but that such actions don't make one an unjust man (1135b20–24). Indeed, one only becomes an unjust man by doing unjust actions from choice.

Regardless of whether or not one thought Ramirez was purposefully acting poorly, or doing so because it seemed most fun at the moment, in Aristotle's schema Manny would be committing unjust actions either way. Red Sox Nation seems to concur with Aristotle that voluntarily doing unjust actions was unforgivable. And unlike Williams's failing to recognize the fans, Ramirez's failings impacted his play on the field—the place where we most need our ballplayers to excel.

Forgiveness and the Fenway Faithful

So why do we forgive some but not others? It seems clear that larger character-driven aspects and lifelong habits will go far in forgiving a player. Thus we forgive Williams but not Ramirez. But even this aspect seems to fall short in explaining Buckner's error lingering in the Red Sox fan's psyche. Like Wakefield, he otherwise put up exceptional numbers. Yet Buckner remains the scapegoat of 1986—the year we could've won it all.

I think that by returning to the type of action itself we can come to see what makes *the* error so prone to blame. Buckner's play wasn't just any error. It was the World Series losing error (because Game Seven would never have occurred without *the* error). This is a lot different from a pitch that brings about a loss to *those* Yankees—even in a League Championship Series. We have lost lots of pennants. And we remember those plays as well. But just as we remember Bucky Dent as a villain, we don't blame Carl "Yaz"

Yastrzemski for fouling out to end the game. A pennant is not a World Series. Wakefield is not Buckner.

It may seem odd for those who don't perceive something grander in Red Sox baseball to properly see implications for a wider understanding of forgiveness. But, where else outside of the confines of our team can we really come to think about what it means to forgive, who we can forgive, and why forgiveness is so important. We have loved the Red Sox for so long that they are a part of us, and our continual forgiveness (sometimes with bitterness) and anticipation of future heartbreaks was understandable. Our lamenting the game-changing moments that shaped our outlook on the world is normal. We recognize these ballplayers as part of our lives—through newspaper, radio, television, and watching games in person. My decision to forgive a ballplayer is more than my decision to forgive the guy who cut me off in traffic. The Red Sox are family to the members of Red Sox Nation. We need to understand what it means to forgive the players and the team. But in doing so, we come to understand what it means to forgive.

With two new World Series championships under our belt, on April 8th, 2008 as the 2007 World Series banner was unfurled at Fenway, Bill Buckner threw out the ceremonial first pitch. He received a four-minute standing ovation from the fans. Perhaps twenty-two years later we were finally able to understand that a misadventure was just as forgivable as a mistake. Bucker will long be famous for *the* error. But maybe, just maybe, we can forgive him. Just don't ask us to forget it.

Forgiveness

ANDY WASIF

To err is human, to forgive divine.

—ALEXANDER POPE

To err is human, to err during the playoffs is intolerable.

—Anonymous Red Sox fan

Throughout history, the concept of forgiveness has driven a stake through the usually uniformed beliefs of Red Sox Nation. To forgive or not to forgive, that is the question.

Many times, those who are forgiven shouldn't have been blamed in the first place. *The Eastern Sports Philosophical Network* (ESPN) has done specials on the subject of blame and forgiveness. Is it moral to decide one's perceived legacy over one play? Who are we to blame? Therefore, who are we to forgive? What causes us to forgive? What's it to you? You wanna make something of it? You think I'm scared of you? All valid questions save for the last few.

Take Bill Buckner, for example. No, really. Take him. Please! . . . is what people *would've said* in 2003. But in 2004, in a collective act by the Nation, he was granted forgiveness. He had previously perpetrated a grievous sin of the highest magnitude in that he was left in the game by his manager (John McNamara) and put in a position by two pitchers (Calvin Schiraldi and Bob Stanley) where a ball hit to him by a speedy runner that would've beaten him to the first base bag anyway got by him thereby ending a game that his team wouldn't have won regardless. Simply inexcusable on his part.

And yet he wasn't to be forgiven until *another* incarnation of his team, years after his retirement and relocation to Idaho where he took to publishing a weekly newsletter, *The What the Heck do Red Sox Fans and Media Know Anyway? Times*, finally won the prize for which he was competing.

So it might be theorized that winning a championship is the only thing that absolves one of blame. However, that presumption would be proven incorrect by Mary, er, Johnny Damon.

The flowing-haired center fielder *did* win the championship and *then* needed to be forgiven. It's this reversal that's philosophically divergent from the previously revealed policy. Rising to cult hero status in Boston, fans routinely asked the question, "What would Johnny Do?" And the answer was: "Run to New York for more money."

His actions demonstrated a desire to take the best offer on the table and not to hurt the citizens of the Nation, which is usually justifiable given his resume's glowing highlight, that of "curse-ender." However, Johnny forsook the Golden Rule and chose the Yankees as his new employer, thus solidifying his place as "Enemy of the State." Is there anything he can do to one day gain forgiveness? Well, there would be if Johnny were still alive, but at this point, most of Red Sox Nation just considers him dead.

This shows that the rules on forgiveness can be akin to flipping a coin. The fans have yet to establish solid guidelines and continue to assess each case individually. On the contrary, they're much more rigid in their practice of blaming. They divide the blame equally amongst the manager, players, and general manager, each deserving one hundred percent of the blame. You could probably throw an extra hundred percent at the media as well.

The topic of forgiveness has always been a touchy subject in Red Sox Nation. Most All-Time rosters they compile are put into two categories: "Dead to us" and "Skating on Thin Ice."

Fenway Faithful

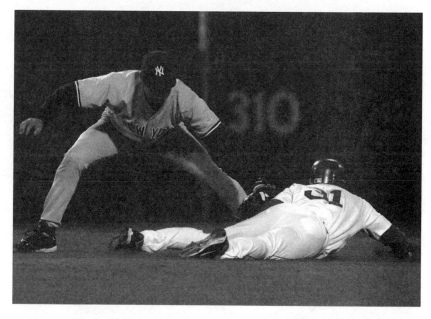

Dave Roberts steals second base during Game Four of the 2004 ALCS.
Courtesy of the Boston Red Sox. Photo by Cindy Loo.

9

Wicked Faithful

PATRICK TIERNAN

To depict a baseball game as a religious experience may be considered blasphemous. After all, what could possibly be sacred about bench-clearing brawls, foam finger souvenirs, and awkward bonding moments like watching your hot dog travel down a row of strangers? Yet there's something ineffable about walking through the corridors of Fenway Park: the indelible hue of green that permeates the architecture; the old-school, hand-operated scoreboard; and the vague sense that you're somewhere incomparable in the baseball pantheon. To simply stand in the shadow of Fenway Park is regarded by many to be a religious experience, to witness something so majestic that even the most erudite poet can't capture it in words. Being at a Red Sox game, one cannot help but think of the historical memories of doubt and redemption that have captured the essence of what it means to be part of the Fenway Faithful. Belief for this group is a personal and communal ritual practiced every spring at the cathedral on Yawkey Way where petitionary prayers are offered in the hope they will be heard.

Religious Diamond in the Rough

Faith means belief in something concerning which doubt is theoretically possible.

—WILLIAM JAMES

Anyone from New England knows that baseball is religion. With slogans such as *Fenway Faithful*, and *Believe in Boston*, and *Keep the Faith*, religious language permeates the culture of Beantown

like no other. It's a sentiment that's universal for members of Red
Sox Nation while its experience is different for each individual. My
love for the Red Sox is different from my father's. He fondly
remembers being at Fenway to see Ted Williams hit a home run off
Bob Feller during his Triple Crown season in '47. His passion for
the team he grew up with is timeless, evidenced by the youthful
delight he exhibits whenever he's able to watch a Sox game from
his home in California. Even my mother, who bleeds Dodger Blue,
has converted to the church of the Sox. These moments and the
relationships they forge are ecstatic, where you stand outside of
yourself and revisit experiences and memories as if they were in
the present.

This ecstatic state parallels what William James called a "mystical state of consciousness," in which an individual encounters the
sacred. In his great work, *The Varieties of Religious Experience*,
James describes this mystical state as exhibiting certain qualities.
The first is ineffability, where the experience must be firsthand and
can't be transferred or imparted to others, defying any verbalization
of the memory. Remembering Vin Scully's call ("There's a little
roller up along first . . .") as the potential final out eluded Bill
Buckner during Game Six of the 1986 World Series is a moment
many of us shudder to recall. While this may not at first glance
seem like anything religious, it does convey the indescribable
nature of that gut-wrenching experience. Contrast this with Dave
Roberts's steal of second base during Game Four of the 2004 ALCS
and how many of us to this day regard that as the moment that
turned around the fate of the Red Sox. Second, this mystical state
has a noetic quality, namely that it offers insight into certain truths
that remain authoritative, such as how Red Sox teams throughout
the years evoke feelings of destiny and fortune. Third, there's the
notion of transiency, or the fact that the mystical state cannot be
sustained. A blowout game, or one besieged by poor pitching, can
definitely negate this feeling of bliss! Fourth is the characteristic of
passivity, that we're somehow grasped by a higher power or feeling that we can't control.

For James, these characteristics presume that we have the will
to believe in the first place. In many ways we are drawn into the
enchantment of America's pastime. The complexity of religious
experience is captured in Rudolph Otto's book *The Idea of the Holy*
(Oxford University Press, 1958), where he describes the *mysterium
tremendum* or, the awe of what is holy:

The feeling of it may at times come sweeping like a gentle tide, pervading the mind with a tranquil mood of deepest worship. It may pass over into a more set and lasting attitude of the soul, continuing, as it were, thrillingly vibrant and resonant . . . It may burst in sudden eruption up from the depths of the soul with spasms and convulsions, or lead to the strangest excitements, to intoxicated frenzy, to transport, and to ecstasy. (p. 1)

Being part of the Fenway Faithful requires one to accept the peaks and valleys of victories and defeats, to be elevated or disheartened into a state of awareness that only a Red Sox fan can identify with.

Wait 'Til Next Year . . .

It's like déjà-vu, all over again.

—Yogi Berra

Belief is central to understanding the psychology of Red Sox Nation. What we believe in frames what we hope for in the season. Spring training showcases rookies, new acquisitions, and grizzled veterans while everyone in New England takes a collective breath and prays for a winning year. The spring offers a new beginning new possibilities and provides for one of baseball's more aesthetic moments. "This *could* be the year and this *could* be the team that wins it all," becomes a common refrain. The fact that the starting lineup for the Red Sox changes more often than the drummer for Spinal Tap (albeit not under the same unfortunate circumstances) does not cause consternation amongst the Faithful. After all, the mantra "Keep the faith" is recited as if our livelihood depends on whether or not the Sox have success in the postseason.

So what are we keeping the faith *in* anyways? Can anyone genuinely ascribe their hometown sports team's victory to some divine presence? It sure doesn't bode well for the losing team! Many people think of faith as some disposition toward something—having faith in some ultimate force or law that transcends our existence. But another way of looking at faith is to see it not as a possession but as a state of being. In this manner, faith isn't a set of beliefs but an innate disposition or mindset. It's something we are in, standing in relation to ourselves and others. It's a universal characteristic of the human condition. The symbolism behind the phrase "Fenway Faithful" assumes this collective sense of awe and wonder at what's possible in any given season. Seen in this way, faith is an activity one engages in, not merely something one has or loses from time to time.

Psychologist of religion James Fowler, in *Stages of Faith* (1981), suggests that faith progresses in complexity throughout stages in our lives. One of these stages, the mythical-literal stage, exemplifies the childlike faith many in Red Sox Nation live out season to season. At this level, narratives become genuine markers of what's real for the believer. There's the simple but not necessarily naive view that virtuous actions are rewarded and evil deeds are punished in a linear sort of way. This could explain why the monumental losses of the Red Sox over the past decades are so unfathomable to fans because it betrays this innate sense of what's just. We trust that the human spirit will endure, as seen in this modified prayer posted in a local souvenir store:

> Our Father, who art at Fenway
> Baseball be thy game.
> Thy kingdom come,
> The series needs to be won
> On earth and then on to the
> Cask 'n' Flagon . . .
> And lead us not into desperation,
> But deliver us from any losses.
> For thine is the power and the glory
> Forever and ever . . . The Yankees suck . . . Amen

Although this worldview is akin to bargaining with the universe—"Please, if you let the Red Sox win just one World Series, I'll do anything."—it does underscore the need for stories and for those individuals who have a penchant for storytelling—heroes overcoming great obstacles (Curt Schilling's infamous bloody sock), legendary myths (Ted Williams being able to see the stitches of the ball being pitched), the cruelty of the gods (numerous lost postseason opportunities) and reversal of fortunes (coming back from an 0-3 deficit against the Evil Empire). What's the legacy of the Faithful if not a Greek tragedy?

One (Red Sox) Nation Under Fenway

You should enter a ballpark the way you enter a church.

—BILL "SPACEMAN" LEE

The international recognition of Red Sox Nation exemplifies how a sports team can transcend its local fan base and respective culture. Who else can make road games look and sound as if they were playing back home? It's a case study of sociological cheerleading for sure. As a religious community bounded in the historical misfortunes and accomplishments of the team formerly known as the Americans, the social gathering of fans can have experiences that bind them across generations. The commonly accepted etymologies of the word religion operating here come from the Latin *religare*, "to bind back" and *religio*, "a bond between humanity and the gods." These experiences are what the sociologist of religion Peter Berger, in his book *A Rumor of Angels* (1969), calls "signals of transcendence" (pp. 52–75), phenomena found within our reality but appear to point beyond it. The commonly ordinary experiences of order, play, hope, damnation, and humor are all applicable to the Fenway Faithful. They speak to the sacred experience of being on Yawkey Way, witnessing a franchise that inspires and brings together families and friends.

We all have a need for order. Amid the hectic confusion of daily obligations and commitments, humans have an intrinsic need to establish certain patterns of behavior. Baseball in Boston accomplishes this through the consistent and very rigorous rituals of the baseball season. For example, "Truck Day" on Yawkey Way is the first harbinger of the new season, the spring ritual of watching the Red Sox equipment being packed up for Florida. Another rite of passage is how Opening Day is conveniently scheduled for the middle of the workday so dedicated employees can call out unexpectedly. The game of baseball itself creates an order that allows its fans the opportunity to engage in escapism, a psychological diversion that gives us a reprieve from the duress of our everyday lives.

What we watch then is just as important as how we celebrate it. Play, as it pertains to the baseball diamond, is the capacity to live, if only for a moment, outside of time. When you enter Fenway Park, you experience a sentiment that is reminiscent of Little League snack time on a Saturday afternoon. It even seems like public prayer is permissible—or rather, necessary—when rooting for the boys from Beantown.

The human propensity for hope is another signal of the sacred for a community. In the words of the theologian Jürgen Moltmann, from his book *Theology of Hope* (1993): "What would become of

us if we did not take our stand on hope, and if our heart did not
hasten beyond this world through the midst of the darkness . . .
?" (p. 19). Hope is seen on the face of every Red Sox fan who ever
was or will be—the desire for their team to be the one. It offers
an awareness of a future latent with possibility, however many
shortcomings there've been! This is the irony behind chants of
"1918," as if the past somehow influences the present. Yet we still
believe in something beyond ourselves, in spite of the chants and
lingering moments where the specter of the Bambino lurks in the
shadows.

We can also take solace in knowing that damnation is one of
Berger's signals of transcendence. It's the other side of hope and
provides a condemnation of those transgressors against humanity:
Bucky "Bleeping" Dent, Aaron Boone, A-Rod, and George
Steinbrenner. Damnation upholds the value of justice against the
backdrop of sheer evil. Red Sox games throughout time are fraught
with examples of derogatory and slanderous epithets yelled from
bleacher seats, or printed on shirts sold on Brookline Avenue
(insert favorite A-Rod/Derek Jeter joke here). Here, a simple slogan
becomes the judge, jury and executioner of past traitors against Red
Sox Nation: Roger Clemens, Wade Boggs, and Johnny Damon,
among others. These cathartic statements echo the understanding
that the argument from damnation points to a realm beyond our
experience. In damning the other, we affirm the collective solidarity that is Red Sox Nation. By establishing a nemesis, group cohe-
sion is built and sustained. The popular shirt that reads, "I support
two teams: the Red Sox and whoever plays the Yankees," captures
this sentiment perfectly.

The last signal of transcendence, humor, is so broad, that it may
appear ludicrous. How does laughter relate to divine reality? First,
and foremost, it forces us to remember that watching a game is
meant to be playful. The "Cowboy Up" refrain of the 2003 season
demonstrates this point. The dances in the dugout, the celebratory
high-fives that lasted for minutes, and the overall sense of cama-
raderie exhibited by the club showed the world that for a child's
game, baseball can have ultimate consequences. More importantly,
by finding humor within the game we're able to lose ourselves in
the realm of possibilities. This band of brothers, the idiots of New
England, came together to face the Evil Empire, Major League
Baseball's manifestation of corporate greed, arrogant pride, and
financial avarice—enough to make Satan blush.

The chorus from the infamous song "Tessie," sung by the Royal Rooters during the inaugural World Series against the Pittsburgh Pirates, perhaps best captures this collective experience of Red Sox Nation in 1903:

Tessie, you make me feel so badly;
Why don't you turn around.
Tessie, you know I love you madly;
Babe, my heart weighs about a pound.
Don't blame me if I ever doubt you,
You know, I wouldn't live without you;
Tessie, you are the only, only, only.

What else can sum up the borderline obsessive passion Fenway believers exude? One hundred and one years later, doubting through it all yet never giving up hope entirely, the Dropkick Murphys would revive the song into what would become the new mantra of Red Sox Nation.

It's Always Darkest before the Dawn

Doubt is not a pleasant mental state, but certainty is a ridiculous one.

—Voltaire

1946 . . . 1967 . . . 1975 . . . 1978 . . . 1986 . . . 2003. Why does merely glancing at these years create an emotional reaction among the Faithful? No other sequence of dates can foster so much resentment from so many. Each is painful for different reasons altogether. In the spirit of existential angst, the playoff history of the Red Sox has been absurd. In Homer's *Odyssey*, we encounter the Greek king Sisyphus who, before being punished by Hades, was stronger than Death himself. His condemnation was to roll a massive stone to the top of a mountain only to have it fall back on its own weight, akin to how the New England hopeful forge through any talk of fate or punishment.

This legacy of turmoil is collectively referred to as the "Curse of the Bambino," a historical stigma on the Boston Red Sox franchise. To understand its impact, one must recall the religious origins of the New England colonies and the influence of Puritanism. Its origins can be traced back to the sixteenth century Protestant movement that originated in England. Early New England settlers fled from persecution to establish a colony grounded in respect for freedom of religious practice but adhered to strict moral guidelines that regulated behavior. The most well known writer of the movement was the French theologian John Calvin, who remarked that, "you must submit to supreme suffering in order to discover the completion of joy." Because of the reality of sin, grounded in the selfishness of the ego, humanity was condemned to suffer with only a predetermined number of genuine believers to be saved in the afterlife.

Over four hundred years later, this same sense of persecution remains. According to *Boston Globe* sports columnist Dan Shaughnessy's book *The Curse of the Bambino* (Penguin, 1990), the "Original Sin" in Red Sox folklore was the infamous trade of Babe Ruth to the Yankees after the 1918 season by then owner Harry Frazee. Since then, Boston's beloved baseball team has suffered through an epic series of tragedies and misfortunes that was ended, many believe, when the Red Sox won the World Series in 2004. The Curse of the Bambino is the definitive illustration of belief for Red Sox Nation.

But is the Curse just a figment of our collective imagination? A convenient excuse for failing to win it all? The eighteenth-century agnostic David Hume was skeptical about religious experience. In his essay "Of Superstition and Enthusiasm" (*Writings on Religion*, 1992), Hume suggests that superstitious beliefs are the manifestation of feeble-minded people:

> In such a state of mind, infinite unknown evils are dreaded from unknown agents; and where real objects of terror are wanting, the soul, active to its own prejudice, and fostering its predominant inclination, finds imaginary ones, to whose power and malevolence it sets no limits. (p. 3)

However imaginary or genuine, the power of the Curse has been subjugated to numerous attempts to have it exorcised from the memory of Red Sox history. Hume continues by noting how various rituals only reinforce the naiveté of such beliefs:

> [They] consist in ceremonies, observances, mortifications, sacrifices, presents, or in any practice, however absurd or frivolous, which either folly or knavery recommends to a blind and terrified credulity. Weakness, fear, melancholy, together with ignorance, are, therefore, the true sources of superstition. (p. 4)

While the metaphysical debate over whether or not there's some tangible hex on the storied Red Sox franchise is one for another time, it has not stopped those determined (some might say paranoid) fans who attempted to remove it through alternative methods. From sage-burning ceremonies and exorcisms to the highest mountain and the lowest depth of a New England lake, Sox fans have engaged in ritualistic behaviors in an effort to purge the pain and anguish. After consulting with a lama (a Tibetan teacher), one fan ascended Mount Everest and placed a Red Sox hat at the peak of the mountain and later burned a Yankees hat in effigy at the base camp.

Another group of devotees scoured a pond near a cottage Babe Ruth used to rent when he played for the Red Sox. According to legend, during a night of imbibed revelry Ruth pushed a piano out of his cottage, down a hill, and out onto the frozen pond where the party continued through the night. The piano, too heavy to be pushed back up the hill, was left and eventually fell through the melting ice. Some fans believed that if the piano could be recovered and repaired, the Sox could "fine tune" their postseason performance. However no piano was ever found and the mystery remained.

Hume would have a field day with the rationale behind these rituals. The connection between superstitious beliefs and the practices intended to remove their effects commits what's known in logic as the fallacy of causation (*post hoc ergo propter hoc*—"after this therefore because of this"), whereby it's believed that an action, or behavior, directly causes a particular consequence to occur, when in fact there's no causal connection. In the case of the Curse of the Bambino, the assumption that any ritual could have influence on Boston's chances of winning the World Series is illogical. Then again, New Englanders just may rebut that the passion of being a fan and the emotional nature of seeing the 2004 championship banner being raised trumps any form of logic.

Even if Hume's definition of superstition and all its naiveté is correct, it stands to show how the faith embedded in the New England psyche transcends any one ritual, prayer, or condemnation. In an important sense, these examples provide a window into human nature. By providing even the illusion of control in an otherwise erratic and bewildering spectacle such as baseball, belief in the Curse"and the attempts to remove it demonstrate the hope and determination that characterizes the human need for religious practices.

Monstah Moments

Religion becomes a state of mind achievable in almost any activity of life, if this activity is raised to a suitable level of perfection.

—ABRAHAM MASLOW

Before the 2004 season, terms like "miraculous" and "unbelievable" were more apt descriptions of the charitable works of Mother Teresa or the illusion of levitation by Criss Angel. For eighty-six years, the Red Sox suffered a series of pitching and fielding mishaps that fed the phenomenon of the Curse of the Bambino. During the 2003 play-offs against the dreaded Yankees, doubt, much like a December nor'easter, enveloped Fenway believers like no other time before. "Is this going to be it, is this going to be our year?" But, alas, Tim Wakefield would walk off the mound that night after giving up the winning run to the reincarnation of Bucky Dent: Aaron Boone. "But there is no joy in Mudville," so the poem goes, and the little that was left had vanished from the hearts of Red Sox Nation.

Somehow, the 2004 season felt different, as if the demons had finally been exorcised. The year ended hopeful with the Sox winning the Wild Card. But then, quickly, the playoffs began to feel like the gods weren't yet done toying with the prayers of New England. Down 0–3 to the Yankees in the ALCS, the Red Sox had all but sealed their fate as the team that never would. I remember that Sunday morning as if it were yesterday, thinking to myself, at least if they win tonight, they wouldn't get swept. That afternoon, as if he had read my mind, Kevin Millar (Mr. "Cowboy Up" himself) reminded the world about the significance of a win that night: "Don't let us win tonight. . . . Don't let the Sox win this game." And after Dave Roberts's legendary steal and David Ortiz's epic clutch hitting, the dream had been preserved. Apparently the Yankees didn't heed Millar's warning.

Game Five provided a similar dynamic of extra innings and high tension and gave the Faithful pause for thought: is it possible? Curt Schilling's epic performance during Game Six provided a palpable sense of redemption for the pitcher who remarked, "I'm not sure I can think of any scenario more enjoyable than making fifty-five thousand people from New York shut up." Neither can I. After Schilling made good on his promise and the Sox embarrassed the Yankees in the ultimate Game Seven of all Game Seven's, many of Fenway's devotees experienced what the humanist psychologist

Abraham Maslow dubbed a "peak experience." The almost anticlimactic sweep over the St. Louis Cardinals in the World Series was practically an afterthought after the historic comeback over the Yankees. Yet, no matter if you believed, or dismissed, the Curse of the Bambino, it had been reversed and no longer held any rhetorical weight. A religious experience on Yawkey Way? There's no other way to describe it.

Maslow believed that peak experiences could be felt by individuals and groups who had become self-actualized. After basic physiological and emotional needs are met as part of a hierarchy of needs, individuals develop an acute sense of what an authentic existence looks like (from "A Theory of Human Motivation," *Psychological Review* 50, pp. 370–396). Being self-actualized allows you to view the world as full of possibilities. These peak experiences are sudden feelings of intense happiness and well-being where one becomes aware of an ultimate meaning or truth in life. As a type of mystical experience, it can be witnessed in a non-supernatural context such as a baseball park; it makes the believer more accepting and less neurotic about the anguish experienced in life's various moments. Maslow even recognized that a peak experience is an individually defined heaven in a natural surrounding. This form of religious experience allows for a broad interpretation of faith in which glimpses of the divine can be seen in the most beloved sport of our nation, where grown men become the boys of summer all over again.

I personally had two peak experiences in 2004: marrying my wife Anitza and witnessing the Red Sox become World Series champions. Both have made me a more authentic believer of what's possible in a world marred by doubt and confusion. But then again, the magical thing about the Red Sox is that everyone has their own story, their own conviction about what's possible when you keep the faith.

Do You Believe It?

The heart has its reasons which reason knows not of.

—BLAISE PASCAL

The day after the Red Sox lost the 1975 World Series to the Big Red Machine of Cincinnati, *Boston Globe* sports writer Ray Fitzgerald wrote, "This was a set of baseball games that almost transcended winning and losing, a string of pearls to be tucked away in a drawer and brought out from time to time to bring back a memory or two." He might as well have been speaking about the 2004 Red Sox. The collective experience of the Fenway Faithful during that mythic period of time in October transcended the anguish of the last century. More precious than a string of pearls, we now possess two World Series trophies since the dawn of the new millennium. They are not just artifacts of two championship victories but symbols of this believing community. These golden prizes have been immortalized in the pictures of thousands of fans across the country as icons of faith and hope. What baseball can teach us is, in part, biblical in nature,

> that we might witness the fall of the mighty and the rising up of the weak [and] we may not see the final outcome of that transformation in our lifetimes, but the signs are there . . . to connect faith and the national pastime is not to argue that baseball is something more than a game; it is to affirm that baseball is a game. (Christopher H. Evans and William R. Herzog II, "The Faith of Fifty Million: A Kingdom on Earth?" in *The Faith of Fifty Million: Baseball, Religion and American Culture*, 2002, pp. 220–21)

So why do we remain faithful believers as citizens of Red Sox Nation? We believe because we have to. We believe because of the Puritan paradox that suffering gives way to joy. We believe because the Red Sox symbolize more than a game or a collection of pennants. We believe because baseball beckons us to hope in something greater than ourselves. Perhaps it's a stretch to say that being a believer of the Red Sox can be a religious experience or that superstitious beliefs may be a sign of divine intervention. Then again, maybe it's not up to us to decide either way. Now that's wicked.[1]

---

[1] I am especially grateful to my brothers Kevin, Dennis, and Timothy—honorary citizens of Red Sox Nation and lovers of wisdom in their own right—for their suggestions and feedback on earlier drafts of this chapter.

10

Why Red Sox Fans Are Moral Heroes

KAROLINA LEWESTAM and
ORLA RICHARDSON

"They killed our fathers and now the sons of bitches are coming after us"—this is not a cry of a war-scarred nation under siege, but an exclamation of a Red Sox fan after his team lost a playoff game to the New York Yankees, in October 1978.

This strikes a non-fan as a surprisingly dramatic claim. "They killed"—is losing to the Yankees comparable to death? And if it is, surely it's the team on the field that gets killed and not the fans in the bleachers ("they are coming after us")? How can a game become more than a game: an epic that engages generations (first our fathers, now us)? And finally, why so much rage, and why such a strong sense of doom?

Mike Barnicle, a *Boston Globe* columnist would say that the answer is simple: "Baseball isn't a life-and-death matter, but the Red Sox are." There are indeed only a few other teams that inspire such strong feelings of loyalty. For true Red Sox fans the Sox are the most stable element of their lives—more often forgiven than errant friends, more permanent than most jobs, and less likely to be divorced than unfaithful wives. There are people that leave their families and abandon their children, but a Red Sox fan that switches allegiance, or, even worse, becomes a Yankees fan, is more rare than a trout in the Mystic River.

Red Sox Fans—A Breed Apart?

The passion of a fan, unlike so many passions today, is obsessive, enduring, and isn't for sale. And if you're an obsessive lover, you're never fully at rest: Mike Lowell's hips, Daisuke's ERA, Jason

McLeod's draft strategy, all these things keep you up at night. And when the team we love loses, we lose a bit of ourselves. We suffer and we feel anger; we blame everything and everyone, we replay crucial moments, and finally we indulge in "what-if? scenarios"— what if Grady Little had pulled Pedro before the eighth inning, what if Buckner had grabbed that ground ball in the 10th inning and made the out. Ultimately, we hate our fate as fans. But we endure the defeat and remain loyal, because this is what it means to be a sports fan. The Red Sox fan, burdened by both what he has seen and what he knows from the history of baseball, stomached eighty-six years of defeat. That's a lot of losing for one nation.

Think about this particular kind of loyalty for a moment. For Red Sox fans this kind of unyielding commitment is normal, but it's nothing short of extraordinary in today's world. In fact for many it's not only unique, but also disturbing and obsolete. In America we believe that a person has the right to walk away from anything he or she wishes to leave behind. In liberal democracies this is how we understand progress: the extending of our freedom to manage, create, and change our lives. Before democracy, it was obvious to most that the journey of our life would be determined by our class, our social group, our parents' wealth, and professions. However, we can say that things have changed. Today our inherited biography is not so definitive. We believe that just because Jacoby Ellsbury was born in Oregon to a Navajo mother, doesn't mean that he has to stay in Madras and become a forester on the reservation like his father. Jacoby is free to dream big; if he's talented and hard-working, he should be able to become whomever he wishes—for instance, center fielder for the Boston Red Sox.

Jacoby's success story represents the beautiful face of freedom, but there are other faces of freedom that seem a little less agreeable. For example, freedom has gradually eroded our ability to be unthinkingly loyal. Traditionally, in the worst of times it's loyalty that has enabled us to gather together and endure, but now, we can walk away when inconvenience strikes. We can always move on, make a different choice, change, cut ourselves off—whether it's our home, our family, our work, even our psychological past (that is, after all, what we use therapy for: to "free" ourselves from the effects of traumas, past relationships, past mistakes). We live in a society characterized by a form of rampant individualism that transcends personal history; an individualism that believes any loyalty can be forsaken. In such an environment it's easy to understand why someone would continue to support a winning team: for example, the St. Louis Cardinals in the '40s, the Oakland Athletics or the Cincinnati Reds in the '70s, the New York Yankees anytime before 2000. But the commitment found at Fenway Park (pre-2004) is incomprehensible, incomprehensible but exceptional.

The ability to be fiercely loyal isn't the only important quality that Red Sox fans display. The fan is also intimately acquainted with the power of fortune. Not wealth, but fate, chance, luck, and with those happenings that cannot be controlled. Our contemporary individualist—who will not accept that chance could keep him in Madras, trapped by his family's social status—used to care about luck, but now he just buys insurance. When he slips on an icy sidewalk, it's not just bad luck, it must be someone's fault—and thus he sues the city. Equipped with weather forecasts, Google maps, and warnings about hot liquid in MacDonald's cups, he will, for once, be really surprised by his own death.

And for the Red Sox fan? There's no insurance against the heartache of an Aaron Boone homer in the 11th inning or the sale of Babe Ruth to finance a dog of a Broadway play. There's no reason to sue Tim Wakefield or DeMarlo Hale. No way to make Big Papi wear a T-shirt saying, "Warning: No home run today." Every game is unpredictable. Every game is an arena for the Moirai, the ancient goddesses of fate, who cold-heartedly spins the thread of victory, only to cut it when they please. Each game brings the possibility of loss, of despair. And this despair has to be endured, as much as the joy after a game that's won has to be lived. The spirit can't fail; the fan has to be there at the next game, again hoping for victory. Red Sox fans specialize in fate and they know how to take it. What others think of as the absurd part of life, what others try to shield themselves from—the absurd doings of luck—becomes the axis around which a fan's life revolves.

Jim and John

Red Sox fans are different from ordinary people for two reasons: because they have the ability to be loyal and because they constantly face the uncontrollable power of fate. Now, how do these reasons help them? Do they make them better people? Can others learn from them, and if so, what would be the object of this learning? Before we answer these questions, let's meet two people.

One of them is named Jim, the other one John. They both work in the same bank. On Thursday, October 16th, 2003 they both get up at 8:00 A.M. They both brush their teeth and pack their bag in the morning. They both forget to eat breakfast, which isn't a recommendable thing to do, because a healthy breakfast can keep you going for the whole day. They take the same bus to work and reside in neighboring cubicles. At the end of the day, Jim comes back home and goes to sleep unperturbered, reminding himself to eat breakfast the next morning.

John, on the other hand, wakes up with a terrible premonition that the Red Sox will lose today. And there was absolutely nothing he could do to make them win. It didn't stop him from trying: he wore his lucky shirt, kept his baseball cap with him all day, repeated his routine to mimic exactly his movements from yesterday, when the Sox had beaten the Yankees in Game Six. He believed all day that they would in fact not lose, not this time. After work he rushes to the bus and runs to his TV. He watches the game and witnesses a season ending defeat. It was a terrible day, but he thinks next season will be better. Next season we might win. The next morning John wakes up again. . . .

Now, since we already know John (and some of us probably see themselves in him) we can move to more serious business. Human beings often ask: How should we live? Philosophers, thinkers, novelists, radio hosts, hermits and prophets, songwriters and filmmakers have attempted to answer this question for centuries. We think a good answer to this question must openly acknowledge the fact that living is often filled with undeserved hardships. It must be able to help us recognize the fundamentally absurd nature of the human condition. Yet it must also caution us against using this absurdity as an excuse to quit, or to refuse to make a stand when such action is required of us. If our attitude is right we can live in the face of these fears, and live fully.

Living Fully

We shouldn't deceive ourselves about the human lot. Living is, for the most part, a trial. We fail ourselves and others. We fall victim to sickness and to loneliness. Realistically, there is little chance that there's a heaven. Most of us work all day at unfulfilling jobs that keep us from our partners, our children, and our friends. Others don't have jobs at all; some of them live in poverty. Someone loses her loved one in a car accident, another person's life will never be the same since her child was born with a genetic illness. We're inevitably trapped in our bodies, and they betray us in old age, and when betrayed we face death. That these things happen is only part of our woe; that they happen unannounced is the main worry. It is, for us rational animals, the heart of the tragedy: that the thief doesn't knock at the door and that death doesn't blazon her coming. Things that we think we control, we have no real power over. Anything can happen to you in the next five minutes. Tomorrow. Or now. Isn't it simply absurd?

The trick is to *know* that life is absurd. Around every corner there's an Aaron Boone or a hundred-game losing season. That most likely life makes little sense. That yes, you're only a speck of dust, tormented by unpredictable winds. But knowing all that, you should still live to the fullest. Even though we know that love will end, we still love, and love passionately without hesitation or regret. Even when Clemens and Duquette fall out, or even when Damon leaves us for the Yankees. Remembering that your life might stop, keep building a boat, writing a book, mowing the lawn and organizing your records. Act as if the sky was clear, even on a rainy day. But look at the clouds and be prepared for the rain. But forget about them. But know they are there. See them. But don't see them. "Now, this is even more absurd that the absurdity of life!" you might say, "let alone impossible." Yes, but absurd does not mean bad! Sometimes an absurd thing is exactly what one should do. "Impossible," you say! Well, maybe. But there was at least one person, who managed to consciously walk under clouds, believing that the sky is clear. A person who knew that his dearest wish was impossibly cursed but yet he believed in its fruition.

The Story of Abraham

The story about this man is a story you know well. It's not about Carl Yastrzemski though it is about another impossible dream. It's not about Ellsbury stealing home though it feels like a snapshot of an improbable moment that freeze-frames in our minds. It's not the story of Bill Buckner and his eighteen years of hell, but it is the story of a man who carries a terrible burden. This is the story of biblical Abraham, a story re-told most poignantly by a Danish philosopher Søren Kierkegaard. In this story we find a lesson that may seem out of place in the modern world yet this lesson tells us about a life well-lived. And this lesson in living is one we think is also present in the story of the Red Sox fan.

Abraham and his wife Sarah have waited into old age for a child. A miracle occurs and Sarah gives Abraham a son—Isaac. The story of Abraham could naturally close here, with its moral lesson intact: wait faithfully and you shall receive what is due to you. However, having given Abraham the thing that he has waited most piously for, Abraham's God now instructs him to take his son and sacrifice him. What must Abraham think? What kind of cruel joke is this? He gathers up provisions for the journey, and heads to Mount Moriah with his only son, knowing he must kill him. The journey is long: three full days. For three full days Abraham knows that he will sacrifice his son. How is he able to walk? How does the desert look to the old man? Do they talk a lot in the meantime? Do they stop to eat or to drink? Is Isaac perhaps cold and Abraham passes him a coat? When they arrive at Mount Moriah, Abraham ties Isaac and takes the knife. And then God stops him and tells him to free Isaac and go home in peace.

Kierkegaard writes: "Abraham was greater than all, great by reason of his power whose strength is impotence, great by reason of his wisdom whose secret is foolishness, great by reason of his hope whose form is madness, great by reason of the love which is hatred of oneself" (*Fear and Trembling and the Sickness unto Death*, Anchor, 1954, p. 31). But we must wonder: how can we understand the greatness of a man ready to murder his only son?

Abraham receives an order from God, and God's orders cannot be reversed or denied. He sets out for Mount Moriah. Every step of the way is marked with infinite pain. Every conversation with Isaac, every sight of his son is a terrible torment. Abraham is going to kill his own son: the killing is painfully real to him. Is he resigned?

Kierkegaard would say that he's "infinitely" resigned—resigned to the point of irony, to the degree where we crave detachment from whatever caused our resignation. When someone we love is leaving, when something we cherish is vanishing, the pain can be so strong and the sense of injustice so poignant that we might want to stop caring—because indifference would give us peace and rest. We can see that given the terrible nature of Abraham's situation this resignation, this detachment is a thoroughly acceptable stance to take. Those of us who are faced with such tragedies may have no other livable choice but to sit back and joke about the absurdity of life or the impossibility of happiness. To be resigned is a very rational step to take. The fan should say: "the Red Sox will lose, they have done so for the last eighty-six years." The human being should say, "I, my descendents, and my achievements will pass away, as all human beings, and the things they create, do." However, Abraham refuses to remain in a perpetual state of resignation—he rejects this "life's a bitch and then you die" attitude.

Abraham, or at least the Abraham in Kierkegaard's story, never stops loving Isaac. Not for a moment is he detached. He moves beyond resignation, to the realm that Kierkegaard calls "true faith." In the same time he knows both that Isaac will be killed and still believes that he will live. Resigned to the future yet full of belief that this future would not obtain, certain that God would take Isaac from him, certain too that his faith would make this requirement unnecessary. In other words, he's like someone whose father is suffering from cancer: this person knows that her father will die, and yet instead of remaining resigned, she moves beyond this phase. She hopes and believes, she loves and does not give up, right up to the very last moment. This belief is absurd, preposterous, and yet it's this kind of belief that makes human beings great. This is what it means to have true faith; this is what it means to be a moral hero. We must show strength of character and freedom to put ourselves in the vulnerable position of recognizing the hopelessness and impossible nature of the human condition, and then transcend this realization to live and act.

The Lesson

For most, the ability to pass beyond resignation, to believe and to live fully in the face of a terrible drama is a question of innate strength, or a natural talent one might say. We all know people that are talented in living. They seem to take challenges both more seriously and with more lightness. But there's a person, who is better prepared to be dared by fate than most of the regular crowd. It's the guy you see on the Red Line, or somewhere by Kenmore Square; or maybe he was sitting two rows behind you at Fenway. John, our Red Sox fan from earlier, is well trained in this manner of living. Of course he's no Abraham. But there's a structural similarity in their experiences of the absurd and in their commitment to living through such events. Recognizing the point of similarity between the two brings us closer to our claim that John is, in fact, a kind of moral hero.

John knows that the Curse of the Bambino makes it impossible for the Red Sox to do anything other than lose, and of course to lose in painful, almost inhumanly cruel ways. The certainty of this loss is a terrible expectation—and terrible in a way that others can't quite understand. Yet John, like Abraham, cannot simply choose some other way out. He cannot simply walk away. He knows the full horror of his situation; he knows that it's rational to be resigned to loss and even more rational to isolate himself from the consequences of such loss. Yet not only does he remain in the way of such a horrible destiny, he performs an almost acrobatic turn of simultaneous acceptance and belief—acceptance of the inevitability of loss and the strange hope and commitment to the belief that things will be otherwise. To the outside world—to his co-worker Jim—our John is as incomprehensible as Abraham on the mountain poised to sacrifice his son.

Perhaps this feat of faith is best expressed in the words of David Ortiz. Big Papi recounts how he felt after winning Game Four of the 2004 ALCS:

> One day I was driving from my house to the stadium . . . and I saw a big sign on the street that said, 'Keep the faith.' And I saw it was a photo of Manny, it had the big smile. I just parked in front of the photo and I just sat down for a minute and just thought about it, you know, we've been through the whole year. Then I went to the field and I just expressed myself to my teammates about what the Boston nation has been waiting for us and what they expect from us. So it doesn't matter if we are down 3–0. We just have got to keep the faith . . . because the game is not over till the last out.

Red Sox fans know how to keep the faith. They have been tested. Cursed for eighty-six years. Eighty-six years of losing could get the best of us bitter and indifferent. But instead they chose to believe and they choose to believe over and over again. To be capable of such faith is a virtue; this virtue is what one can learn from sports, where loyalty has to persist through loss. And since a loyalty so strong and a loss so frequent is hardly present anywhere else, Fenway Park remains the best university for learning how to live fully, how to believe and how to stay engaged in the presence of uncertainty, in the face of defeat.

Some will protest, and with a hint of intellectual snobbery will deny baseball this important role. Theater (they might say), great novels, reading Kierkegaard—this is what teaches us how to live, not a bunch of grown men throwing a ball around. If we saw a great play about Abraham's journey to Mount Moriah, it surely would teach us more about faith and strength than even the best game of the season. It might often be true. But sports have one great advantage over theater. You can go to the theater on a Sunday evening, maybe every couple of months. But you aren't just a Red Sox fan on a Sunday evening; you live the life of your team, their presence is always with you.

And sometimes just one play, one moment in a game can tell you more about who you are, and who you want to become: when Curt Schilling pitched with that bloody torn tendon we understood something of the human ability to persevere, when Jon Lester delivered that no-hitter we all experienced the possibility of courage and the denial of fear in the face of cancer, and when we watched Ted Williams hit we realized that hard work makes everything possible.

11

We Are Family: The Self and Red Sox Nation

CHELSEA C. HARRY

Don't get me wrong: These people love the Patriots. But they wake up and want to know what happened to the Red Sox. I mean, they really care. It's unbelievable. I've never seen anything like it.

—Terry Francona on Boston fans

My husband recounts his own story of conversion as an event that was inescapable if he wanted to be accepted by my family. He grew up in New Jersey (you know what that means), and as we sat beside each other on the couch in 2004, watching the Red Sox play the Cardinals in the World Series, we were cheering for different teams. This was unfathomable to me. Seriously? *Seriously?* I called my dad. Chris and I were only dating at the time, but the situation seemed to be some sort of test, a possible turning point. I briefed my dad and handed the phone to Chris. My dad, Tim, is one of those infinitely kind, warm-hearted, animal-loving, do-anything-for-you kind of guys. Chris remembers the person on the other side of the phone sounding more like Tony Soprano.

"Chris," he said, "I don't like what's going on." My dad's characteristic jovial tone had changed to something more severe. "In this family we root for the Red Sox, and it would really be better for you if you started rooting for them also." I'm not sure if it was this phone call or the fact that I ate meat that night—breaking over twelve years of vegetarianism in an effort to offer something up to the bargaining table—but Chris has been a proud member of Red Sox Nation ever since.

As we laughed together remembering that day, it occurred to me that we Red Sox fans embody and unsheepishly promote a

131

team spirit unlike any other group of fans. Sure, teams like the Yankees, the Cubs, the Steelers, even our own Patriots, have an unwavering fan base, but we Red Sox fans act as if we're actually part of the team. As Francona says above, *we really care.* Is this a crisis of identity, or something more like a philosophical movement? Defying my realist New England upbringing, I'm going to go with the latter possibility.

While critics on Red Sox discussion boards find it both awkward and hilarious that we call ourselves a "nation," in so doing we have blurred the distinction between team and fan, and we have thus called into question the age-old dichotomy between "us" and "them"; "me" and "you"; "self" and "other." After all, most of us don't play for the team, personally know anyone who plays for the team, or otherwise concretely contribute to the season's successes or failures. And yet families like mine—nurturing, understanding, tolerant groups of people—have a difficult time identifying with those who cheer against the team, as if the "team" isn't simply a playful affiliation, but *who we are.* Tim Wakefield himself has said that Red Sox fans are the team's twenty-sixth player.

Be the Team

The phenomenon of an American baseball team that has created a community across familial, state, and national boundaries, aptly called "Red Sox Nation," calls into question our Western conception of individualism and personal identity. Arguably, our notion of the "self" began to develop in the works of the Ancient Greek philosopher, Plato, who in the fifth century B.C. wrote that justice was each individual doing her part for the greater whole. Fast-forward approximately eight hundred years, and Saint Augustine argued that the good person acts in accordance with God's will. But, it wasn't until the seventeenth century that we adopted our modern secular notion of "self" in the West. Specifically, René Descartes's now famous pronouncement, "I think therefore I am" redirected our idea of self to what we now consider the all-important "I." In contemporary Western society, we often find that the "I" (or in most cases the "me") trumps all—"I have to do what's best for me"; "It's not about you; it's about me"; "I have to look out for myself and my needs"; "No one understands *me*!"

The Boston Red Sox and their fans challenge this egocentric concept of self, which has at this point proliferated in Western society for nearly five hundred years. Themes of interconnectedness, mutuality, and unity bring Red Sox Nation closer to an Eastern concept of self than its Western counterpart, the exclusive "I." Perhaps this is why Terry Francona has described working in Boston as simultaneously thrilling and very difficult. He isn't simply dealing with a ball club trying to win games; he is dealing with all of us, too.

In Eastern philosophy, "self" is not necessarily synonymous with "I" or "me." For example, the Chinese concept of self is based on the belief that there's a fundamental unity between man and nature, which promotes a spirit of interdependence among all beings. The Pre-Confucian period, which dates back to Ancient China prior to the eighth century B.C., teaches that one's "self" is a part of a greater whole, which includes one's immediate and extended family in addition to one's community. Chinese philosopher Chung-ying Cheng, in *New Dimensions of Confucian and Neo-Confucian Philosophy* (1991), explains that it isn't our personal experiences and our individual thoughts that determine who we are, but communal thinking and experiences (p. 3). For this reason, it's impossible to think of an individual person divorced from his relationships within his family and community or outside of the context of what is going on around him historically. Such a belief is in sharp contrast to the Cartesian legacy many people still hold on to today in the United States.

Descartes believed his existence, which he proved based on the fact that he was aware of his own thinking, to be the first, and possibly only, indisputable truth. On the foundation of Descartes's "I think," we understand ourselves as autonomous self-contained units. And we use what we believe to be our unique mental lives to organize, judge, and rationalize all that is "other" around us. In this way, we affirm the dichotomy between "self" and "other" and "I" and "you." Confucians, on the other hand, believe that we're first and foremost a part of a greater whole and that we become ourselves only after we become a part of our context.

Cheng coins the term *naturality* (from the Chinese word *hsing*, meaning human nature) to deemphasize the historically Western link between the individual and rationality (*New Dimensions*, p. 12). Naturality doesn't deny the importance of human rationality, but instead demotes it from being our most prized human function and incorporates it as one component among many of the human self. Naturality isn't about the power and ability of a single person, but about the interrelatedness and unity of various human functions among all people in a community.

It seems strange that the Western emphasis on individual achievement is rampant even in team sports, but in a society where prestige and money largely define our worth, it appears to be par for the course. In most ballclubs, each player is first concerned about his own career and stats, and, from there, is interested in how he can use those in order to further his name and reputation. The public recognizes these individual players because the players seek outside endorsements, and we consequently see them plastered on billboards and appearing in TV commercials.

They gain personal notoriety not for their athletic ability or team spirit, but because they stand behind some corporate giant in an effort to meet their selfish desires for excess wealth and individualized attention. Their actions epitomize a classic Cartesian obsession with a person's inner life, or what Descartes called the "*Cogito.*" Who one "is" amounts to one's private thoughts, and thus to whatever materializes from these thoughts. Increasingly in Western society, we have attributed a certain amount of ownership to whatever develops from these thoughts; sometimes we even patent them as intellectual property. The attention we consequently place on property and ownership in the contemporary West has in many respects become what we value about individuals. We ask "Who is he?" and what we usually mean is: "What does he do?" and "How much money does he make?" And, generally speaking, if we want to be considered successful by Western standards, we conduct our lives in a way that promotes our self-image. It is no different for most ballplayers. A-Rod, for example, caught the public's eye in recent years when his face wound up on the cover of tabloids more often than on the cover of sports publications.

Boston defies this norm. Sox players who act in this way aren't placed on a pedestal, traded as a commodity, or paid more; they are criticized and thought to lack sportsmanship and team ethics. Think about the recent departure of Manny Ramirez, for example, after months of reported temper tantrums and egoism, he was promptly shipped off to the Los Angeles Dodgers; his incredible hitting record of no consequence. Our actions in Boston model an Eastern sensibility. While it may seem unnatural for a Western mind to think that "self" means something much larger than the inner-life of an individual person, this is precisely the Confucian ideal Cheng writes about. According to this ideal, who someone *is* depends on the relationships he has with his community and not on what he thinks, produces, or does for self-promotion. This idea is not foreign to us in Boston; it's the Sox way. After all, our feud with the Yankees has everything to do with the way they play the game— as a bunch of self-loving pseudo celebrities.

Confucianism and Team Spirit

My doctrine is that of an all-pervading unity.

—CONFUCIUS, *Analects*

There's an informal fallacy in Western logic called "composition," and it states that it's false to conclude that a collective entity will be good just because its individual members are good. Applied to baseball, this means that just because all the individual players on a team are All-Stars doesn't necessarily mean that the team will be an All-Star team. While surely this can happen, and it does, it's not simply because such a group of players are together that creates the success of the whole. Instead, it's the indefinable aspect of the way the players work together, the *je ne sais quoi* (I know not what) of the team, which allows them to excel as a unit. It may seem ironic then, that in the US we regularly treat team sports as if they're about the individual members on the team. The draft is all about acquiring the top players at top dollar instead of searching out individuals with team spirit and drive to improve the greater whole. These latter qualities are pejoratively referred to as "intangibles" and are considered secondary to a player's stats. This isn't to suggest that the Red Sox don't care about an individual player's stats. Of course they do. But they care about something else too, and it's this "something else" that makes the comparison between the Sox and Eastern philosophy so natural.

Confucianism was one of the three major schools of Chinese philosophy that arose from Ancient Chinese origins. It's best known as a system of morality. Today, it still influences Chinese government and politics. Confucian teachings, including the *Analects,* the *Doctrine of the Mean,* and the *Great Learning,* are a mix of theory and practice. Not only do they tell us what it means to be the best person one can be, but also they provide concrete suggestions as to how one becomes that person, through self-sacrifice, love, and team loyalty.

Take One for the Team

The man of perfect virtue, wishing to be established himself, seeks also to establish others; wishing to be enlarged himself, he seeks also to enlarge others.

—Confucius, *Analects*

Confucianism begins with the belief that what's external to us (*t'ien*) is the same substance that's inside us (*te*). Our skin isn't a hard and fast boundary between our egos, or whoever we are inside, and the rest of the world. Instead, we are intrinsically relational, defined by our interactions and associations, and not by our individual accomplishments or attributes. Because what is external to us is inseparable from that which is internal to us, it's as if everything is one and the same. Inside *is* outside, and outside *is* inside.

As a consequence, who we become as people develops out of the way we relate to others and not from our individual accomplishments. Likewise, the ways in which we become "good" or "virtuous" ultimately depend on how we treat others instead of how much money we make or on how well we're hitting this season. While it may seem ironic to say that becoming oneself is a matter of letting go of selfish desires, this is precisely what Confucius's writings teach us. In becoming who we are meant to be, we must recognize and honor who we are to others, in addition to thinking ahead to what we could be for them. And so, becoming good means to act in harmony and unity with others, working toward collective accomplishments instead of improving individual skill sets.

"Confucian virtue" and "Sox virtue" are indistinguishable. The first rule for both is that self-sacrifice is the beginning of self-cultivation, or working to actualize one's individual potential. Red Sox games are full of self-sacrifice, and as commentators have pointed out, Sox baseball isn't about each player increasing his stats at the expense of the team. On the contrary, players work together for team success. This is evidenced in players who have taken "hometown" discounts to stay with the Sox. They sacrifice a potential increase in personal wealth and take a less lucrative arrangement in order to remain in Boston. We saw this with fan-favorite Mike Lowell in 2007. Despite the fact that he was named World Series MVP in 2007 and had filed for free agency, he signed for less money to return to the Sox.

Sox fans will never forget two other extraordinary examples of self-sacrifice, where players put not just their wallets, but also their health on the line in order to support the Nation. In the '78 playoffs between the Red Sox and the Yankees, a thirty-nine-year-old Carl Yastrzemski fought through extreme back pain and aching wrists in order to sustain his unwavering support for the Sox. As Richard Bradley reports in *The Greatest Game* (2008, p. xii), Yaz was supposed to be hospitalized, to sit out the season, but he fled the hospital and started swinging around a shovel he found on the streets of Boston. He just couldn't wait to swing a bat again.

The game in '78 was not unlike Game Six of the ALCS in 2004 when Curt Schilling pitched untiringly against the Yankees despite a severe ankle injury. Night after night we all tuned in to see if he would make it through another game. The Sox came out on top during that series, and we'll never forget how we got there. By the end, Schilling's sock was soaked in blood.

Love the Team as Thyself

If a man sets his heart on love and benevolence, he will be free from evil.

—Confucius, *Analects*

But actualizing our interconnectedness isn't just about self-sacrifice. For Confucians, love and benevolence (*jên*) is the virtue that underlies all others. As individuals, we can connect ourselves to our inherent interconnectedness through acts of love and benevolence. This isn't a virtue that Sox players or fans would need to be taught. Acts of love and benevolence are part of every game at Fenway.

In a 2009 interview, Jason Varitek, Tim Wakefield, and David "Big Papi" Ortiz attested to the love and support they get from fans. Wakefield talked about being up on the mound while the bases are loaded. Just when his nerves are starting to get the best of him, Sox fans stand up. They cheer him on and encourage him; they lend him support in such a way that it's almost as if they're a part of him. He says it always helps him get through rough times to know that so many loyal and loving fans believe that he can do it.

Likewise, Ortiz talked about being up to bat and hearing Fenway fans cheer him on. He claims it to be like no other feeling in the world. He knows he's loved, and out of mutual love and a desire for reciprocity he swings like he never would without that support. He doesn't want to let them down. Sox baseball is first and foremost about honoring this inextricable relation to a long history of fan loyalty and heartfelt support, and in this way the Sox emphasize their Confucian sensibilities.

In the Confucian text *Doctrine of the Mean* (which is generally attributed to Confucius's grandson), we're instructed that love and benevolence is "exercised in loving relatives." Where Confucius talks about one's "parents" or when his grandson mentions "relatives," we can substitute "fans," "managers," "players," or "coaches." For Red Sox Nation, this translates to team pride, even when things aren't going so well. And when they aren't going so well, our prideful sentiments turn to deep empathy.

Many of us have encountered fellow fans wearing their Sox gear while traveling, or living, outside of New England. There's an instant bond. "Go Sox!" I have yelled to strangers, and I have experienced people yelling the same to me. We all know what that feels like! I was living in Hawaii during the 2003 season, and I have a fond memory of watching the playoffs with a group of virtual strangers, huddled around a smallish TV on the University of Hawaii campus. My brother has experienced something similar living out in California. On game days, he meets his buddies at the local Red Sox bar. Reading various homemade Sox web pages, I noticed that many Sox fans have never even lived in New England. One fateful trip to Fenway was enough to inspire them to join the Nation.

When I taught at Bridgewater State College, I expected the majority of my students to be wearing their Sox jerseys and hats on game days. My mom isn't the kind to wear team merchandise, but her Sox shirt is an exception. And talking about how Dustin Pedroia, Jacoby Ellsbury, Big Papi, Kevin Youkilis, or Mike Lowell did last night with some lady in the checkout line at Stop & Shop is more like talking about one's brother or father, and not about an anonymous player on the hometown team.

Put the Team First

A man should say, I am not concerned that I have no place, I am concerned how I may fit myself for one. I am not concerned that I am not known, I seek to be worthy to be known.

—Confucius, *Analects*

It's not surprising, then, that Confucianism places a strong emphasis on the family. The family was considered the smallest unit of society, and what one thought or felt was not expressed in terms of his or her individual self (*ch'i*), but in terms of his or her family. Who people were, then, in terms of how we know them or characterize them, had to do with who their family was. Red Sox Nation is a family.

Red Sox Nation is borderline notorious for their team loyalty. Big Papi remembers playing at Fenway before he was traded to the Sox. From the visitor's dugout, he recalls, all he could see were the throngs of Boston supporters—the ballpark is always sold out—fans cheering and chanting for their team. According to Papi, at times it was so intimidating that he felt as if, setting foot onto the field, someone was going to come out and physically attack him.

For Boston fans, player honor and loyalty are similarly etched indelibly into our minds. My eighty-four-year-old grandma Fay recalls bringing my dad and uncle to the '67 World Series—she and my late grandpa, Tom, let them skip school to go. Those were Yaz's glory years, she tells me. When asked, she admits that Yaz was one of her all-time favorite players. But, she adds, not just because he was a great ballplayer, but because of his team spirit and career long dedication to the team. My dad interjects to say that Yaz was also active with many Boston charities, including the Jimmy Fund. And today, Yaz's legacy with the Sox lives on in his grandson, who was signed to the team mid-way through last season.

In the *Analects*, this kind of team loyalty is translated as "filial piety." Recounted conversations among Confucius, state officials, and philosophers help to explain its meaning. To one, he defines it as "not being disobedient," which he clarifies as meaning, "that parents, when alive, should be served according to propriety; that when dead, they should be buried according to propriety." To another, he remarks that, "the filial piety of now-a-days means the support of one's parents." Confucius teaches that we should all have the highest reverence for our family. Not only are we indistinguishable outside the context of our family and community—literally, we are nothing—but also we define ourselves by the way we treat those in our families and communities.

There's nothing that Red Sox Nation loves more than a player who plays out his career with the Sox. This love of loyalty is built into our guidelines for retiring numbers. Whereas other teams retire numbers willy-nilly—the Yanks are on number 16!—the Sox only retire numbers when a player has both been inducted into the Baseball Hall of Fame and also played with the team for at least ten years. At this time, we have retired only seven numbers: Jackie Robinson's #42 (retired by all teams), Carlton Fisk's #27, Jim Rice's #14, Ted Williams's #9, Carl Yastrzemski's #8, Johnny Pesky's #6, Joe Cronin's #4, and Bobby Doerr's #1. Pesky was exempted from the criteria mentioned above because of his exceptional multi-faceted loyalty to the Sox. He spent over eighty percent of his career in baseball with the Sox, as a player, a coach, and as a broadcaster. And so while we obviously are a team that values success, we're just as committed to honoring team loyalty. This should explain why players like Johnny Damon are touted as "traitors." I'll never forget going into Boston after he joined the Evil Empire and seeing his face scratched out of Sox team posters. Damon is to us what some ungrateful, self-obsessed, loner Confucian would be to his village: a great disappointment.

One with the Team

> The mind of the superior man is conversant with righteousness while the mind of the mean man is conversant with gain.
>
> —CONFUCIUS, *Analects*

While the wise Confucius never declared, "Yankees Suck," he sure did seem to know why we hold such disdain for a team so dissimilar to our own sensibilities. Members of Red Sox Nation work for the whole, not for themselves, which brings us closer to Chinese virtue or righteousness than to the typical Western egoism represented well by the Yankees and others. And so what about that *je ne sais quoi* of which I spoke earlier? What I have intended to say here is that Red Sox players, and fans alike, possess this indescribable quality, which tends toward a commitment to unity and a concept of self that's defined by our interrelation with others around us. For this reason, we find it difficult to include those who don't include us, to assimilate the "I's" when we are one big "We."

Richard Bradley touches on this idea exactly when he states that the Red Sox and the Yankees represent two different ways of seeing the world (*The Greatest Game*, p. xii). In Boston, it's simple—we're all in this together. Through the exercise of something akin to Confucian benevolence, we're each able to cultivate ourselves first and foremost as members of a great community. By way of self-sacrifice and the habitual undermining of our selfish desires, team members, managers, coaches, and fans (I ate meat, remember?) instead identify with the larger picture. If the whole suffers while one succeeds, truly no one succeeds. But, as we know in Boston, when each individual works so that the whole succeeds, all benefit and prosper.

12

Thou *Shalt* Steal! How the 2004 Boston Red Sox Reconciled Faith and Reason

JOEL W. CADE

Everything you know about baseball is wrong.

Everything you think makes a player great is rubbish. Instead of wins, the value of a pitcher lies in his strikeout per nine innings and his groundball to fly ball ratio. A hitter's value lies not in his batting average but in his ability to get on base. A team's ability to win isn't based on offense, pitching, and getting along in the clubhouse; instead, wins are directly related to a team's ability to score runs. At least this is what we're told in Michael Lewis's book *Moneyball* (2003).

Moneyball claimed that the traditional way of doing things is misguided. Traditionally, a baseball team was comprised of speedy leadoff men and power-hitting position players. Michael Lewis's book exposed the Oakland Athletics' model for creating a winning team based on key statistics, such as "on-base percentage," or how often a player gets on base. This model is known as Sabermetrics.

Which approach is better, the one that favors traditional roles and managerial intuition or the one that favors the rigorous absolute of statistics crunched by sabermetricians in their basements? This, for better or worse, is the current debate in Major League Baseball.

Baseball's debate is similar to the philosophical debate between faith and reason. A faith-based approach is based on the belief that the traditional way of playing the game yields the best results. This belief is based on intuition without any rational justification. Opposed to this is the rational approach. This approach is based on statistical research defining exactly what styles of play and types of players produce the best results. In philosophy, the faith versus reason debate explores how humanity can live the best possible life. Which line of thinking, then, leads humanity toward the good life—faith or reason?

One place where this debate has been resolved is the front office of the Boston Red Sox. By resolving the debate between faith and reason, the Boston Red Sox were able to overcome their opponents, reverse the curse, and win the 2004 World Series. They also opened up new possibilities for living the good life.

Traditionalists and Sabermetricians

Baseball theorists break down into two camps. Baseball traditionalists argue that the game of baseball has a time-honored approach that has historically defined the game. This approach is defined by certain strategies and methodologies. For example, baseball traditionalists will argue that the sacrifice bunt is an excellent means of scoring a runner from third base. Even though the run is coupled with an out. The out is considered a *productive* out because a run is scored in the process. Also, traditional decisions are often based on intuition or "gut-feelings." A perfect example is Grady Little's decision to leave Pedro Martinez in the game during the 2003 ALCS. The traditional approach claims that baseball is at its best when the time-honored approaches like the bunt and "gut" decisions are employed. These approaches give the game a human element that cannot be replaced. These elements must be respected, preserved, and passed on to the next generation of fans.

Sabermetricians, commonly known as "Moneyballers," employ statistical analysis to predict outcomes of both individual players and overall team performance. Using statistical analysis, they derive the best possible approach to any given scenario. Whereas a traditionalist might call for a sacrifice bunt to score a runner from third, a sabermetrician would argue that the best approach would be to allow the batter to hit freely. The sacrifice results in an out, but sabermetricians argue, the out significantly reduces the chances of the team to score more runs beyond the runner at third. By allowing the batter to hit freely, the chances of scoring the runner from third and the possibility of scoring more runs increase significantly. Using mathematics as their model, sabermetricians seek the underlying rationality behind the game to create a winning team.

Which approach leads to the best results? Baseball is now embroiled in a controversy over which method yields the best results on the field. In the same way, philosophy has been debating a similar question for thousands of years. Does faith—based on unprovable beliefs, or reason—based on logical delineation, lead to the best possible human life?

Tertullian and Joe Morgan

Tertullian of Carthage, your typical anti-intellectualist cult leader, proposed a solution to the debate between faith and reason. His solution is summed up nicely in the following: "What indeed has Athens to do with Jerusalem? What has the Academy to do with the Church?" For Tertullian, reason had no business in matters of faith. Faith can stand alone without recourse to rational verification. For example, when debating a non-Christian over the validity of the Christian faith, Tertullian argued that non-Christians didn't have the right to quote the Bible in the debate. His argument was that the Bible is the property of those who believe. Non-believers, by virtue of their non-belief, had no rights by which they may reference the Bible. For Tertullian, the Bible and faith stand so radically apart from rational discourse, that those who would rely on reason don't have the means or right to properly interpret the Bible. Tertullian's solution to the faith versus reason problem was to rely on faith to the neglect of reason.

Joe Morgan, Hall of Fame second basemen, member of the 1975 Cincinnati Reds, and current ESPN analyst, seems to agree with Tertullian. His views sharply criticize any approach to understanding baseball that deviates from baseball tradition. His motto could be: "What do computers have to do with baseball? Or math with bunting?" He is so set against any rational analysis of the game that he even refuses to read any books on the subject. When asked why he has never read *Moneyball* he responded, "I don't read books like that. I didn't read Bill James's book, and you said he was complimenting me. Why would I wanna read a book about a computer, that gives computer numbers?" ("Say-It-Ain't-So-Joe," *San Francisco Weekly*, July 6th, 2005).

The Tertullian-Morgan approach to faith and reason simply ignores the problem by claiming that faith is right and reason has no place. This approach breeds conflict. For baseball, the conflict splits baseball into two camps that simply ignore each other. Philosophically, this approach breeds religious fundamentalist ideas opposed to any rational approach to religion and leaves faith and reason antagonistically divided.

St. Augustine and Ted Williams

St. Augustine of Hippo, patron saint of beer drinkers and avid sports fan, proposed a different solution to the debate between faith and reason. His approach is summarized in the statement: "Faith seeking understanding." One begins with faith and attempts to use reason in order to understand why faith makes it claims. For Augustine, reason can be used in order to define and defend the claims of faith. Augustine illustrates this point by describing the despoiling of the Egyptians. In his book, *On Christian Doctrine*, Augustine explains that when the Israelites left Egypt, they took all the riches of Egypt with them. Using this as an allegory, the riches of Egypt stand for the truths of reason that the faithful can use in defense of their faith. Some claims of reason are true and, as such, they should be used in service of the Christian faith.

Ted Williams took a similar approach. Although he already knew how to hit well, Williams took an obsessive interest in the mechanics or "science" of hitting. In his book, *The Science of Hitting* (Fireside, 1986), Williams details the science of the proper swing and the mental approach to hitting. He employed reason for the purpose of perfecting the part of his game in which he already had faith. He never deviated from the traditional approaches to the game, but, in a fashion similar to Augustine, he employed reason to enhance and better understand those traditional ways.

The Augustine-Williams approach seeks to reconcile faith and reason. They begin with faith, or baseball tradition, and seek to understand it by the use of reason. For sabermetricians and traditionalists this model shows that the tradition, rather than being discarded, can be explained through reason. Philosophically, the claims of faith are initially accepted and are rationally explored to discover their meaning for human life.

St. Thomas Aquinas and Wade Boggs

St. Thomas Aquinas, patron saint of students and theorist of how many angels can dance on the head of a needle, also discovered a way to reconcile faith and reason. His solution can be summarized in the slogan: "Faith completes reason." Aquinas argued that reason gives us the truth. But only to a certain point. When reason cannot determine the truth of things, faith intercedes. For Aquinas, reason can make valid claims regarding faith and God. However, rational knowledge of religion is not adequate to encompass the totality of faith. Like a house without a roof, reason takes humanity only so far. The roof of the house must be finished by faith. Where reason fails to grasp the totality of faith, faith must supply the truth. Faith completes the work begun by reason.

The superstition of Wade Boggs is a perfect example of the Aquinas model. Wade Boggs perfected Ted Williams's science of hitting. By perfecting the rational approach to hitting, Boggs won five batting titles. However, they didn't call him "The Chicken Man" for nothing. Although Boggs took an extremely rational approach to hitting, he also relied on irrational superstition, religiously following a strict routine that included eating chicken on every game day. This devotion to routine supplied the finishing touches to Boggs's approach that gave him the confidence to hit well. Without the chicken, Boggs would be incomplete as a hitter (well maybe). Nevertheless, his rational approach was completed by a religious devotion to routine.

The Aquinas-Boggs approach also reconciles faith and reason. They employ reason in order to arrive at the best possible approach. Where reason is unable to find the truth, faith fills in the gaps. For baseball, sabermetricians and traditionalists are reconciled insofar as sabermetricians can look to tradition for answers regarding things that can't be explained statistically. Philosophically, reason is employed to determine the good life, but where reason is lacking faith fills in the gaps.

Faith, Reason, and the Stolen Base

So far, the culture of Major League Baseball has taken on the Tertullian-Morgan approach to faith and reason. Baseball traditionalists either discount or simply ignore sabermetricians. Likewise, sabermetricians feel embittered by their apparent excommunication from the baseball community. This has created a divisive culture of mistrust when trying to construct a winning baseball team.

Philosophically, the Tertullian-Morgan approach divides reason against faith. This approach is exemplified in the faith versus science debate. Religious fundamentalists claim the literal truth of their holy books in the face of obvious rational evidence to the contrary. Science claims the truth of their findings without considering religious evidence to the contrary.

The current culture of Major League Baseball regarding faith and reason is no more apparent than when discussing the stolen

base. The stolen base has been around since the beginning of baseball. Its virtue lies in moving a runner into scoring position. Its vice
lies in that the would-be base stealer might be thrown out. If successful, the stolen base gives the team at bat a better chance to
score. If unsuccessful, the team at bat loses an out and a runner on
base. Although a potent ally, the stolen base can be a dangerous
enemy.

Not surprising, traditionalists and sabermetricians disagree
about the effectiveness of the stolen base. For traditionalists, the
stolen base is an effective weapon to be employed by the top of
the batting order. It's designed to move the runner into scoring
position so that the middle of the order can drive them in. For a
traditionalist, in a perfect world the leadoff hitter would get on
base, steal second, advance to third on a sacrifice bunt and be driven in by the third hitter. For sabermetricians, the stolen base is an
antiquated relic from the dark ages of baseball. The stolen base can
potentially move runners into scoring position, however, the risk of
the steal isn't worth its reward. For the stolen base to be an effective weapon the would-be base stealer must be successful a Rickey
Hendersonesque seventy-four percent of the time. Unfortunately
for the traditionalist, there was only one Rickey Henderson. For
sabermetricians, the only thing a stolen base is good for is creating
outs and ruining scoring opportunities.

Reconciling Faith and Reason

The 2004 Boston Red Sox reconciled faith and reason by following
a different model than the current culture of Major League Baseball.
Instead of setting up sabermetrics against baseball tradition, general
manager Theo Epstein and the Red Sox front office took an inte-
grative approach similar to that of St. Augustine and Ted Williams
and St. Thomas Aquinas and Wade Boggs. However, Epstein's
approach was a modified form of the "faith seeking understanding"
and "faith completes reason" methods. Epstein's motto might be
"understanding justifies faith."

Epstein's staff combined both sabermetrics and the traditional
aspects of baseball when putting together the 2004 Boston Red Sox.
His plan was largely based on the *Moneyball* approach. In his first
two years as GM, Epstein acquired players with high on-base per-
centages and pitchers with high strike-out totals and ground-ball
ratios. This enabled the 2003 team to finish first in the Major League

in runs scored and helped them make the playoffs only to suffer at the hands of Grady Little and Aaron "freakin" Boone. However, in 2004, Epstein was willing to "think outside the *Moneyball* box." Instead of relying totally on reason, Epstein was willing to explore the possibilities of when a bunt or stolen base would be an effective weapon.

The contrast between the 2003 and 2004 Red Sox is enlightening. Grady Little, who went with his "gut" and left Pedro Martinez in the game, was replaced by Terry Francona. Francona's success, according to *Baseball Prospectus 2007*, was a result of his adoption of a rational approach. Where Little went with his "gut" and employed traditional strategies like the bunt and stolen base, Francona's approach was much different. Between the years of 2004 and 2006, the Red Sox were last in the majors in sacrifice bunts and stolen bases. However, as noted by the authors of *Baseball Prospectus*, Francona liked to use speed off the bench in the form of pinch-runners. In other words, Francona employed the stolen base when it was most effective. With Terry Francona came a manager who embraced the approach taken by the Red Sox front office.

Understanding Justifies Faith: Trading for Dave Roberts

On July 31st, 2004, Epstein made a rather unusual acquisition. He acquired Dave Roberts from the Los Angeles Dodgers. What makes this trade unusual, in *Moneyball* terms, was that Roberts had a poor on-base percentage and wasn't a home-run threat. Roberts didn't fit the *Moneyball* mold whatsoever. Roberts was nothing more than a pure base-stealer. Why would Epstein acquire a base-stealer?

A shift had occurred in the Red Sox front office. Instead of relying purely on on-base percentage and home runs, the Red Sox staff began to understand when and how to employ the stolen base as a potent weapon. Roberts, who had been working diligently with Dodger Hall of Fame shortstop and prolific base stealer Maury Wills, was the best candidate on the market. All it took to get Roberts from the Dodgers was the decision by GM Paul DePodesta, who figured prominently in the book *Moneyball,* to accept career minor leaguer Henri Stanley in return. In Roberts, the Red Sox acquired insurance just in case they came across a situation in which they absolutely needed a stolen base.

As I said earlier, "understanding justifies faith," the unique approach employed by the Red Sox management, is a combination of the Augustine-Williams approach and the Aquinas-Boggs approach. Like the Augustine-Williams approach, reason is employed to enhance traditional baseball categories in order to determine the best possible means of winning baseball games. Like the Aquinas-Boggs approach, reason is employed to confirm the usefulness of traditional approaches within well-defined contexts. For example, Boggs used a well-defined, almost religious, routine of eating chicken on game days. This routine works within the context of Boggs's rationalistic approach to hitting. In this approach reason confirms the value of faith.

Epstein's "understanding justifies faith," then, is an approach in which reason is employed to determine the best possible means of winning baseball games. In the process, it openly explores and confirms the value of traditional approaches when used in the correct circumstances. In 2004, the Red Sox front office used understanding to justify the need for a base-stealer. They employed reason to understand when and how to employ the stolen base. By doing so, the Boston Red Sox gained a critical advantage over its opponents.

The Steal

> Maury Wills once told me that there will come a point in my career when everyone in the ballpark will know that I have to steal a base, and I will steal that base. When I got out there, I knew that was what Maury Wills was talking about.
>
> —DAVE ROBERTS, *Boston Globe* interview, 2005

The Red Sox reconciled faith and reason, but how did this reverse the curse? The significance of the Dave Roberts trade didn't become apparent until Game Four of the ALCS on October 17th, 2004.

It was the bottom of the ninth inning and the Red Sox were down 4–3 with Mariano Rivera on the mound. Rivera, who was almost invincible, hadn't walked a batter in the playoffs since the 2001 World Series. Yet, inexplicably, Rivera walked Kevin Millar on five pitches. This walk set up what would become known throughout Red Sox nation as "The Steal."

Everyone knew what was coming. We only needed to actually see it happen. Out from the dugout came the seldom-used Dave

Roberts. His only true asset to the team was his ability to steal bases. And during his time with the Red Sox he didn't have many opportunities to do that. But that night was different. Everyone knew he was going to steal second base—even Jorge Posada and Mariano Rivera.

With Roberts on first and the whole world knowing what was about to happen, Rivera began his delivery toward home. "But Roberts was already gone, digging toward second, erasing the past with every step" (Steven Goldman, *Mind Game*, 2005).

From a purely sabermetric point of view, Dave Roberts should have never been on the 2004 Boston Red Sox roster. His skill set doesn't match those of a player who can positively contribute to a winning ball club. From a traditional point of view, Dave Roberts's steal was a confirmation of exactly what traditionalists had been saying all along. The genius of the Red Sox was that they were able to reconcile faith and reason. They were able to rationally determine under what conditions the stolen base would be most effective. Having done their homework, the Red Sox were in position to utilize Dave Roberts's most valuable asset.

Reversing the Curse

"The Steal" put Dave Roberts on second with nobody out. The next batter, Bill Mueller, singled to center scoring Dave Roberts. The Red Sox won on an extra-inning home run by David Ortiz. This victory gave the Red Sox their first victory of the series, but they were still down 3–1. No team had ever come back from a 0–3 deficit to win the ALCS. But this year was different. The Red Sox had found a way to overcome all the odds; they had reconciled faith and reason. The Red Sox then embarked on an amazing eight-game postseason winning streak, which included a sweep of the St. Louis Cardinals to win their first World Series in eighty-six years.

Rounding Third and Heading for Home

The culture of Major League Baseball has approached the problem of faith and reason along the same lines as Tertullian and Joe Morgan. Dividing themselves into "camps," GM's are labeled as traditionalists or sabermetricians. Both traditional and sabermetric GM's hire coaches sympathetic to their respective approaches. They also tend to sign players that embody the virtues their system's value. Sabermetricians have several "favorite" players, like Ted Lilly, Marco Scutaro, and Scott Hatteberg that get bounced around teams with statistic friendly GM's. Likewise, traditional GM's tend to keep players around that, according to sabermetricians, provide little or no value to their team like Juan Pierre, Corey Patterson, and Tony Pena Jr. These approaches are exclusive and have divided baseball along the lines of the specific skills that each system values. This division creates two markedly different styles of baseball.

Instead of playing into this exclusive culture of Tertullian and Joe Morgan, the 2004 Boston Red Sox took a reconciliatory approach. They conceded that traditional methods might be useful if they were employed in the proper situations. Following their own "understanding justifies faith" model, they used statistics to discover the value inherent within taboo traditional strategies like the bunt and stolen base. This approach gave the Red Sox a marked advantage over their opponents, especially the Yankees.

The Boston Red Sox model provides hope that faith and reason need not always be enemies. Using reason to explore the validity of religious ideals justifies their usefulness in determining the good life. It also allows religious ideas to challenge and enhance a rationally determined good life. The Boston Red Sox reconciled faith and reason to pull off a miracle by winning the World Series. Maybe their approach can pull off another one. Maybe it can get persons guided by faith to reconcile with persons guided by reason and likewise. Miracles do happen.

Breaking the Eighth Commandment

Would St. Augustine steal second base? Even though it breaks the Eighth Commandment, I believe St. Augustine would steal second base like a bushel of pears! By reconciling faith and reason, the Boston Red Sox prove that within the right conditions breaking the Eighth Commandment is both a rational and Holy thing to do.

Thou *Shalt* Steal!

13

The Primitive Mysticism of Red Sox Fans

PETER KREEFT

2004 was an apocalyptic event. In 2004, the eighty-six year curse that Dan Shaughnessy in *The Curse of the Bambino* conclusively proved to be real, and not merely mythical, by unimpeachable empirical evidence and statistical calculations, was broken. The Red Sox world championship of 2004 transformed Red Sox fans from losers to winners, from Charlie Browns to Lucys, from Christians to lions, from Jews to Philistines. The result of this apocalyptic event: a massive identity crisis.

The degree of difficulty the cosmos experienced in assimilating this apocalyptic event was made visible by two meteorological events. The first was that at the precise moment that the Sox won the fourth and last game of the World Series, in St. Louis, there was a total eclipse of the moon. (I kid you not. Check it out.) Many Red Sox fans at that point expected to see the skies to roll back like a scroll and to hear a voice sounding suspiciously like Charlton Heston's announcing: "Now, children, this is the one thing you know I never allow to happen on Earth. History is over. You're home."

The second meteorological event was the fact that the winter of 2004 was the severest in Boston's history, if severity is defined by multiplying cold, wind chill, and snow together by a certain formula. This was no surprise to Red Sox fans: Hell froze over when the Red Sox won the Series.

We now live among the aftermath of this apocalyptic event. And we have to choose between two opposite definitions of "Red Sox fan": pre-apocalypse or post-apocalypse.

I'm tempted to choose to define the post-apocalypse Red Sox fan, because that would be choosing to focus on the present rather than the past. But instead I choose to define the past, the classic 1919–2003 version of "Red Sox fan," for five reasons.

1. We don't really quite *know* what our new identity is yet; we're still just trying it out, like a stiff, new suit.

2. It may not last.

3. It's not as *unique* as our old identity.

4. It's not as *miraculous* as our old identity, and therefore not as *interesting* as the old one.

5. It's not as *lovable* as our old identity. (Everybody loves Charlie Brown more than Lucy.)

So I will define our old identity even though it is apparently dead and buried, because sometimes the dead are more interesting than the living. And sometimes they rise from the grave and haunt us.

What Philosophical Categories Fit the Red Sox Fan?

Philosophy asks many questions, but these questions are grouped into sets of questions, which create the basic subdivisions of philosophy. The four that are usually regarded as the most basic and important are *epistemology, metaphysics, philosophical anthropology,* and *ethics.*

Epistemology asks what knowing is. It asks how we *do* it and how we *should* do it. For instance, how do, and how should, the senses and the reason interact? Is certainty ever possible? And why do so many smart philosophers and horror writers love the Red Sox?

Metaphysics asks what is real. It seeks the laws and principles of all reality. For instance, are matter and spirit both real? Is causality real? Was the "curse" real? Can immaterial things like curses cause material things like gopher balls?

Philosophical anthropology asks what *we* are. As Socrates famously said, "Know thyself." Are we angels, ghosts, animals, computers, chemical equations, gods in disguise, or just extraterrestrials? Was Bill "Spaceman" Lee human?

And *ethics* asks about good and evil, right and wrong, rights and duties. For instance, does the end justify the means? Is it wrong to blow smoke in the umpire's eyes? What if he's Larry Barnett?

Three other important divisions of philosophy are *aesthetics*, *philosophy of history*, and *philosophy of religion*. (Philosophy is applicable to everything, so the number of possible subdivisions labeled "philosophy *of____*" is in principle unlimited.)

These divisions are classifications of the types of *questions* philosophers ask. What about the *answers*? They are classified into various philosophical schools of thought, some major and some minor. The major ones, such as Platonic Idealism, Aristotelian Commonsense Realism, Skepticism, Rationalism, Existentialism, Materialism, and Mysticism, give answers to the basic questions in *all* of the subdivisions.

There are also subdivisions within the schools. For instance there's Scientific as well as Philosophical Rationalism; there's Marxist as well as Freudian Materialism, there's theistic as well as atheistic Existentialism and there is Primitive as well as Philosophical Mysticism. Primitive Mysticism is still found in places like Papua New Guinea, the Kalahari, the inner part of Outer Mongolia, and Fenway Park.

The "bottom line" of this chapter is that the philosophy of the Red Sox fan is Primitive Mysticism, in all eight of the subdivisions of philosophy distinguished above.

The Epistemology of the Red Sox Fan

Three main questions of epistemology are:

1. How does ordinary knowledge work?

2. How can we attain *wisdom*?

3. How can we attain *certainty*?

Primitive Mysticism's answer to the first question is: by tradition and authority. We trust our shamans and witch doctors, no matter how absurd or outrageous they seem. The shamans for Red Sox fans are sports writers and sports radio talk show hosts. They're our supreme authorities. For they know our history, and our present and future are determined by our fate, which is made visible in our past history. For instance, we know that the one thing that's always infallibly predictable, each season, is the unpredictable.

When I say fans get their ordinary knowledge "about *reality*" from tradition and authority, I mean by "reality," of course, *not* the universe outside Fenway Park. Red Sox fans don't usually care much about trivial things like wars and depressions and alien invasions—unless the aliens deposit their young on earth and we can sign them as free agents, as we did with Manny. Even "baseball in general" is too general to be a topic of supreme importance for most Red Sox fans. There used to be a sign in the tunnel in Fenway Park that read: "Baseball is only a game. The Red Sox are serious."

That saying is a perfect example of Red Sox logic, which isn't subject to ordinary logical laws like the law of non-contradiction. Mystics, both primitive and philosophical, usually insist that reality transcends the law of non-contradiction, even though that very statement, if it also transcends the law of non-contradiction, means what it does *not* mean; so "reality transcends the law of non-contradiction" really means, "reality does *not* transcend the law of non-contradiction."

Following ordinary logical rules, the conclusion from the two premises that baseball isn't serious and that what the Red Sox do *is* serious, is that what the Red Sox do is not baseball. Some Red Sox fans would embrace that conclusion. They'd say it's *not* baseball: it's exquisitely choreographed sadism, terminating in cardiac arrest, clinical depression, or philosophical wisdom.

Which brings us to our second question, about wisdom. "Philosophy" means, literally, "the love of wisdom." Boston is a city of philosophers, and thus of wisdom. The Boston area, with its two-hundred-plus institutions of higher education, has ten times more philosophers than New York City, even though New York has ten times more people than Boston. The reason is clear: philosophy is the love of wisdom, wisdom comes through suffering, and New York has had the Yankees while we've had the Red Sox.

Before 2004, Yankee fans used to hold up signs reading "26–0," which was shorthand for the fact that the Yankees won twenty-six World Series between 1918 and 2000, while the Red Sox won zero.

In Boston, fathers take their young sons to Fenway Park for the same reason butchers take their sons to slaughterhouses: it is their initiation into "the way things are." It is Enlightenment.

Regarding the third question, the way to certainty, there are four possibilities:

1. Certainty is impossible (Skepticism).

2. Certainty is possible by reason (Rationalism).

3. Certainty is possible by experience (Empiricism).

4. Certainty is possible by Mystical Intuition.

Obviously, the Red Sox fan's epistemology embraces option 4. The Red Sox fan *just knows*.

One of the things the Red Sox fan *just knows* is the truth of Murphy's Law ("If anything can go wrong, it will.") For instance, if the wind *can* blow Yastrzemski's apparent home run shot to left back onto the field for a pop fly out, in the Greatest Game Ever Played (October 2nd, 1978), and then, an inning later, suddenly turn and blow Bucky "Bleeping" Dent's pitiful little pop fly *out* of the park and into the net for a three-run homer, it most certainly *will*.

But our mystical epistemology goes beyond Murphy's Law and the laws of logic: we also *just know* that if something *can't* go wrong, it still will. For instance, if that dippy little dribbler *can't* possibly go through Billy Buckner's legs (it couldn't even go through my three year old grandson's legs), and bring in the winning run for the Mets in the infamous sixth game of the Series in 1986, it nevertheless *will*. It will happen not because it can but because it can't. (The laws of logic now dimly appear in our rear-view mirror.)

The night after that game was called the *Night of the Living Dead* because thousands of Red Sox fans shuffled through the streets like zombies. Even though the Sox had another chance the next day in Game Seven, everyone *just knew* what had to happen. Even after the Sox led 3–0, no one was foolish enough to hope that victory was possible.

No one *except* our heroes. They're actually *surprised* when the impossible happens. For instance, there was a genuinely surprised expression on his face during that eternal half second when short-stop Johnny Pesky held the ball relayed to him from center field while Enos Slaughter scored the winning run for the Cardinals all the way from first base on a single to win the World Series in 1946. (Dom DiMaggio, the Sox regular center fielder, would have caught the ball on the fly, because he always played very shallow. In fact, he was frantically motioning, from the dugout, to his replacement in center to move in, but to no avail.)

Our managers are also sometimes ignorant of truths every fan *just knows*. The most notable example was the supernatural brain-cramp in the grainy little managerial mind of him-who-must-not-be-named when he refused to remove Pedro Martinez even though everyone else in the world knew he was tanked after one hundred pitches. This eventually allowed the Damnyankees (that's one word in Boston) to win Game Seven of the 2003 ALCS by Aaron Boone's home run.

This is our road to certainty: the infallible sense—almost a kind of *smell*—that something bad is going to happen. This philosophy is nicely summarized by the words of a sign that a fan used to bring to every home opener: "Wait Till Next Year." We are Macbeth, muttering his "Tomorrow and tomorrow and tomorrow" speech, and that hope is necessarily shattered by the tautological fact made famous by a small, female, teenaged, orange-haired philosopher named Annie: "Tomorrow is always a day away."

That is, until 2004, when the laws of time changed and tomorrow became today. But that was the most tragic of all examples of Murphy's Law, because it deprived us of our identity. Our greatest failure was our success, another paradoxical truth that flouts the law of non-contradiction.

The Metaphysics of the Red Sox Fan

This *identity problem* gets us into metaphysics, for it's a metaphysical problem how any thing can lose its identity. Old Parmenides figured this out back when Socrates was still in diapers. It must be *the same thing*, the same X, that once had its identity and that loses it. But to say that "X has lost its identity" is to say that now "X is not X," that X has lost its X-ness, and that's logically self-contradictory. Among all the philosophical schools, only Mysticism embraces logical self-contradictions.

The God problem is another task for metaphysics. Metaphysicians make maps of reality, of all reality, of reality as such, and most people's metaphysical maps have three places on them, usually called *world*, *self*, and *God*. Philosopher Immanuel Kant called these three ideas "ideas of pure reason" and tried to prove that we all had to think them, though he said we could never know whether any one of the three actually existed outside our consciousness.

Theravada Buddhists believe all three are unreal, or empty ("sunya"). Vedanta Hindus believe that the world is empty or illusory ("maya") and that the self and God are at bottom the same ("tat tvam asi," "thou art that"). A few philosophers in the West, like

David Hume, believe not only that there is no God but also that there is no self. Many more philosophers believe there is no God. So it's the God idea that's the most controversial in the West, and the most interesting to philosophers.

Agnostics believe that we cannot know (or at least that *they* cannot know) whether God exists or not. Even believers in God who aren't agnostic about His (or Her or Its) *existence*, are agnostic about His *nature*. Is He a person, as in religious Judaism and Islam, or three divine persons in one Being, as in Christianity? Or is God only a force, like fate or destiny?

Alcoholics Anonymous' "higher power" is a conveniently generic God that merely distinguishes atheism from any kind of theism. For those who claim that God is a person almost always claim that He is also a force. And nearly all who believe that also say that one of the names for that force as it affects human lives is destiny or fate or predestination or divine design. So I will focus on the metaphysical issue of whether or not there exists a divine, or superhuman, force called fate.

Apart from this single issue, Red Sox fans come in all theological sizes and shapes, but all of them believe in fate, even those who are atheists. (If you object that there cannot logically be a divine force called fate if there's no divine source or cause of it, you are still thinking in pre-mystical logic.) We can call this force the "nameless dread," or we can tame it with cute names like "the curse of the Bambino," but it makes no difference; it's there, like a force field, or a rotten weed. Names don't exorcise it. A fate by any other name will smell as sour.

Once fate is admitted, there are three possible philosophical explanations for it:

1. There only seems to be a God behind it. It's really only the form in which random chance appears to us, or the face we project onto it.

2. It comes from a wise and benevolent God.

3. It comes from a Being whose proper name is not God but Satan, or Steinbrenner.

All Red Sox fans *just know* that #3 is the true explanation.

One of the classic metaphysical problems is the reconciliation of fate with free will. Most people believe in both, and all interesting stories that human beings ever tell always combine both somehow. For if there's no free will, then the stories are not about choices, and are boring. We don't tell, or read, stories about machines. But if there's no fate, no "higher hand" at work, but only randomness, then there's no author, and no story, really. No story was ever produced by an explosion in a print factory.

But though storytellers effortlessly *show* us the presence of both fate and free will in every story they tell, philosophers have problems *explaining* it, since the two ideas seem to contradict each other. Are we the causes of our own choices, or are we caused to choose by another? Do we pull our own strings or are our strings pulled by a higher (or lower) puppet master?

Red Sox fans, however, have no problem with that dilemma. They always believe in fate. If they also believe in free will, as most people do, they see it as strictly subordinate to, and a servant of, fate. We can indeed choose—among tortures. We can often choose *how* we die but not *whether* we die. Playing out our baseball season is like living out our lives: there are many ways it could get to the end, and there's much freedom to choose among these many ways, but it's always fated to end in defeat.

The Philosophical Anthropology of the Red Sox Fan

We can define human nature either structurally of functionally. Structurally, there's nothing distinctive in the Red Sox fan's philosophy of human nature. They're not materialists, like Marxists, who deny the reality of the soul. For that would deny the reality of soul-categories like agony, hope, insanity, frustration, and enlightenment. Nor are they Theravada Buddhists, who deny the objective reality of the body and matter. For that denial would, paradoxically, have the very same effect.

But functionally, Red Sox fans have a unique definition of man, and it's that of Primitive Mysticism. And that uniquely mystical functional definition of man is that of the tragic hero on a mystical quest. In the typical ancient epic, the hero (Gilgamesh, Siegfried, Ulysses, Oedipus, Aeneas, Frodo) endures incredible sufferings on his journey to hell and back. He struggles to conquer his unconquerable antagonist fate, and eventually *fulfills* his fate precisely by his impossible but heroic struggle to overcome it.

On the eighty-six-year-long mythic journey, our archetypal Red Sox fan has endured not only more than human nature can bear, but more than it can believe. We perform the self-contradictions of bearing the unbearable and believing the unbelievable, because we're mystics. (My definition of mysticism is also self-contradictory, for it's an attempt to define the indefinable, to eff the ineffable.)

The Ethics of the Red Sox Fan

The most serious and important question in ethics is traditionally thought to be the question of the "summum bonum," or greatest good, or ultimate end and purpose of human life. This was the great question for all classical ethical philosophers like Plato, Aristotle, Augustine, and Aquinas, and also for existentialists like Pascal, Nietzsche, Kierkegaard, and Sartre, although most contemporary philosophers modestly confine themselves to smaller questions like defining rights and duties, and the moral permissibility of specific practices like capital punishment, abortion, animal vivisection, waterboarding, or taking your innocent children to Fenway Park.

The greatest good, and the ultimate meaning of life, for Red Sox fans, is beating (and preferably humiliating) the Damnyankees. Red Sox fans are Manichean dualists. They believe in a single absolute good and a single absolute evil. And it's not so much the attainment of the good as the defeat of the evil that is their ultimate purpose and happiness. Thus it was the great Yankees choke of 2004, when they lost a 3–0 lead in the playoffs to the Sox, that was seventh heaven to Sox fans. The subsequent World Series triumph was mere dessert.

Primitive Mysticism always sees the eternal conflict between good and evil in concrete terms. Evil is not an abstraction, or a lack of good, or a lack of obedience to a law. Evil is the Yankees. End of story.

The Aesthetics of the Red Sox Fan

Aesthetics is about beauty, and our mysterious love of it. For instance, Plato's *Symposium* is about these two things. Mysticism in aesthetics is the claim that beauty and our love of it, though obviously very real, transcend rational explanation.

This fits Red Sox fans to a T, because no one can say why the Red Sox are beautiful, or why we fall in love with them, any more than Dante could logically explain why Beatrice was the goddess he made her out to be. Only the lover can see, only the lover has opened his "third eye," the eye of the heart. "The heart has its reasons which reason does not know," said Pascal.

Freud confessed that beauty was a mystery that surpassed the present ability of all of his new scientific psychology to explain. He hoped that psychology would explain it in the future; but if he were alive today and felt the fervor of the Fenway Faithful, he would just shake his head and say "Ach!" Come to think of it, Red Sox fans do that too. Freud the Stoical pessimist would have made an excellent Red Sox fan.

One feature of beauty that the mystic can accept more readily than more logical thinkers is its paradoxical relation of mutual dependence with ugliness. Beauty itself is not the most beautiful thing in our experience; the drama of beauty versus ugliness (read Sox versus Damnyankees) is. This is true *even if beauty loses,* if only the loss is sufficiently dramatic, artistic, impossible, and at the same time weighted down with destiny, doom, and predestination, as in 1978. Even Stephen King couldn't have written a more nightmarish script than that year's plot. Yet it was in a way the most *beautiful* season in Red Sox history—in the same way as the most beautiful of all earth's mythologies is Norse mythology, in which the beautiful gods go down to final defeat at the hands of the ugly, evil frost giants.

Why are there far more beautiful Civil War stories about the army of the South than the army of the North, about Lee than about Grant? Because we love the hero who loses more than we love the hero who wins; because deep down we know that the highest and most precious achievement of the artist is to break the heart of his audience. (For the only fully whole heart is a broken heart.) Well, the Red Sox have attained this pinnacle of aesthetic achievement more often than any other team, even the Cubs. For no one *expects* the Cubs to win a World Series, but Sox fans, being primitive and irrational mystics rather than rational or philosophical mystics, actually expect success each year, at the same time as they expect failure—another logically impossible feat that only mysticism renders possible.

The Philosophy of History of the Red Sox Fan

History's most important philosopher of history is probably Georg Hegel. Hegel is famous above all for two claims about history: that it's necessary (or, in more familiar theological terms, predestined) and that it's rational. Sox fans know he couldn't be more right about the first of those two claims and that he couldn't possibly be more wrong about the second. When a Sox fan reads Hegel's famous claim, in his *Philosophy of History,* that "history is the history of reason," that "reason rules history," and that "the real is the rational and the rational is the real," he or she always breaks out into hysterical laughter.

For the Sox fan's philosophy of history depends on the same logical paradox we saw with regard to beauty: defeat is really victory and heartbreak is really satisfaction. The (pre-2004) Sox were the Jews of baseball: the chosen people, chosen by an all-powerful, all-wise fate—to suffer!

The fate of the Red Sox has always turned on some tiny irrational thing—like Lou Piniella twice playing fifteen feet off his usual position in right field on October 2nd, 1978, for no reason at all, so that he was able to catch the two balls that would normally have driven in runs and won the game—and without seeing either one (by his own admission: blinded by the sun, he said he just put up his glove to decoy the runner and then suddenly felt the ball nestle inside it). That's how history moves; as Pascal said, "Cleopatra's nose: if it had been a quarter inch longer, the whole history of the world would have changed."

Hegel believed that history was written by an all-rational, all-controlling absolute spirit. Red Sox fans believe that history is written by an insane, drunken, demon-possessed leprechaun.

The Philosophy of Religion of the Red Sox Fan

The most pervasive philosophy in the world is religion. About ninety-five percent of all human beings today, and a greater percentage in the past, believe in some religion. Among religions the most pervasive is Judeo-Christian-Muslim theism. Half the world believes it.

The most important challenge to this religious philosophy is the problem of evil. Indeed, it's the atheists' trump card. If an all-good and all-powerful God exists, how can evil exist? Since evil exists, it seems, God cannot. The history of the Red Sox turns this argument around on the atheist. For this history furnishes strong probable proof for the existence of God. That such systematic torture could occur merely by chance is extremely unlikely.

The problem for religion here is that it's difficult to justify distinguishing this God from the "insane, drunken, demon-possessed leprechaun." All attempts to placate, worship, influence, and win the favor of this God, passionate and pervasive as they were, were uniformly rebuffed for eighty-six years for no apparent reason. (Fenway Park was also exorcised twice before 2004, to no avail.) Believers see this not as a problem that refutes their religious hypothesis but as a divinely designed test of faith and an opportunity for virtues like courage and perseverance. (Annie Dillard wrote of a man who lives on an island in Puget Sound who is trying to teach a stone to talk. That's the kind of "perseverance" we're talking about here.) Red Sox fans count the radical *unreasonableness* of their history as *reason* to believe. For, they say, if we could rationally discern the mind of the baseball God that would make its mind no more God-like than our own.

So Red Sox Nation has done great service to philosophy in giving the definitive answer to the only definitive refutation of the most important claim of the most pervasive philosophy in the world, and doing it from the premise that the atheist considers his strongest. Only Primitive Mysticism could possibly do that.

Some Red Sox fans believe, some doubt, and some disbelieve, in God and heaven. But if there's a God and a heaven, every Red Sox fan, when they get to heaven, will ask God the same two questions: Why were you a Damnyankee fan for eighty-six years? And, what prompted your repentance and conversion in 2004?

True to their philosophy of Primitive Mysticism, Red Sox fans expect that the answer will not be expressible in words. My own prediction is that they will *see* the answer in the smile on God's face, and if you asked them to put it into words would say only: "Mona Lisa!"

Red Sox Future

It remains to be seen what new identity will emerge from the new modern "Enlightenment" philosophy of the Red Sox that has brought them such sudden success. It's a philosophy of rational optimism, rational investments, rational trading, rational medical services, rational teamwork, rational strategy, and rational effort that has displaced the old irrational mysticism. The old identity seems to have simply disappeared like a dandelion in the wind. Soon there will come a day when no one but the old will remember the old Sox and their mystical "curse." Will that be a day for rejoicing or for mourning? Or (with fitting paradoxicality) for both?

In my dreams I hear my son trying to explain to his son the old mystical mystique. It sounds like Mr. Spock admitting: "No, it is not logical. But it is true."

IV

The Rivalry

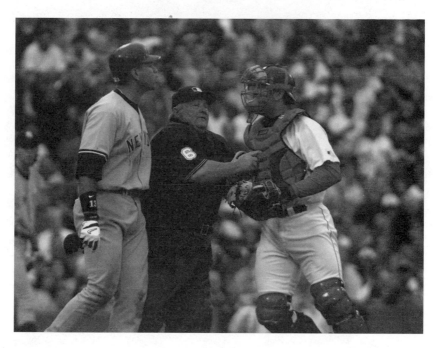

Alex Rodriguez is about to get a face full of Jason Varitek's catcher's mitt.
Courtesy of the Boston Red Sox. Photo by Brita Meng Outzen.

14

On the Genealogy of a Rivalry

NOLEN GERTZ

> Yankees suck!
>
> —Red Sox Nation

My friend Sara knew a guy who knew a guy who could get us tickets to Game Two of the 2003 ALCS and though I went, I didn't want to go.

The Red Sox had won Game One and I had that same feeling that every one of us who grew up a Sox fan felt—there was no way we were going to win two playoff games in a row at Yankee Stadium. Of course I didn't just fear that the Sox were going to lose, or that the Sox were going to lose to the Yankees, but that I was going to have to deal with the taunts ("Got rings?") and the chants ("1918!") and every unbearable expression of superiority from every Yankees fan on the subway, in the streets, and in the stands. Just as we knew the Sox couldn't win that game, they knew the Yankees couldn't lose. While they walked around the stadium before the game high-fiving with a shared sense of entitlement, we walked around—wearing lucky shirts, lucky hats, lucky underwear—nodding silently to each other while trying to hide our shared sense of defeat. Long before Nick Johnson would give the Yankees the lead, long before Jorge Posada would put the game seemingly out of reach, and long before Mariano Rivera ended it, we already experienced what Aaron "F-ing" Boone would soon make a reality—the Red Sox were going to bring us once more to the brink only to leave us still tearfully waiting for "next year."

Though 2004 seemingly changed everything, I still find myself often thinking back to that October night and asking the same questions I did then. Questions like: Why do we put ourselves through this much misery generation after generation? What makes us hate the Yankees and their fans so much? And why do we have such a propensity for using religious language[1] when talking about the Sox and the Yankees? To try to answer these questions, let's see if Friedrich Nietzsche—the philosopher who not only tried to understand the war between good and evil but tried to understand what "good" and "evil" actually mean—can help us to figure out why the Sox-Yankees rivalry is the greatest in all of sports, why a Yankees loss is almost as satisfying as a Sox win, and why it felt so good to watch Varitek shove his catcher's mitt into A-Rod's face.

Masters versus Slaves, or Yankees versus Everyone Else

Friedrich Nietzsche could perhaps best be described as the Manny Ramirez of the philosophy world. Much like Manny, Nietzsche's natural gifts easily placed him at the top of his field, but his eccentricities, his continuous flouting of conventions, his ability to aggravate traditionalists, and his being linked to the most objectionable influences (Nazis rather than steroids) have turned him into something of the "bad boy" of philosophy. And when people try to figure out why he wrote works with titles such as *Hammer of the Gods*, *Twilight of the Idols*, and *Antichrist*, the only answer that seems to make sense is that it's just "Nietzsche being Nietzsche." And while Manny has left us with two World Series championships and enough memories of his hijinks to last a lifetime, Nietzsche has left us with Superman, the idea that whatever doesn't kill us makes us stronger, and a body of work that has influenced individuals as diverse as George Bernard Shaw, Sigmund Freud, Woody Allen, and Goth bands everywhere.

In his *On the Genealogy of Morals* (Vintage, 1989), Nietzsche argues that the story of morality that we were all taught growing up—that there's a "right" and a "wrong" and that there's a proper way to live your life—is only half of the story. The other half of the story is what happened long before our half, during the time when the world was divided into masters and slaves. Nietzsche likens the masters to lions, or "blond beasts," who ruled not because they

---

[1] "The Curse," "Good versus Evil," "David versus Goliath," "The Evil Empire," "Faith Rewarded," not to mention Johnny Damon going from "Jesus" to "Judas."

were the wisest, the oldest, or the most well-liked, but because they were the strongest, deadliest, and most fierce. These warriors, who enjoyed killing, raping, and pillaging, were also rather stupid, and thus superficial, recognizing those who looked like themselves and acted like themselves as "good" and those who didn't look like them or act like them as "bad." As Nietzsche writes:

> . . . the judgment "good" did *not* originate with those to whom "goodness" was shown! Rather it was "the good" themselves, that is to say, the noble, powerful, high-stationed and high-minded, who felt and established themselves and their actions as good, that is, of the first rank, in contradistinction to all the low, low-minded, common, and plebeian. It was out of this *pathos of distance* that they first seized the right to create values and to coin names for values . . . *that* is the origin of the antithesis "good" and "bad." (First Essay, Section 2)

Nietzsche's point is that the values created by the masters were not moral values, measuring the quality of one's soul, but rather values befitting warriors, measuring the quality of one's sword. By "good" and "bad" therefore they meant nothing more than "strong" and "weak."

Similarly, the Yankees' organization and their fans don't care about playing the game the right way, having a strong farm system, going after players who have good character or who are fun to play with and root for. They care about winning. As George Steinbrenner once said, "Winning is the most important thing in my life, after breathing. Breathing first, winning next" (baseball-almanac.com). The Yankees and their fans expect to win the World Series every year, and if they don't then the season is considered a failure. Much like Nietzsche's masters, the Yankees identified players by whether they looked like and acted like the Yankees, that is to say whether or not they were focused on winning above all else. This is why for years they sought out every available free agent superstar they could get their hands on, regardless of what it cost in salary or prospects, as they had no interest in trying to make the most of what they had while developing minor-league talent like every other team in baseball. The Yankees didn't want to be like every other team, they wanted to be superior, lording their championships and their superstars and their payroll over everyone else.

If any other team got lucky and happened to have a good veteran ballclub with one or two once-in-a-generation prospects that could get them to the playoffs, their fans knew that it was only a matter of time until the Yankees would come and steal their prospects (and maybe even their veterans) away from them. This is why fans of other teams, and even other organizations, would begin to behave in ways similar to how Nietzsche describes the behavior of the slaves. For while the masters saw the slaves as "bad" because they could neither fight nor defend themselves, the slaves began to see themselves as "good," telling themselves and each other that it was good not to fight, and that those who did fight were instead "evil." It is thus with the slaves that we first see something like a moral system of values. Whereas the value system of the masters started out from how they saw themselves and their actions, and only later included how they saw those beneath them, the value system of the slaves had the opposite development, starting out from how the slaves thought of the masters, and only then moving to how they thought of themselves.

According to Nietzsche, the reason for why these value systems oppose each other both in development and in meaning is that the masters are defined by action while the slaves are instead defined by reaction. While the masters' actions are fueled by their bloodlust, the slaves' reactions are driven by what Nietzsche calls "*ressentiment*." Though it is often confused with resentment (as that is the literal meaning of the French word), Nietzsche has in mind something far more insidious, far more hateful, and far more dangerous. Nietzsche writes:

> The slave revolt in morality begins when *ressentiment* itself becomes creative and gives birth to values: the *ressentiment* of natures that are denied the true reaction, that of deeds, and compensate themselves with an imaginary revenge. While every noble morality develops from a triumphant affirmation of itself, slave morality from the outset says No to what is 'outside,' what is 'different,' what is 'not itself'; and *this* No is its creative deed. (First Essay, Section 10)

It's *ressentiment* that leads children who have been bullied to doodle the demise of their bullies in their notebooks, survivors of war-torn regions to hang and burn effigies of their enemies, and baseball fans to hope that free agents signed by the Yankees turn out to be busts while demonizing any players from their team that go to the Yankees. Masters do not experience *ressentiment* because, unlike slaves, they can and will attack anyone who gets in their way. That's why masters value bloodshed and power while slaves value peace and humility, and why the Yankees have no qualms about doing whatever it takes to win while other teams want steroid testing and salary caps so that the game can remain clean and fair. But of course the *ressentiment* that the Yankees arouse in fans around baseball is nothing compared to the *ressentiment* felt by Red Sox fans.

Masters versus Priests, or the Steinbrenner Code versus the Yawkey Way

While it's certainly true that fans of other teams don't like it when the Yankees win, don't like the way the Yankees go about trying to win, and don't like the amount of media coverage that the Yankees get whether or not they're winning, Red Sox fans simply hate the Yankees. This hatred tends to confuse other fans as they see the Red Sox and the Yankees as being remarkably similar to each other, with both seemingly having the most money, the most All-Stars, and the most success in all of baseball. And yet Red Sox fans are confused by such comparisons, arguing that the Yankees' money comes from being in New York while the Red Sox money comes from having a devout fan base, that the Yankees buy their All-Stars while the Red Sox develop them, and, most importantly, that the Yankees have had championships while the Red Sox have had the pain of perennially coming up just short. To understand how the Red Sox could think like slaves and act like slaves while at the same time looking like masters to the rest of the slaves, we need to return to Nietzsche and his discussion of a third category of people: priests.

As Nietzsche points out, it wasn't always the case that those in power were a race of warriors who prized conquest and bloodshed, as there was also an elite race who instead prized abstinence and cleanliness known as priests. Though their value system was similar to that of the masters in that theirs was also based on superficialities, the priests didn't use the categories "good" and "bad" to distinguish themselves from those they considered to be beneath them, but rather "pure" and "impure." In the beginning, "purity" meant nothing more to the priests than simply such practices as bathing, eating certain foods, and avoiding bodily fluids. However, these seemingly innocuous lifestyle choices took on a new dimension, a new layer of meaning, when the priests came face-to-face with the masters, and were forced to enter into either competition or battle with them. For while the masters saw the slaves as little more than weaklings that they could enjoy destroying, the priests saw the slaves as people that they could educate, mold, and use to their advantage. Nietzsche writes:

> The knightly-aristocratic value judgments presupposed a powerful physicality, a flourishing, abundant, even overflowing health, together with that which serves to preserve it: war, adventure, hunting, dancing, war games, and in general all that involves vigorous, free, joyful activity. The priestly-noble mode of valuation presupposes, as we have seen, other things: it is disadvantageous for it when it comes to war! As is well known, the priests are the *most evil enemies*—but why? Because they are the most impotent. It is because of their impotence that in them hatred grows to monstrous and uncanny proportions, to the most spiritual and poisonous kind of hatred. (First Essay, Section 7)

Though it's with the priests that humans began to evolve beyond their animalistic nature and that life first came to have any meaning—as they were the ones who introduced the concepts of God, the Soul, and Heaven and Hell—these advances only took place as part of the priests' grand scheme to not just defeat the masters, but to convert the masters to their new religion. For no longer would there be the religion of the masters, with many gods who demanded sacrifices and warfare and who could be blamed for human failings. The priests would replace such "heathen" myths with the "true" religion, the one that believes that the "meek shall inherit the Earth," that we should "love thy neighbor" and "turn the other cheek," and that there's one God who's always watching us and will reward us for our sacrifices (living like a slave) and punish us for our sins (living like a master).

At this point you're probably saying to yourself, "What does this have to do with the Red Sox? We don't think of ourselves as 'pure'! We don't value abstinence or cleanliness! And we certainly don't share any religious beliefs or want to convert the Yankees!" And yet, as a loyal Red Sox fan myself, I can certainly remember taking pleasure in the news that Giambi and Sheffield had used steroids—not to mention A-Roid—and accusing the Yanks of cheating. I remember growing up being proud of Sox legends like Ted Williams for being a war hero and Yaz for playing hard for the Sox his entire career, while mocking Yanks legends like Ruth, Mantle, and DiMaggio for being as famous for what they did off the field as for what they did on it. And I remember how every Sox fan I knew had rituals for watching games that we all thought would somehow affect the outcome, that we were always on the lookout for bad omens whenever it looked like the Sox were doing well, and that we always prayed for a miracle as soon as it looked like the Sox were going to lose, again.

Of course there are fans everywhere who think that their favorite team and their favorite heroes are more "pure" than those of their rival, and these fans have their own rituals, their own omens, and their own prayers. So what separates the Sox and their fans? We've already seen Nietzsche's answer: "It is because of their impotence that in them hatred grows to monstrous and uncanny proportions, to the most spiritual and poisonous kind of hatred." For the Sox, eighty-six years of losing, combined with the Yankees winning thirty-nine pennants and twenty-six championships over that span, culminated in a feeling of powerlessness that manifested itself in beanings, brawls, and an organizational strategy that essentially consisted of trying to beat the Yankees by copying everything the Yankees did (trading away prospects, offering free agent veterans absurd contracts, and creating a media-driven empire out of NESN and Fenway that could rival YES and Yankee Stadium).

But the real impotence, the truly "poisonous kind of hatred," came from Red Sox Nation. The players could take out their feelings on the field, or they could simply leave and play for another team. The organization could take out their feelings by spending more money on a free agent than most teams could spend on their roster, or they could simply leave and run another team. The fans, on the other hand, could do nothing. We couldn't start brawls like Fisk, we couldn't throw inside like Pedro, we couldn't toss money around like Duquette, and most importantly, we couldn't leave. All that we could do was scream "Yankees Suck!" anywhere and everywhere, wear "Yankee Hater" hats, mock Boggs for riding on the back of that horse, and get excited when Clemens was brought down.

The powerlessness that we felt was so far-reaching and so long-lasting that we didn't just hate the Yankees, but deep down we even hated the Red Sox. For evidence, just listen to any WEEI call-in show, look at sonsofsamhorn.com or bostondirtdogs.com, and think about how quickly we turned on Foulke, Manny, Varitek, and Ortiz—arguably the core of our 2004 championship team—as soon as they stopped performing up to our expectations. The Sox so commanded our attention, our devotion, and our lives that watching them play baseball stopped being fun and became a duty. And when they played the Yankees this duty would become an obsession, so much so that every hit given up, every runner stranded, every botched double play would leave us feeling outraged to the point where we wouldn't just curse the heavens for not letting the Sox win but secretly curse our parents for not saving us from becoming Sox fans.

The Joy of Self-Destruction, or How the Yankees Discovered They Have a Farm System

There are two problems at the heart of Nietzsche's *Genealogy*. The second we'll get to shortly, but the first is: How could the slaves, those pitiful creatures who were "denied the true reaction" and were left with nothing more than their "imaginary revenge," have ever escaped from under the foot of the masters? How could the priests—who were incapable of displaying any inborn power by sacrificing others to please their gods, and thus instead could only preach self-sacrifice as a way to be given power by their all-mighty God—have successfully led the "slave revolt in morality," which didn't just defeat the masters, but wiped them off the face of the earth? Or to put this problem back into our version of this story: How did the Red Sox finally defeat the Yankees, retire Steinbrenner, and demolish "The House that Ruth Built," and how could the most tortured fanbase in sports have become Red Sox Nation?

The solution to this problem, according to Nietzsche, can be found if we realize that the priests couldn't have won by getting the slaves to rise up and become masters themselves, as any direct confrontation would've simply ended in the slaves' destruction. Thus their victory was achieved instead by using their cleverness—the one advantage gained by years of weakness, pain, and servitude—to get the masters to destroy themselves and become slaves. To explain how something as seemingly paradoxical as masters becoming slaves could have happened, Nietzsche provides us with the following famous parable:

> That lambs dislike great birds of prey does not seem strange: only it gives no ground for reproaching these birds of prey for bearing off little lambs. And if the lambs say among themselves: "these birds of prey are evil; and whoever is least like a bird of prey, but rather its opposite, a lamb—would he not be good?" there is no reason to find fault with this institution of an ideal, except perhaps that the birds of prey

might view it a little ironically and say: "*we* don't dislike them at all, these good little lambs; we even love them: nothing is more tasty than a tender lamb." (First Essay, Section 13)

The lambs in this story refuse to accept that it's natural for the birds of prey to swoop in and eat the lambs whenever they get hungry. Rather than recognize that the birds of prey are simply acting on instinct, the lambs "reproach" the birds of prey for this behavior, creating the idea that the birds of prey don't have to eat the lambs, but that they *choose* to eat them and that it's this choice that makes them "evil." This idea is based on the same error in judgment that leads us to believe that because some effects require a cause then all effects require one, which is why, as Nietzsche points out, we say things like "lightning flashes" as though the lightning and the flash were two separate things (or how we say things like "Yankees suck" as though these were two separate things). Therefore, Nietzsche concludes, it's

no wonder if the submerged, darkly glowering emotions of vengefulness and hatred exploit this belief for their own ends and in fact maintain no belief more ardently than the belief that *the strong man is free* to be weak and the bird of prey to be a lamb—for thus they gain the right to make the bird of prey *accountable* for being a bird of prey. (First Essay, Section 13)

Along with the idea that the masters could be held accountable for their actions—that they enslaved those who were weaker than them not because they were naturally stronger but because they were choosing to be "immoral"—the priests introduced the corresponding idea that future punishments for such actions would greatly outweigh any possible rewards in the present. By combining the belief that behind our physical nature there's an invisible and immortal soul that is the "true" self with the belief that beyond the physical world there's an invisible and eternal realm that is the "true" reality, the priests convinced the masters that they had to change their evil ways or risk the wrath of the invisible and omnipotent "true" God.

But it wasn't just the fear of God that motivated the masters to become more like slaves, as they discovered that their new slavish existence still allowed them to feel the same destructive pleasures that they craved, though with a slight twist. As Nietzsche writes:

All instincts that do not discharge themselves outwardly *turn inward*—
this is what I call the *internalization* of man: thus it was that man first
developed what was later called his "soul." The entire inner world,
originally as thin as if it were stretched between two membranes,
expanded and extended itself, acquired depth, breadth, and height, in
the same measure as outward discharge was *inhibited.* . . . Hostility,
cruelty, joy in persecuting, in attacking, in change, in destruction—all
this turned against the possessors of such instincts: *that* is the origin of
the "bad conscience." (Second Essay, Section 16)

It was by this invention of the "bad conscience" that the priests
were able to complete the conversion of the masters into slaves, as
their desire to inflict harm on others came to be redirected back
against themselves and felt instead as what we typically call the
"sting of guilt," that pain that children feel when their parents get
them to stop burning ants and finally start becoming upstanding
members of society, or that pain that we hoped Yankees fans
would feel after the Mitchell Report was released.

Now that we've covered how Nietzsche explains the strategy
that the priests used to overcome the masters, we can see how well
this explanation fits the situation between the Red Sox and the
Yankees. While Sox fans certainly invoked such priestly ideas as
karma, baseball gods, the soul of a team, and fan hell to try to scare
Yankees fans so that they would stop being so smug and instead
be as nervous and insecure as the fans of every other team, the Red
Sox organization used a somewhat different approach to scare the
Yankees into changing their ways. When Theo Epstein was brought
in as the new Sox GM, he and the rest of the new front office introduced the "Moneyball" ideas of focusing on speed and defense
over slow-moving sluggers, replacing aging superstars with
prospects, and using statistical analysis rather than relying on gut-
based scouting. And it was during the 2004 ALCS that the Yankees
got to see the results of this new approach firsthand, as the Sox
came back to win in historic fashion not by simply slugging
homers, but with pitching, defense, situational hitting, and of
course "The Steal."

What's important to recognize here is that whereas the substance of Theo's strategy to defeat the Yankees was different than
that of the fans, the underlying logic of the two strategies was the
same. Both the fans and the front office were trying to convince the
Yankees that success for one season isn't worth selling your hopes

for future success, that what you've done is meaningless compared to what you could achieve, and that the possible rewards of filling your team with free agent superstars couldn't outweigh the risks whereas the difficulties in the short-term of playing prospects would ultimately pay off. What this boils down to is the belief that what we can see in the here and now (things like championships, win-loss records, batting averages, runs scored) is just an illusion that can't be trusted, and that what we can't see but can only have faith in (things like projections, advanced scouting, conditioning programs, and video analysis) is the true reality in baseball. And just as the masters were terrified of the eternal damnation that the priests threatened would befall them if they didn't adopt their religion, the Yankees were terrified of the threat of being dominated by a younger, faster Red Sox team that was built to contest every season while they got older, slower, and needed to restock their team with new free agent superstars every season.

It was no surprise then that after the Yankees were beaten in 2004 they suddenly adopted the new "sabermetric" religion of the Red Sox and were starting to bring up guys from their farm system like Cano, Chamberlain, and Hughes to try to match Youkilis, Papelbon, and Lester. Much like the masters discovered upon their conversion, the Yankees found that this new approach allowed them to redirect their desire to impose their will on the rest of baseball and instead impose their will on their own team, as for the first time they were able to play, bench, or send down their young players whenever they wanted to rather than being held hostage by the contracts and expectations of their free agents. When they replaced their aging superstar Bernie Williams with some kid named Melky, when they let Joe Torre go and brought in Joe Girardi after he had achieved a reputation for developing youngsters and pitching, and, most shockingly, when they kept their prospects and let Johan Santana go to the Mets, we knew that the reign of Steinbrenner was over and that the Yankees had suddenly started to look a lot like every other team in baseball.

The Will to Nothingness, or What Happens when the Red Sox Win

This brings us to the second problem at the heart of Nietzsche's *Genealogy*: After the destruction of the masters, why did the slaves still seem to be just as wretched as they were before, if not worse?

The victory of the champions of "good" over the forces of "evil" led to the creation of such advances as civilization, nation-states, culture, art, science, and philosophy, but it also led to the creation of a disease that has largely gone unnoticed, even though it continues to plague all of us to this day. Nietzsche writes:

> Read from a distant star, the majuscule script of our earthly existence would perhaps lead to the conclusion that the earth was the distinctively *ascetic planet* . . . here rules a *ressentiment* without equal, that of an insatiable instinct and power-will that wants to become master not over something in life but over life itself, over its most profound, powerful, and basic conditions; here an attempt is made to employ force to block up the wells of force; here physiological well-being itself is felt and *sought* in ill-constitutedness, decay, pain, mischance, ugliness, voluntary deprivation, self-mortification, self-flagellation, self-sacrifice. (Third Essay, Section 11)

How is it possible that though we now live in a world without masters, Nietzsche sees in it "a *ressentiment* without equal"?

The slaves blamed every weakness, every failure, every death on the masters, so imagine their surprise when the "slave revolt in morality" caused the masters to destroy themselves, and yet the slaves discovered that they were still weak, still failures, and still dying. Nothing had changed. Without their former enemies to blame, without an obvious cause that could be the target of their "imaginary revenge," the slaves were forced to turn their *ressentiment* against anyone and anything that could possibly be held responsible for their perpetual slavishness. It was the release of this hatred in all directions—strangers, friends, family, fate, the universe, even God—that led ultimately to the birth of "the 'last will' of man, his will to nothingness, nihilism," the desire for the utter annihilation of all existence just so that we no longer had to live with the realization "that there was no answer to the crying question, '*why* do I suffer?'" (Third Essay, Sections 14, 28).

This sickness of the soul, this incurable and yet almost unrecognizable feeling that there's no meaning to anything, has always afflicted Red Sox fans simply because we're human. But in recent years it has tormented us in new ways because of our success. When the Sox won in 2004 we did everything we could to prevent the feeling of that victory from ever coming to an end. We collected shirts, hats, posters, DVDs, books, magazines, photos, memorabilia, anything that possibly had to do with that championship. We flooded Boston for the championship parade and then flooded every town the trophy made its way to around New England. By defeating the Yankees and winning the World Series everything suddenly seemed right in the world, all of our suffering finally seemed worth it, and we watched *Faith Rewarded* and read *Now I Can Die in Peace* over and over again to prove it. But after the 2005 season started, and after the banner was raised and the rings were handed out (while the Yankees were forced to watch), these feelings started to fade and with every loss we began to suffer all over again. Only this time the "curse" was gone, the eighty-six years worth of demons had been exorcised, and the Yankees no longer seemed invincible. And just as the slaves discovered after the masters were gone, the problem wasn't that we suffered, but that there no longer seemed to be any reason for our suffering.

Though we despised any talk of being "cursed," couldn't stand any reference to 1918, and hated the Yankees, it wasn't until the Sox won that we realized how much we needed our demons, our failures, and our enemies to sustain us, to prevent us from asking those questions that other sports fans asked themselves about the very meaning of being a sports fan. Once the Sox won they became a team that people *wanted* to root for, which created the opportunity for expanding Fenway, starting the "pink hat" phenomenon and marketing an official "Red Sox Nation" around the world that people would actually buy their way into. For the fans who grew up with the Sox, who remembered when you could just walk up to Fenway the day of a game to buy tickets, it no longer felt like a badge of honor to be a Sox fan because it no longer meant that you were willing to stick with your team no matter what; instead it just felt like you were taking up another seat on the bandwagon. We no longer supported the team that wasn't supposed to win it all, we now supported a team like any other that could win, that we expected would win, and were disappointed by when they lost. And after we won again in 2007 and the bandwagon continued to grow, it was no surprise that diehard Sox fans started to wonder if it really was worth the suffering to care so much about a bunch of players that would never stop coming and going, if it really was worth the energy to follow a team when each season seemed less important than the last, and if it really was worth the cost in time and money to watch adults get paid millions to play a kids' game.

It was their unchecked *ressentiment* that led to the birth of the "will to nothingness" in the slaves and their desire for the destruction of the universe, and it was a similar development with Red Sox fans that led to their desire for there to never be another game of baseball played after 2004. Nietzsche diagnoses this nihilistic disease that gnaws at all our souls at one time or another in the hope that we could "overcome" it. To do this, contrary to what some believe, Nietzsche doesn't advocate a return to the original value system of the masters, instead he believes that true health will only come through a "transvaluation of all values," or by transcending the need for any values whatsoever. Therefore, if the only way to be free of the "will to nothingness" is to become free of both the values of the masters and the priests and just enjoy life, then perhaps the only way for Sox fans to be free is to become free of both the old "win now at all costs" way of the Yankees and the new "always be competitive by playing the game right" way of the Red Sox and instead find a way to just enjoy watching baseball.

15

Confession of a Yankees Fan

MATTHEW M. KONIG

> The New York Yankees . . . World Champions. Team of the Decade. Most successful franchise . . . of the century.
>
> —BOB COSTAS of NBC calling the last out of the 1999 World Series

Do Yankee fans really hate the Red Sox? Well, yes and no.[1] Sure, many a crude anti-Red Sox cheer is uttered at Yankee Stadium. Such cheers are heard even when the Red Sox are not in town! The Bleacher Creatures' roll call of Yankee starters at *every* game concludes with the derogatory chant, "Red Sox Suck!" What could cause Yankees fans to dislike the Red Sox so much that they express their hatred for the Red Sox even when the Sox aren't in the Bronx?

Three recent examples (and there are many to choose from) should be enough to answer this question. First, David Ortiz. Why do the Yankees ever pitch to this guy?! Second, the way that Jonathan Papelbon gathers himself before each pitch, leaning in with that glare to receive the catcher's signal, evokes a visceral response of disgust and leaves Yankees fans hoping for a line drive back through the box sending a flailing Papelbon crashing to the ground as the ball streaks into centerfield. (Already I feel a little better just imagining it.) And, finally, it will be a long, *long* time before Yankees fans forgive the Red Sox for coming back to win after falling behind three games to none in the 2004 American League Championship Series. I mean, really, if the Red Sox are

---

[1] "Just what I'd expect a philosopher to answer," I can almost hear you say.

going to beat the Yankees in the League Championship Series on their way to their first World Series championship in eighty-six years, they could at least have the decency to do it in a less embarrassing fashion! Anyway, on behalf of the Yankees, you're welcome, glad we could help. (Like I said, a *long* time.)

So far we have established that Yankees fans are not crazy about the Red Sox. No Yankees fan will be applying for citizenship in Red Sox Nation any time soon. But I've suggested that there exists a sense in which Yankees fans do *not*, or at least *should not*, hate the Red Sox, and it's the purpose of this chapter to explain why that is. What follows, then, is enlightenment for both the Red Sox fan and the Yankees fan whose perspective on the Red Sox could use a little broadening.

Warming Up with a Thought Experiment: The "Big" Game

World Series, Game Seven. You are batting cleanup for the Sox. It is the bottom of the ninth and there are two out, two on, your team trails by a run. The pitcher unleashes his best fastball. You turn on it, whipping the bat 'round with great ferocity, then watch as the white sphere rapidly grows smaller against the night's black sky. You dance around the bases like Carlton Fisk after he waved the ball fair in Game Six of the '75 Series. At the completion of your dance, teammates mob you at home plate. You are a hero for all time. Just then, through the din of the crowd, you hear your dad calling you—calling you in for dinner, that is, as the fantasy breaks. Sure, we have all enjoyed such moments in our backyards or down at the schoolyard or playground, not against major league competition but against our siblings and the other kids in the neighborhood.

So let's consider a variation on such a moment. You and a friend are catching up on summer exploits. Your friend, the captain of the varsity baseball team, recounts, with great enthusiasm and obvious pride, his triumph in the town's summer league championship contest.

"All the kids from the neighborhood turned out at the schoolyard to see the big game," he begins. "The Fenway Nine were pitted against the Yawkey Way Sluggers. The game was played rugged and tight, and at the end of eight and a half, the score stood tied. I spent the game on the bench. The coach had been saving me as his secret weapon, and, as he tapped me on the shoulder, I realized the time for deployment had arrived. I grabbed my bat, the one emblazoned with a streak of lightning that marks the fate of the tree from which it was carved. The crowd let out a collective gasp as I emerged from the dugout and strode toward the plate. Even the Fenway Nine were unnerved by the sight of me. Beads of sweat broke out on the pitcher's forehead, and he nervously ground the ball into his glove. The bases were loaded and he had nowhere to put me. I dug in with much aplomb, and gestured to center field, calling my shot. The pitcher reared back with all the force he could muster and slung forth the fiercest pitch his body could deliver. With an easy turn and flick of the wrists, I sent the ball careering off into the distance, well beyond the center field fence!"

Your awe and admiration for your friend are evident as you slap him on the back and offer words of praise. Suddenly, you stop short. "Wait a minute," you say. "Uh, aren't the Fenway Nine and the Yawkey Way Sluggers in the youth league?" "Yes," replies your friend, "but they are the premier teams." "They're one step above tee-ball!" you reply, without making any effort to mask the shock and chagrin in your voice. All at once, your friend's triumph is bathed in bathos—a comic fall from the sublime to the substandard. It turns out the "big" game was not so big after all.

Now for a Little Philosophy: Play Ball!

Continuing the thought experiment, imagine that in 2003, shortly after Aaron Boone deposited Tim Wakefield's flat knuckler deep into the left-field stands at the old Yankee Stadium, the Red Sox organization hit upon an ingenious plan to bring a baseball championship to Boston. They decide, for the 2004 season, to transfer the team out of the major leagues and into the independent Atlantic League. The plan works: Big Papi hits eighty-three home runs, Jason Varitek bats .438, the newly acquired Curt Schilling wins forty games, and the team finishes with an .896 winning percentage, all on the way to trouncing the Long Island Ducks in the championship series. The Sox, like your friend in the "big" game, may as well have been playing against Little Leaguers.

Now, the question is: would you value a championship achieved by such means—even one eighty-six years in coming? If not, why not? To answer this question we need to do a little philosophy. Our starting ace, Arthur Schopenhauer is warmed up and on the mound, and we're about to begin.

Here's the Pitch: Schopenhauer's Spitball

In his philosophy of pessimism, Schopenhauer describes life as an unavoidable and unconquerable struggle against suffering. The aspect of ourselves that strives to achieve some goal, like getting called up to the majors, is what Schopenhauer calls the will. And when, through the striving of our will, we achieve a goal, we gain satisfaction—imagine how it must feel to walk into the major league clubhouse that very first time! But when our will is impeded by obstacles, like a Triple-A pitcher having to sit out a season recovering from Tommy John surgery, we suffer. No problem, you're thinking, all we have to do is overcome the obstacle to gain satisfaction, and then we're happy—what's this Schopenhauer guy so pessimistic about? After all, no pain, no gain, right?

Well, the problem, as Schopenhauer sees it, is that while over-coming an obstacle and achieving a goal may usher in a moment of satisfaction, such satisfaction does not last and is soon followed by a new dissatisfaction, or a new want or need. No matter how awesome it feels to walk into the major league clubhouse that first time, the feeling fades fairly quickly, and merely having gotten there is no longer enough. Most of life, then, is lived in a state of dissatisfaction, in unhappiness, and is only dotted with fleeting moments of satisfaction, of happiness. Here's Schopenhauer, our starting ace, in his own words:

> For all striving springs from want or deficiency, from dissatisfaction with one's own state or condition, and is therefore suffering so long as it is not satisfied. No satisfaction, however, is lasting; on the contrary, it is always merely the starting-point of a fresh striving. We see striving everywhere impeded in many ways, everywhere struggling and fight-ing, and hence always as suffering. Thus that there is no ultimate aim of striving means that there is no measure or end of suffering. (*The World as Will and Representation*, Dover, 1969, section 56)

So, while the obstacles we face in achieving those fleeting moments of satisfaction cause us suffering, the real joke on us is that even when we persevere and overcome, the payoff is small and is quickly followed by more suffering. We are beset by the awareness of a new desire and are left with little choice but to tend to this new deficiency. Feeling a bit pessimistic now? Fret not! Our starting philosopher may have pitched us into a jam, but we have relief warmed up in the bullpen. Now philosophizing, Richard Taylor.

This Call to the Bullpen Brought to You By . . .

Richard Taylor, tackling the question of whether there's meaning to be found in our lives, argues that meaning is found in activity. We find meaning in activity when it's our will to be engaged in that activity. It's the very engagement of our will in an activity that pours meaning into it. Life, then, is composed of a series of such activities. The most important point, however, is that, for Taylor, there's no such activity that, once we have completed it, signals that we are done living.

Imagine the following scenario. Steve is your best friend. In Little League Steve had a wad of gum in his jaw and black under his eye, and spent hours on the field throwing, catching, running, and hitting. In high school he pitched the team to the State Championship three years in row and along the way spent hours on the field throwing, catching, running, and hitting. In college he pitched a two-hit, complete game, shutout and hit four home runs in the deciding game of the College World Series, an unerring performance to cap four years in which he spent hour after hour on the field throwing, catching, running, and hitting. All the years of hard work—all those hours of throwing, catching, running, and hitting—were directed toward one goal: going number one in the Major League Baseball Amateur Draft. The day finally arrives. Steve is surrounded by family and friends and Scott Boras. The cameras are rolling and his face is all over ESPN. Bud Selig announces, "With the first selection in this year's draft, the Washington Nationals…"—who'd you expect?!—". . . select Steve." Steve, his family and friends, and Scott Boras party throughout the night—there's food and drink and much merriment. As the night winds down, as darkness begins to give way to the dawn, it's just you and Steve.

> "Wow, man, what a great night! Congratulations, again. So what's next?" you ask.
> "Nothing, man, nothing at all," Steve replies.
> "That's cool. Just going to hang out, enjoy the day, bask in the glory. Sounds good. But what about after that? When do you report to the minor league team?" you respond.
> "I'm not going anywhere," Steve says blankly.
> "What do you mean?" you ask. "If you're not going to report, what are you going to do?"

"I'm telling you, man, nothing. I'm done. I accomplished what
I set out to do, I was picked number one in the draft. I'm literally just gonna sit and stare for the rest of my days."

Just as it dawns on you that your friend is dead serious (and
hasn't misused the word "literally"), you hear some noise off to
your left. In the corner, curled up in the fetal position, is Scott Boras
crying his eyes out.

The moral of this story is that to live is always to be engaged in
the pursuit of some goal, or at least to be engaged in some sort of
activity. Rather than see this continuous chain of strivings as a
source of sadness and suffering, as Schopenhauer would have us
do, we should embrace it for what it is—the essence of life. In
Taylor's words:

> The point of living is simply to be living, in the manner that it is your
> nature to be living. You go through life building your castles, each of
> these beginning to fade into time as the next is begun; yet it would
> be no salvation to rest from all this. It would be a condemnation. . . .
> What counts is that you should be able to begin a new task, a new
> castle. . . . It counts only because it is there to be done and you have
> the will to do it. (*Good and Evil*, Prometheus, 2000, p. 334)

Taylor is surely providing us with some effective relief philosophizing. But the game isn't won yet. Schopenhauer's view, that life
is predominantly one of suffering because we're constantly striving
after one thing or another without end, has been replaced by
Taylor's view that while it's true in life that we're constantly striving after one thing or another without end, it couldn't be any other
way—to stop striving is to stop living! But more than that, this constant striving need not be perceived as suffering or as a source of
suffering. It depends on one's perspective, which in turn depends
on one's attitude about what it is they're after.

We all have an uncle who dedicates tremendous amounts of
time and energy to the collecting of stamps. We might not get it,
we might not wish to join in the merriment, but we can see that
our uncle enjoys it, so Godspeed, Uncle Joe. But Uncle Joe isn't
alone in enjoying an activity others don't quite see the value in. We
all have hobbies, activities, goals that others can't quite make sense
of. Does it really make sense for people to throw a ball, swat at it
with a bat, and run around a field chasing the ball? If it makes lit-

tle sense for people to engage in such an activity, it presumably makes less sense for others of us to watch them! But for all that, we love baseball anyway.

Thanks to the relief work of Taylor, we have the lead entering the top of the ninth, but the question from our thought experiment still needs answering. Following Schopenhauer and Taylor, we can now rephrase the question. Why have the Red Sox failed to satisfy their desire for a championship—their striving for a championship—by entering the Atlantic League and winning it all? It's time to call in our closer. We take the ball from Taylor and hand it over to our power pitcher, Friedrich Nietzsche.

Nietzsche Nails It Down

Nietzsche tells us that people do not seek (at least not directly) pleasure and do not avoid displeasure, but rather pleasure and displeasure are mere consequences. What we do seek is to achieve certain ends, certain goals, and in doing so to increase our power. When we achieve a goal, we grow in power, and we experience pleasure as a by-product. When we fail to achieve a goal we experience displeasure as a by-product. But we also experience displeasure simply being aware that there's some end or goal we desire to achieve but have yet to do so. The experience of displeasure then comes upon us as an invitation to pursue power, to exercise what Nietzsche calls our will to power. Contrary to Schopenhauer's pessimistic view of dissatisfaction, the will to power seeks resistance, seeks something to overcome, so that its power may grow. Here is Nietzsche's delivery:

> . . . what man wants, what every smallest part of a living organism wants, is an increase in power. Pleasure or displeasure follow from the striving after that; driven by that will it seeks resistance, it needs something that opposes it—Displeasure, as an obstacle to its will to power, is therefore a normal fact, the normal ingredient of every organic event; man does not avoid it, he is rather in continual need of it; every victory, every feeling of pleasure, every event, presupposes a resistance to overcome. (*The Will to Power*, Vintage, 1968, section 702)

The degree of challenge the obstacle poses—the intensity of the resistance, then, is the crucial factor in determining the increase of one's power. And now the answer to our question presents itself.

There would be little to no value in the Red Sox Atlantic League championship because there is no resistance, no obstacle worthy of the effort to overcome it. Nietzsche strikes out the side, his stuff is just too overpowering.

The Rivalry: A Nietzschean Perspective

During the twentieth century the New York Yankees dominated Major League Baseball. As any Yankees fan will be happy to tell you, whether you ask or not, the Yankees appeared in thirty-nine of the century's ninety-six World Series, winning an astounding twenty-six of them. That's nearly three times as many as the next highest World Series win total—a mere nine times by the St. Louis Cardinals (the Athletics organization, with stops in Philadelphia and Kansas City, and currently in Oakland, also amassed nine championships during that time). But this accomplishment would mean little to a Yankees fan—or at least it should—if it weren't for the rivalry afforded by the very capable Boston Red Sox. This is not to say that there haven't been, from time to time, other teams that have provided a challenge to the Yankees' hegemony. It is to say, however, that no other team has done so in such a sustained and threatening manner as the Red Sox.

Through the 2008 season, the Yankees finished first in their division forty-four times; fifteen of those times—more than a third—the Red Sox finished second. Add to these raw numbers the flavorful episodes that have transpired between these two teams—the sale of Babe Ruth and the Curse of the Bambino; the Ted Williams-Joe DiMaggio rivalry; the Boston Massacre; Bucky "Bleeping" Dent; the Pedro Martinez-Don Zimmer melee; Jose Contreras and the Nicaragua Affair which led Larry Lucchino to christen the Yankees the "Evil Empire" and may have led Theo Epstein to do his best Keith Moon imitation—and you have the stuff of sports legend.

In Nietzsche's philosophy we find the recipe for what Nietzsche scholar Bernard Reginster calls an "ethics of challenge." This ethics of challenge applies well to the world of sports. The point of sports, generally, is to overcome the resistance posed by one's opponent or by the difficulty of the feat (for example, trying to hit more than sixty-one home runs in a season without the help of performance enhancing drugs). The good that is sought in the ethics of challenge is the activity of confronting and eventually overcoming a worthy opponent or attempting and accomplishing a difficult feat; these successes are good only to the degree that the resistance faced is significant. (Here, again, we see why the "big" game wasn't so big.)

The good, then, of the ethics of challenge is found in the *process* of overcoming the resistance, rather than in defeating all resistance once and for all. If the latter were true, then once the Red Sox won the Series in 2004, being fully satisfied with their victory, they would've just packed up and gone home, never to play again.[2] But they didn't. They returned to take on the next challenge, to face more resistance, to try to win again. But for any of this to be worth the effort, for a victory to be valued, worthy enemies must be confronted on the field of battle. This is what the Red Sox and the Yankees have been for each other: very worthy enemies on the fields of battle.

A (Bronx) Cheer to the Red Sox: "Without Whom, Not as Much"

Throughout the twentieth century the Yankees dominated the rivalry, they dominated baseball, but without the Red Sox one might be tempted to view the Yankees as grown men playing against mere boys, which affords little gratification, as we saw in the "big" game and in the imagined Boston foray into the Atlantic League. Again, other teams from season to season have challenged the Yankees, but none have done so with the consistency and liveliness of the Red Sox. The competitive spirit they evinced and the competition they provided were necessary to grant full meaning to what the Yankees accomplished in the twentieth century: thirty-nine American League pennants and twenty-six World Series Championships (you know, in case you forgot). Ultimately, then, the Yankees are not the Yankees without the Red Sox. And for that Yankees fans are forever indebted, whether they realize it or not, to the ballclub that wears red socks and calls Fenway its home.[3]

---

[2] If a Yankees fan likes the sound of that, then he or she hasn't been following along closely enough.

[3] Thanks to Bernard Reginster and also to Michael Macomber, whose fine editorial suggestions transformed this chapter from a solid single through the middle into a double in the gap.

16

We Believe

JOSEPH ULATOWSKI

> The Fool hath said in his heart, There is no God. Corrupt are they, and have done abominable iniquity; There is none that doeth good.
>
> —Psalm 53:1

"We Believe" is, and has been, a popular motto of Red Sox Nation. It has been made famous by the Red Sox faithful who scribbled the words on makeshift posters and by a documentary, *Still, We believe* (2004), of the heartbreaking 2003 season. One should notice there's something peculiar about the motto. It doesn't tell us exactly what it is that members of Red Sox Nation believe. It seems like a legitimate question to ask: Belief in what?

Mere speculation about the famous motto would suggest some of the following candidates of what it is that *we believe*. First, it could be: *We believe* that the Red Sox can win the World Series. Maybe. But the motto continues to pop up even after the Sox have recently won two World Series championships. So it must mean something other than that.

A second candidate might be: *We believe* that the Red Sox can overcome some ill-conceived eighty-six-year curse. Bostonians admittedly are a superstitious bunch. We believe in some screwy myths. For instance, Bostonians tend to believe they're the worst drivers in the world even though research professors and government agencies have debunked that myth. But there's no reason we would want to draw attention to the curse. We aren't bold enough to wear a superstition on our pinstripe-free sleeve. Such an action would amount to confessing that the curse is real. No member of Red Sox Nation would be willing to admit that openly!

A third candidate might be: *We believe* members of the Baseball Writers Association of America and the Veterans Committee are foolish for not voting Jim Rice (hereafter affectionately referred to as "Jim Ed") into the Hall of Fame sooner. Jim Ed deserved to be inducted into the Hall long before 2009, given his superb offensive and defensive skills. His 1978 MVP season alone should have gotten him the nod into the Hall. Anytime we feel others have unjustifiably wronged our players we make it known, whether by boos, by threat, or by whatever means gets our point across. Each year that passed without Jim Ed's election into the Hall of Fame resulted in a collective "BULL . . . SHIT" chant by Red Sox faithful, not a "we believe" chant. So, the motto certainly doesn't accurately represent our frustration with the Baseball Writers Association and the Veterans Committee for not inducting Jim Ed into the Hall sooner.

Perhaps *we believe* in players' loyalty. We love loyal players like Dom DiMaggio, Jim Rice, Ted Williams, and Carl Yastrzemski, who play their entire career with the Red Sox. But this doesn't seem like the right way to interpret the motto either. We treat players who have chosen (albeit unwisely) to abandon us very well too. Think of Nomar Garciaparra's return to Fenway in 2009. His return to Fenway in an A's uniform was greeted by a standing ovation. This is hardly the response you'd expect from a crowd that might harbor hard feelings toward players who have been disloyal.

Finally, it's not too far-fetched to think it means: *We believe* the Yankees suck! The problem with this interpretation is that every Red Sox fan is willing to scream wildly that the Yankees *really* suck! There's no reason for us to hide it from others. The Yankees suck. The Yankees *really* suck! And every member of Red Sox Nation would be willing to say it over and over again (So—in case you haven't been paying attention—the Yankees suck). No upstanding member of Red Sox Nation would refrain from saying the Yankees suck. So, since none of these candidates seem to capture what we mean when we say, "we believe," I will dedicate the rest of this chapter to an investigation of the motto.

Red Sox Fanaticism *Is* a Religion

There's something noticeably religious about the motto. When someone says, "I believe," it's typically a claim that the person believes in the existence of some divine being. Similarly, I will contend that the content of the *we believe* motto must make reference to something extraordinary. I argue then, that the motto conveys that the Red Sox are the one baseball team "than which none greater can be conceived," or the Red Sox are the greatest conceivable baseball team.

In the history of philosophy, there's a reference to a being "than which none greater can be conceived." It arises in the works of the medieval philosopher St. Anselm of Canterbury. Since Anselm argued that there is a being "than which no greater can be conceived"—for Anselm it's God—I will use his argument, as a foundation for my claim about the motto's content.

People have difficulty understanding Anselm's argument because it's based purely on reason. Because it's based purely on reason philosophers have a special name for it. It's an *a priori* argument. Which means that it's one derived from using our minds alone, independent of our experience and observations of the world. The opposite of an a priori argument is an *a posteriori* argument, which *is* based on our experience and observation of the world. Because Anselm's argument is based in reason and not on experience and observation people find the argument hard to understand.

This leads me to say something in the way of clarification. I'll be talking about Boston, the Red Sox, and the players on the team. These are things we may observe and (if we're so lucky) experience. Given that I'll be talking about the Red Sox, the team's players, and the city of Boston, I'm going to overlook an obvious complaint. The complaint is that omnipotence, omniscience, omnibenevolence, and omnipresence, properties commonly associated with a divine being such as God, cannot be ascribed to things like sports teams. There is no *all-powerful* or *all-winning* sports teams. On this count, the Red Sox couldn't be the greatest conceivable baseball team, since they haven't acquired every single great baseball player and they haven't won every World Series championship. To argue, then, for the claim that the Red Sox are the greatest conceivable baseball team it will have to be implied by some other equally good conclusion.

Ultimately, I think the motto refers to the fan's belief that Boston is the sports city "than which none greater can be conceived." After all, Boston is—quite literally—the greatest conceivable sports city. Our belief that the Red Sox are the greatest conceivable baseball team can be derived from an argument for the claim that Boston is the greatest conceivable sports city. Underlying our view of Boston's greatness is the argument drawn earlier from Anselm who proclaimed that from a conception of God, the being "than which none greater can be conceived," God exists. Along the way to the conclusion that the Red Sox are the greatest conceivable baseball team, I will have to address the ~~Yankees fan~~ Fool that has said an equally good argument can be made for New York.

The Starting Lineup

Terry Francona has managed to win a few championships through the development of a strategic starting lineup. Each game he must put in place a good starting lineup before the Red Sox take the field; likewise, a philosophy chapter has to layout a few concepts before it gets to what it's trying to prove. So here I'd like to clarify a few concepts I'll use in the rest of the chapter; think of what I'm doing here as announcing the starting lineup for the game to follow.

The first thing we have to do is try to grasp how "existence" and "possibility" are used in Anselm's argument. First, we should recognize a distinction between things that exist and things that don't exist. The distinction is easy to understand through some examples. Whereas David Ortiz and Jonathan Papelbon exist, Ebbets Field does not exist. Next, we have to clarify a distinction between *possible*, *impossible*, and *necessary* objects.

Possible objects come in two flavors: First, some possible objects exist, even though it's not hard to fathom them not existing. For instance, Alex Rodriguez or objects like my dining room table are "possible objects." These objects might not have existed. After all, it's easy to conceive of a world in which Alex Rodriguez does not exist (*that*, we may say, is a *far* better world than this one). Saying that something *might* not have existed means that these things are "contingent." The second kind of possible objects don't exist, though they could have existed. Think here of unicorns or the fictional detective Sherlock Holmes. These things don't exist but might have existed. There's nothing ruling out the possibility that they could have existed or even may exist in some future time.

Impossible objects are things that don't exist, couldn't have existed and will never exist. Squircles, a thing that is both round and square at the same time, fall into this category. Similarly married bachelors are impossible objects because a bachelor is by definition a man who is unmarried.

Finally, that leaves us with one other category: necessary objects. The kinds of objects that are necessary include only those things that exist and could not possibly not exist. A necessary object *must* exist.

Now Batting . . . St. Anselm of Canterbury

I will now give two variations on Anselm's argument. According to Anselm, God should fall in the necessary category. God must exist and could not possibly not exist. God shouldn't fit into the other categories: possible or impossible objects. Anselm assumed that everyone, atheists included, could conceive of a being "than which no greater can be conceived"; call this, for better or worse, the "greatest conceivable being." If the greatest conceivable being doesn't exist, then there's a being greater than the greatest conceivable being, namely the greatest conceivable being that exists. Therefore, according to Anselm, a being "than which no greater can be conceived" *has* to exist.

Another version of the argument should make clear Anselm's argument. The word "God" means the greatest conceivable being. The idea of God exists in the mind. Even the Fool "hath said in his heart 'there is no God.'" Such an admission by the Fool indicates that she is able to have an idea of God. A being that exists in reality is greater than one that merely exists in our minds alone. If God exists in the mind alone, then God is not the greatest conceivable being. We already know that God *is* the greatest conceivable being, since that is by definition what God is. Therefore, God must not only exist in the mind but in reality as well.

Anselm's argument is *a priori*, which means, knowledge of God's existence doesn't depend on experience or an understanding of the world. The argument doesn't call on our observations of the world around us to prove God exists. Similarly, I think an a priori argument showing that Boston is the greatest conceivable sports city is possible. In other words, we need not have visited Boston to know that it's the greatest sports city. For Boston is the greatest conceivable sports city, whose nonexistence is inconceivable.

Therefore, one can conceive of a sports city "than which none greater can be conceived." Call this the greatest conceivable sports city. If the greatest conceivable sports city does not exist, then one can conceive of a sports city greater than the greatest conceivable sports city, namely a sports city that exists. Hence, the greatest conceivable sports city has to exist—and that city is Boston.

Unconvinced! I thought so. The city of Boston doesn't make its appearance in the above argument until its conclusion, and there's nothing in the argument's premises to suggest that Boston *is* the sports city of which the argument speaks. One could easily replace Boston with Atlanta or, God forbid, New York. None of the premises of the argument rule out such a replacement. So, Boston isn't necessarily the city the argument mentions. Further argumentation is necessary.

I Love That Dirty Water . . .

The greatest conceivable sports city has to be the one at the center of the universe, since the rest of the universe revolves around it. What is Boston? Well, Boston is "the hub of the universe," as Oliver Wendell Holmes claimed in *The Autocrat of the Breakfast-Table* (1859). We could say that a working definition of Boston is "the hub of the universe." Several media outlets support this view by referring to Boston as the "hub" when they run stories about Boston. In fact, I imagine almost everyone has referred to Boston as the "hub" at some point in time. So, it seems like a definition that fits the city best.

Even the most foolish New Yorker, say someone from Queens or Yonkers, would admit that the hub of the universe isn't hard to conceive. Only the hub of the universe could be the greatest sports city. We (and they) can conceive of a point that is the center of the universe just as easily as we can conceive of a point on a particular piece of paper or conceive of a point on a line. It's greater for the hub of the universe to exist in reality and in the mind than to exist in the mind alone. Therefore, if the hub of the universe exists in the mind but not in reality, then Boston is not the hub of the universe. Consequently, Boston must exist not only in the mind but in reality as well. Since Boston, the hub of the universe, *must* exist in reality, it must be the greatest conceivable sports city.

It's an easy move from Boston's being the greatest conceivable sports city to the sports teams of Boston being the greatest conceivable sports teams. If Boston is the greatest conceivable sports city, then the sports teams of Boston must be the greatest conceivable sports teams. The Red Sox play in Boston. Thus, the Red Sox must be the greatest conceivable baseball team.

Objection: Not All of Boston's Sports Teams Are the Best Sports Teams

The Boston Red Sox have had their share of triumphs and defeats. Subsequently, one might doubt whether it follows from the argument above that the Red Sox are the greatest conceivable baseball team, even if they play in Boston, the greatest conceivable sports city. A ~~Yankees fan~~ Fool might argue that it doesn't follow from Boston being the greatest conceivable sports city that the Red Sox are the greatest conceivable baseball team. The ~~Yankees fan~~ Fool might protest that just because the 1961 New York Yankees are considered the best baseball team in history, it doesn't follow that Roger Maris was the greatest right fielder of all time. To argue like this is to commit what philosophers call the fallacy of division. Which is an argument that says what's true of the whole must be true for some or all of its parts.

I agree that we can't say each player on a championship team is good just because the championship team itself is the best in the league. No one would argue that "Pokey" Reese was the greatest player of the 2004 season, even though he played for the World Series Champion Red Sox. Of course that's not my claim. I argued that the greatest conceivable baseball team is the one in the greatest conceivable sports city. What allows Boston to be the greatest conceivable sports city are the sports teams residing there. The Red Sox are from Boston. The fallacy of division is committed only when a person reasons from whole to parts. But it's a priori true that a concept of the greatest sports city must include within it the greatest conceivable baseball team. The relationship between Boston and the Red Sox isn't a fallacy of division; it's one of identity.

Objection: New York Is Just As Good As Boston

Another objection suggests that any city will fit in Boston's place. The ~~Yankees fan~~ Fool hath said in his heart, "Boston isn't the greatest sports city." His reasoning is simple. It's possible to construct an argument with exactly the same form as Anselm's argument that alleges to prove New York is the greatest conceivable sports city. New York must be the greatest conceivable sports city, for if it was not then it would be possible to conceive of a city whose baseball team has won more World Series than it, which is absurd. Hence, New York—and not Boston—is the greatest conceivable sports city.

Therefore, the Yankees must be the greatest conceivable baseball team.

If the ~~Yankees fan~~ Fool is correct, then Boston isn't the greatest conceivable sports city *and* the Red Sox aren't the greatest conceivable baseball team. But the ~~Yankees fan~~ Fool bases his judgment that New York has the greatest conceivable baseball team on the fact that the Yankees have won the most championships of all Major League Baseball teams. In his reasoning, the Fool uses *contingent*, or a posteriori information to support an *a priori* argument. The ~~Yankees fan~~ Fool cannot call on experience to support an a priori argument because a priori arguments use reason alone. We know that the ~~Yankees fan~~ Fool cannot argue a priori to the conclusion that New York is the greatest conceivable sports city because it's not part of New York's definition that it is the hub or center of the universe. Thus, the ~~Yankees fan~~ Fool cannot possibly argue that New York is the greatest conceivable sports city.

There's a second way to explain that it cannot follow from New York's being the greatest conceivable sports city that the Yankees are the greatest conceivable baseball team (besides the fact that it's the Yankees). New York has two baseball teams: the Yankees *and* the Mets. Even the ~~Yankees fan~~ Fool has to admit the Mets *can't possibly be* the greatest conceivable baseball team. So, if the Mets aren't the greatest conceivable baseball team, then New York cannot be the greatest conceivable sports city. That leaves the Yankees out of the running for the greatest conceivable baseball team. So, here we have at least two arguments underlying the claim that the New York Yankees are not and cannot possibly be the greatest conceivable baseball team.

What Makes the Red Sox Great Is More than the Team

Someone trained in philosophy will recognize that contingent things, such as cities, cannot be claimed to be the greatest conceivable anything. After all, there might be a characteristic or property that makes that thing something better; this means that it wasn't the greatest conceivable thing to begin with. What I have argued, however, is that it's part of the definition of "Boston" that it's the greatest conceivable sports city. Since Boston is the hub of the universe and the universe's center must house the greatest sports city, ultimately Boston must be home of the greatest conceivable baseball team.

The Fool—any fool and not just the biggest fool of them all, the Yankees fan—may contend that the Red Sox aren't the greatest conceivable baseball team. The ~~Yankees fan~~ Fool may have twenty-seven reasons for believing they're justified in thinking that some other team isn't the greatest conceivable baseball team. The ~~Yankees fan~~ Fool, however, hasn't accounted for many things that comprise what constitutes the greatest conceivable baseball team. What about the greatest fans? What about the greatest ballpark? What about the greatest legends? What about the greatest mascot (Oh yeah, if any of you players attempt to accost Wally like that Pirates player assaulted the racing sausage at the Brewers game, consider yourself lucky if you're able to leave the city alive)? Do any other teams have this kind of aura surrounding them? All of these factors contribute to the Red Soxs greatness; in fact, they account for Boston's greatness.

I have argued that the Red Sox are the greatest conceivable baseball team. Such a conclusion was drawn from the greatness of the city in which the Red Sox play—Boston. A city steeped in patriotism and emanating American history couldn't help but be the greatest conceivable sports city. *We believe* because of this city's greatness. The motto, then, refers to the sports city "than which none greater can be conceived." If Boston is the greatest conceivable sports city, then the sports teams of Boston must be the greatest conceivable sports teams. Other fools cannot argue that their city is the greatest because it's not part of the definition of their city that they are hub of the universe. The Red Sox and everything about the team seem to indicate that they are indeed the greatest conceivable baseball team.[1]

---

[1] I am very grateful to Jeff Lockwood, Michael Macomber, Josh Schexnider, Elaine and Joe Ulatowski, and Joe Zogalis for their comments, criticism, correspondence, ad conversation about previous versions of this chapter.

17

Why Are They *Our* Red Sox?

SANDER LEE

Why do normally sane adults root for the Boston Red Sox? The most obvious answer would be that we support such teams simply because they happen to play within an acceptable geographical distance from one's home and their proximity allows us to go to their home games. But we all know this isn't true. Fenway Park only holds 39,928 fans and many of those are well-off season ticket holders and corporate sponsors. The vast majority of fans rarely go to the ballpark to see games. For most of us, whether we live in Boston or somewhere else in the greater New England region (or in the geographically unlimited Red Sox Nation), the closest we ever get to a game is by way of radio, television, or Internet. In fact, many of the Red Sox most loyal fans, me included, live in states other than Massachusetts. From my home in southwest New Hampshire, it takes me approximately three hours to drive to Boston, park, and take the T to Fenway Park. Furthermore, it's impossible to claim that we support the Red Sox because they uniquely represent our region. As we all know, most of their players and coaches don't come from New England and don't live here during the off-season.

Ultimately, the answer to this question is frighteningly similar to the answers we must give to many of the basic questions about the way we live our lives. Those of us who root for the Red Sox do so because we choose to. My wife sometimes asks me why I allow myself to feel bad when the Sox lose. She accepts that it might be fun to feel good when they win, but why torture myself when they lose? There's no good way to explain the pleasures and pains of the true fan to those who choose not to enter the magical realm of sports. In this way, being a fan is a little like making the "leap of faith" discussed by the Danish philosopher Søren Kierkegaard. Kierkegaard claims that the only life worth living, and capable of delivering us from despair, is one that results from a "leap of faith," despite the fact that society may ridicule those of us who make such a choice, and that no empirical evidence exists to prove such a choice is justified.

The faith of Red Sox fans over the hard years of 1918–2004 recalls the tale of Abraham and Isaac, the story of a man who decides, against both his desires and his reason, to blindly follow God's command to sacrifice the life of his son. This story was used extensively by Kierkegaard to illustrate his belief that a willingness to sacrifice one's own hopes and even the hopes of one's children may be necessary to find redemption. It's no accident that one of the most common signs held up by fans at Red Sox games simply reads: "We Believe."

Who Are the Red Sox?

Because of their decades of losing, their heated rivalry with the "Evil Empire," and the much-discussed "Curse of the Bambino," interest in the Red Sox phenomenon transcends the sports world and has entered other areas of popular culture.

For example, in the TV show *Lost,* the myth of the cursed Red Sox was used by one character, Christian Shepard, to persuade his son Jack to accept his fatalistic outlook. Symbolic of these views is his use of the motto, "that's why the Red Sox will never win the World Series." In saying this, Christian is claiming that events in life are beyond our control. It doesn't matter what the Red Sox do or which players they put on the field; it's their fate to be eternal losers. They might come one strike away from winning the World Series (as they did in 1986), but fate will inevitably intervene to destroy their hopes. Those who superficially appear to be the causes of these failures are not really responsible. So Red Sox fans must forgive Bill Buckner and there's no reason to hate Aaron Boone or even Bucky F. Dent. Ironically, these references to the Red Sox fate took place only a few weeks before the team reversed the curse and won their first World Series in eighty-six years.

Before 2004, many fans shared Christian Shepherd's view of the Red Sox. Despite the fact that the people associated with the team (the players, managers, owners, and fans) have been replaced multiple times since Harry Frazee sold Babe Ruth to Colonel Jacob Ruppert's Yankees on December 26th, 1919, it became conventional wisdom to claim that the Red Sox franchise possessed an inherent essential nature that required the team to endlessly repeat the same futile pattern of disappointment.

While this theme may be associated with more than one worldview, it shares many elements of the philosophy of Arthur Schopenhauer. Schopenhauer believed that everything that exists is a manifestation of a force he calls the "will." This will is fundamentally spontaneous and irrational. There's only one will and it pervades all reality while determining every action. By making these claims, Schopenhauer is opposing his philosophy to those of Immanuel Kant and Georg Hegel, the most influential German thinkers of his time. For Kant, the inner will is rational. By following our common intuition of duty (which derives from the will), all of us are freely able to act morally. In Hegel, this force becomes an all-encompassing rational spirit, which drives human history progressively towards a better, more moral future.

Schopenhauer reacts negatively to such optimism. Turning these ideas upside down, Schopenhauer's will is made up of our worst impulses, the irresistible violent and sexual drives that most of us try to hide behind a veneer of civility. These impulses are evil and overpowering. While we like to pretend that we're strong enough to overcome these instincts through rational action, the sad truth is that we can never escape their grip. The most we can do is lie to ourselves that all is well when we know in our hearts that it isn't.

In this sense, Schopenhauer could be described as a "masochistic determinist." A determinist believes that we have no free will. Everything that happens must happen exactly as it does and there's nothing any of us can do to change events. In the case of Schopenhauer (and many Red Sox fans prior to 2004) this determinism is masochistic in that one continues to hope against hope that things will turn out better even when you know for sure that they won't.

In the archetypal version of this pattern, Red Sox fans begin the spring filled with hope, believing that this is the year we win it all. As the season progresses, the team justifies this optimism showing signs of brilliance, outplaying their opponents, even the Yankees, with grit and stamina. Following the All-Star break, with some of their best players suffering injuries or falling into inexplicable slumps, the Sox start to slip, looking nothing like the team that raised our hopes just a few weeks before. However, despite their problems, and with the help of fine performances on the part of relatively unknown fill-in players, the Sox stay competitive until they reach the inevitable season-end showdown with the Yankees. While this showdown may take many forms (a season-ending series, a one-game playoff, or a seven-game playoff series) the end result is always the same; the Red Sox snatch defeat from the jaws of victory and the Yankees win, plunging the fan into the abyss of despair (often accompanied by the agonizing sounds of Frank Sinatra singing "New York, New York").

In his essay *The Myth of Sisyphus,* the French thinker Albert Camus describes the fate of a man doomed to endlessly repeat the same meaningless task over and over again. Camus suggests that Sisyphus's fate mirrors that of the ordinary person forced to repeat the same patterns of behavior in the face of an irrational world empty of meaning, and we may use this metaphor to describe the experience of the average Red Sox fan from 1918 to 2004.

I was inducted into this collective mindset when I moved from Washington, DC to New Hampshire in 1986. Growing up in Dallas, Texas in the 1950s and 1960s, I was deprived of a local Major League Baseball team. My only experience as a baseball fan came, appropriately enough, in the summer of 1964 when my family moved temporarily to Philadelphia to be near relatives. There I was exposed to my relatives' enthusiasm for the Phillies who, unusually, were having a marvelous year. I began rooting for them, living and dying with each game. Nursing a six and a half game lead over St. Louis with twelve games left to play, the Phillies famously went on a ten-game losing streak in one of the most shocking collapses in sports history. While this was a gut-wrenching experience, it was not enough to destroy my usual optimism. It took the Red Sox to do that!

I arrived in New England in 1986 in time to experience another marvelous season, even getting the chance to see Roger Clemens pitch in person at the height of his powers. From my new home in rural New Hampshire, I followed the season and then the playoffs with increasing intensity. When Don Baylor hit his historic home run in Game Five of the ALCS against the Angels, I yelled alongside my brother as we watched on TV. My wife, who was gardening, came in and asked what had just happened because, she told us, she had just heard screams coming from every direction despite our remote location and the fact that the closest houses were out of eyesight.

Like all members of Red Sox Nation, October 25th, 1986 was one of the worse days of my life. I watched in horror as the Sox came within one strike of winning their first World Series since 1918 only to see it all fall to pieces as that infamous ball went through Bill Buckner's legs. The next day, when I entered my local general store wearing my Red Sox cap, the owner asked me how I could stand to wear it today of all days. When I told him that the Sox could still win Game Seven, he just shook his head sadly and murmured, "You poor fool." The following evening I understood what he meant and completed my transformation into a true Red Sox fan, one who dreamed that the Sox would succeed despite my inner fear that all such hopes were an affront to Schopenhauer's cruel will who would inevitably destroy them in the most agonizing possible manner.

Thus, on October 16th, 2003, I watched again in tortured dread, but no surprise, as Grady Little squandered a 5–2 lead in the seventh game of the ALCS. As most members of Red Sox Nation screamed in protest at their TV sets, Little made the obviously dangerous decision to leave an exhausted Pedro Martinez in the game in the eighth, allowing the Yankees to tie, and, finally, win on Aaron Boone's homer in the 11th against an exhausted Tim Wakefield (who clearly deserved better). This ending, perhaps even more than 1986, or the Bucky Dent game of 1978, epitomized the Red Sox experience with all of its inevitable horror, and the despair that follows each collapse, a despair reminiscent of the expression on the face of the man in Edward Munch's famous 1893 painting "The Scream."

Yet, even then, despite the apparent inevitability implied by these events, I believe most Red Sox fans, including me, could be better described as "existentialists" rather than masochistic determinists like Schopenhauer. For most existentialists, the world has become a meaningless and terrifying place without rational purpose in which the individual is free to choose how to live. While that individual is completely responsible for those choices, there exists no objective external moral authority (such as a purposeful God) by which those choices may be accurately gauged.

Realization of this condition usually results in an emotion described as despair or "anguish." Anguish is the apprehension that comes from the realization that one is continually faced with situations in which a choice must be made—not to choose is a choice in itself—and there's nothing to guarantee the validity of one's choices. Out of this anguish there arises what the French philosopher Jean-Paul Sartre calls "bad faith." This occurs when a person lies to oneself and thereby refuses to accept his freedom and the responsibility that goes with it. No one can successfully lie to himself, as it's impossible to totally deceive one's own consciousness. Such a person is necessarily aware of his own inconsistency and refusal to take responsibility.

Analyzed from this existential perspective, I would argue that even on October 16th, 2003, most Red Sox fans didn't really believe that defeat and humiliation at the hands of the Yankees was always and forever predetermined. By the same token, I would argue that most Red Sox fans also ultimately rejected the claim that such defeats were the results of Harry Frazee's selfish acts of greed in dismantling the 1918 champion Red Sox and handing the best players, including Babe Ruth, over to the Yankees.

Thus, efforts to blame specific defeats on the Red Sox inevitable destiny are really forms of Sartrean "bad faith" in which the actual failures of specific individual players and management are denied in a hypocritical attempt to evade genuine responsibility. Proof that most Red Sox fans agree with this analysis lies in the fact that offending players and managers such as Bill Buckner and Grady Little were held individually responsible for their acts. Following their blunders, neither was retained for the next season.

While some argued that the fiasco of the sixth game in 1986 was really manager John McNamara's fault for leaving an aging and injured Buckner in the game instead of bringing in Dave Stapleton as he had done so many times before, I have never heard a Red Sox fan argue that "Billy Buck" shouldn't be blamed for his error because it was inevitable that the Sox would lose. For this reason, when Buckner was invited to throw out the first pitch in the home opener against the Detroit Tigers on April 8th, 2008, the fans gave him a four-minute ovation to show that, with two World Series victories under their belts, all was now forgiven.

Who Are the Yankees?

While Frazee's actions do help explain our historic hatred of the Yankees who built their initial success by robbing Boston fans of their best players, they don't justify the punishment built into the

"Curse." How could it be fair to punish the fans of New England for the acts of an owner, himself from New York, who betrayed their trust by selling off their beloved players? If curses really existed, and if, unlike Schopenhauer's will, they were fair, it would be the Yankees who were cursed by their evil acts of theft, not the Boston fans who were the victims of their crimes.

This claim is undoubtedly the foundation of New England's vehement hatred of the Yankees and is the basis of their characterization of them as "The Evil Empire." A famous cliché of the 1950s says, "rooting for the Yankees is like rooting for U.S. Steel or General Motors" (James Murray, *Life Magazine*, April 17th, 1950). While neither U.S. Steel nor General Motors are doing that well today, we all get the point. Like other big successful corporations, such as Microsoft today, the Yankees buy rather than earn their victories at the expense of the "little guy." Red Sox Nation sees Yankees fans as big money celebrities and snobs who don't have the patience to suffer the years of defeat required to earn eventual success. Like the city they represent, the Yankees must always be the biggest and the best with all the arrogance that implies. There's a story (perhaps apocryphal) that a Yankees player was once asked about the rivalry with the Red Sox and he replied, "there is no rivalry. In order to have a rivalry the other team has to win occasionally."

While the characterization of the Yankees as a team who tries to buy championships may still be accurate, most Red Sox fans realize that they're not immune from similar criticisms, especially in the wake of highly publicized bidding wars over players like A-Rod, Dice-K, and Mark Teixeira, to name but a few. On the other hand, Red Sox fans feel no ambiguity in hating players who abandon the Nation in order to make more money by joining the enemy. While former players who go to other teams are usually greeted with cheers when they return to Fenway (players like Kevin Millar, Orlando Cabrera, Dave Roberts, or Nomar Garciaparra to name but a few), players such as Roger Clemens or Johnny Damon who voluntarily join the the "Evil Empire" automatically vie for the role of Darth Vader himself. Such players have no excuse. Having been already exposed to the loving and virtuous embrace of Red Sox Nation, there can be no moral justification for allowing mere money to motivate such a betrayal. On the other hand, there are some Yankees that even the most hardened Red Sox fan can't help but admire.

Johnny Pesky, the patron saint of the Nation, once said of the Red Sox–Yankees rivalry as it existed in the 1940s and 1950s: "Truthfully, I think there was affection. There was hard, tough competition but there was respect. If you didn't love Yogi Berra or Phil Rizzuto, there was something wrong with you" (Harvey Frommer, *Baseball's Greatest Rivarly: The New York Yankees and the Boston Red Sox*, 1982, p. 54). The same might be said today for a Derek Jeter or a Joe Torre (especially now that Torre has expiated his sins by writing a tell-all book about his former team).

On the other hand, the hatred for the very idea of the Yankees is so great in the Nation that no compromise may be tolerated. In the weekly feature "Tales from the City" in the May 24th, 2009 Sunday edition of *The Boston Globe Magazine* a reader named Michelle T. Perillo from Stoneham, Massachusetts contributed the following under the heading "No Deal":

> In a sale bin at a local Marshalls, I came across a name-brand package of girls' underwear with a faint pink pattern. Feeling proud about finding a bargain others had missed, I looked again: The pink design was a Yankees logo. I, too, dropped my "bargain" like a hot potato.

Even if no one other than herself ever saw or knew about her underwear, Michelle Perillo, like any other good Red Sox fan, couldn't live with such a blasphemous item of clothing on her body.

The word "Yankee" itself raises a minor philosophical issue. The British philosopher Bertrand Russell is famous for pointing out that some words or phrases have ambiguous references that may fundamentally confuse their meaning. Such phrases, such as "the present king of France" or "the evening star" must be clarified before true meaning may be conveyed. In another context, calling someone a "Yankee" might have a very different meaning than it does for the Nation. To the British, any American may be accurately referred to as a "Yank" as in the patriotic tune "Yankee Doodle Dandy." In addition, even a resident of California may be said to display "Yankee ingenuity."

Ironically, when used to refer to a resident of a particular region of the United States, as opposed to the whole country, the word most often refers to someone from New England. The well-known regional publication *Yankee Magazine* has its offices in Dublin, New Hampshire and describes itself as "the only magazine devoted to New England." A humorous aphorism attributed to E.B. White summarizes these distinctions:

> *To foreigners, a Yankee is an American.*
>
> *To Americans, a Yankee is a Northerner.*
>
> *To Northerners, a Yankee is an Easterner.*
>
> *To Easterners, a Yankee is a New Englander.*
>
> *To New Englanders, a Yankee is a Vermonter.*
>
> *And in Vermont, a Yankee is somebody who eats pie for breakfast.*

Are These World Series Champions Really *Our* Red Sox?

As we all remember fondly, in the ALCS of 2004, the Red Sox reversed the "curse" by coming back from a 3–0 deficit to overcome the Yankees and went on to sweep the Cardinals in the World Series. Then in 2007, proving that they were no fluke, the Red Sox repeated the miracle coming back again from a 3–1 deficit (this time against the Cleveland Indians) and again sweeping the World Series (this time against the Colorado Rockies). This change in status from perpetual losers to repeat winners could've had a devastating impact on Red Sox Nation.

If it were true, as we discussed earlier, that the Nation really believed in Schopenhauer's determinism with its accompanying acceptance of the "curse," an essentialist view of the team (regardless of its personnel), and an evil will that heartlessly and unfairly mandated cyclical humiliations at the hands of the hated Yankees, then these winning Red Sox might be unrecognizable. From this perspective, one could argue that the resurrection of the winning team last seen in 1918 marked the end of the Red Sox narrative and that the new team which emerged as world champs in 2004 was not the *real* Red Sox at all, but an entirely different animal which will need to craft a new identity.

Evidence that some fans do indeed accept this approach comes from the multiple reports of long time fans that passed away soon after the Series with their relatives quoting them as saying that now they could finally die in peace. It's even possible that some living former fans have turned their backs on the Red Sox, or even on baseball altogether, justifying their actions with the assertion that the events of 2004 finished the story and thereby ended their interest.

However, returning to the existential perspective, I would argue that this is most definitely not the view of the majority of the Nation. While speculating about curses and franchise identities may be good fun, an entertaining way to divert ourselves during the long "hot stove season," when it comes down to it, we all know that everyone possesses the free will to choose our actions and the responsibility for the consequences of those actions.

In the beginning of this essay I asked why are they *our* Red Sox? They are ours because each of us chooses to care about them, chooses to follow them, even when they are losing and despite their changes in personnel. We do this, not because anyone really thinks that the team has a metaphysical essence that transcends history, but instead because each of us decides that it's valuable to have faith in a team for the sake of the journey through which we travel each season.

Some seasons that journey is depressing from beginning to end. Other seasons have their ups and downs and end in final defeat. And, every once in a while, that season is a miraculous trip to the stars that enriches our imaginations and gives us the strength to survive the disappointments that will always lie ahead of us somewhere.

Good versus Evil

ANDY WASIF

A couple of questions that have kept philosophers occupied for centuries are "What is good?" and "What is evil?"

Although usually a road uniform-colored gray area, one of the benefits of being a Red Sox fan is that the distinction between these two questions falls into somewhat of a more black and white, or more specifically, navy blue and white-pinstriped area. As a Red Sox fan, I can tell you quite unequivocally that the Yankees are evil and everything else is good.

The parallels that have been drawn to the classic film *Star Wars* are uncanny. The Yankees are the "Evil Empire"; they wear black masks, and speak with the help of a ventilator. (All right, so the parallels aren't quite so dead-on, but you get the picture.)

The Red Sox, on the other hand, are the rebel uprising. And who *doesn't* love an uprising? They're the ones that everyone roots for in battles with the Empire. How can you not like the handsome heroes coming from the Tatooine district of Boston? They're obviously the "good" in the equation.

If you expand it further to include "the good," "the bad," and "the ugly," then you can start talking about Philadelphia fans, but for now, we'll keep it between the first two.

Let's examine this judgment through three philosophical concepts: Relativism, Objectivism, and Subjectivism.

Relativism

What's evil depends on the particular culture involved, so no set standards exist by which a culture may be judged good and evil. This leaves it up entirely to you. So what standards are you basing your judgments on? Should a ballplayer be clean shaven or shaggy-headed? Shall players be developed in one's own farm system or overpaid for? Are hats to be worn or set on fire?

Narrow-minded Yankees fans try to hide behind this manner of reasoning. They see the world as the opposite of the way we Red Sox fans see it because they see their culture as better than ours. What they don't know is that we are actually better than they are. And, who cares what they think anyway?

Objectivism

There are objective standards of good and evil that can be discovered and that apply to everyone. This is the manner of thinking that is followed by the other twenty-eight teams in the league. If you observe the entire league as a whole, they might say that Red Sox fans are similar to Yankees fans, however, a. They are being subjective and we haven't covered that yet (see below) so it doesn't count, and b. Who cares what they think?

Subjectivism

All moral standards are subjective matters of taste and opinion. So it would appear that what's good to one is evil to another. Sounds a little too convenient for a good ol' fashioned philosophical donnybrook, doesn't it? This is more for the "live and let live" crowd. You will not see any Red Sox fans practicing this type of morality, not where rivalries are concerned. We will stick with objectivism, if you don't mind. Besides, who cares what they think?

So what makes particular actions good or evil? A crazy fan dives into the net behind home plate at Yankee Stadium? (Evil.) Someone takes a swipe at Gary Sheffield as the Yankees right fielder attempts to field a ball against the wall at Fenway Park? (Hey, seemed like the fan was there first and Sheffield shouldn't have rushed over to startle the fan: Good.) A Yankees fan throws a mustard-laden pretzel at a visiting team's fans? (Absolutely evil, especially if it ends up in the poor patron's eyes.) A Red Sox fan throws a slice of pizza at another Red Sox fan. (Hey, that's just how Boston fans "share" food here. Good.)

Views from the Grandstands

Johnny Pesky helps to unveil Jim Rice's retired #14 at Fenway Park on July 28th, 2009.

Courtesy of the Boston Red Sox. Photo by Mike Ivins.

18

The Disenchantment of Johnny Damon

MICHAEL MACOMBER

What was the first thing that you thought about when you read Johnny Damon's name just now? For many Red Sox fans, it would be:

Sell-out! Judas! He sucks! Traitor!

I have yet to encounter a Sox fan who first thought of Damon's mammoth grand slam in Game Seven of the 2004 ALCS. If you are saying to yourself, "That was the first thing I thought of," you're a better person than most of us.[1] I distinctly remember the feeling I had immediately after his grand slam. It was one of cautious exhilaration. As all Red Sox fans remember, it happened early enough in the game so as not to fill us with too much hope and optimism; after all, we were Red Sox fans, accustomed to epic collapses. Still, Johnny Damon filled us with hope. And once the game was over, we all reveled in his role in finally defeating the New York Yankees. Johnny Damon helped bring a championship to Boston after eighty-six years of trying. The same Johnny Damon who now wears Yankees pinstripes, the same Johnny Damon who is mercilessly booed every time he steps into the batter's box at Fenway Park.

Is it fair for Red Sox fans to treat Johnny Damon this way? Was it right for Johnny Damon to join the Yankees, knowing full well what damage it would do to his legacy as a Red Sox player?

---

[1] Or you are lying.

Doom 'n' Gloom versus Stoic Red Sox Fans

Baseball fans can be a fickle bunch, especially Red Sox fans. They tend to react to each game as if it were an isolated experience. There's the fan who experiences a great deal of pain while watching the Sox lose at Fenway. Who could blame him? The cost of attending a game at Fenway Park is painful enough. Then there's the fan that reacts violently to every miscue during a regular season game. How many times have you been in a bar, or at home watching with friends, and someone yells out, "YOU SUCK!!" after Dustin Pedroia misplays a routine groundball? Does Pedroia really suck? Really!? And when Pedroia goes on to get the game winning hit, and the same fan that said he sucked earlier is now yelling out "PEDROIA THE DESTROYAH!!" Well? Which is it? Does he suck or does he destroy?

On the other hand, there's the fan who sits through an entire game quietly, calmly, taking it all in stride—the good, the bad, and the ugly. This fan understands that even the best teams lose at least a third of their games during the season. These fans seem to have a rational explanation for everything that happens on the field, like "What did you expect? He's been playing hurt all season." Or, "Of course he gave up a home run, lefties are killing him this year." These same distinctions are mirrored by some of our favorite ballplayers. For example, we see the sudden upsurge of emotion when Kevin Youkilis strikes out or when Pedroia makes a diving stop up the middle, which is contrasted by the calm demeanors of Jason Bay or J.D. Drew.

With its 162-game schedule and multiple rounds of playoffs, the baseball season doesn't fall neatly into simple categories. It's a long and complex story, with many twists and turns, players coming and going, streaks and slumps. Historically, many Red Sox players have expressed frustration with Boston fans for actively displaying their mood swings, jeering a player who is struggling one week and cheering them when they turn it around the next. Immediate, overly emotional reactions are rarely ever an accurate interpretation of a particular game. In fact, only after the season has finished are we capable of trying to understand what has happened. Only then do we have all of the material we need in order to make a judgment on whether or not it has been a successful year or not.

It's a natural tendency for human beings to try and understand the world around them. After all, there's a lot of material out there.

In order to understand the world, we must grasp the things around us with our minds. We must take the seemingly infinite amount of material that the world has to offer and try to make sense of it. There are two ways this can happen. We can react based on our sensory experience alone, which usually leads to an irrational and strictly emotional response—say Youkilis throwing his bat after a called third strike. Or, we can use our reason to organize the variety of sensory experiences we get from the world in order to get to some sort of reflective equilibrium. I imagine this second option is what's happening in J.D. Drew's mind as he walks slowly back to the dugout after a strikeout.

Mind Over Matter

To use one's reason an individual must experience a series of material things by way of his or her five senses and categorize them under a concept. At the most basic level, this is how we come to understand the world in general, and baseball in particular. For example, on the ground in front of me I see a white sphere that is cut by a continuous curve of many red stitches. Through this sensory experience I determine that this object in front of me is a baseball. What I have done in the brief time it took me to identify the object in front of me as a baseball is something that philosophers have been debating since they first started thinking about the world.

By identifying the thing in front of me as a baseball, I accomplished what philosopher Immanuel Kant calls a determinate judgment. I took in many particular things—the sphere shape, the white color, the red stitches—and determined that all of these things combined represent an object that we call a baseball. Put simply, my mind was able to reduce the many things in front of me to one concept: white, sphere, red, and stitches (sensual particulars)—baseball (concept).

In addition to reducing many things to one, I was able to accomplish quite an amazing feat, one almost as good as hitting a major league curveball. The power of my understanding is such that, by equating white, sphere, red, and stitches to a baseball, I have taken a series of *material* things and categorized them into a concept, something that is *immaterial*. In other words, I have *reduced* the series of particular things in front of me into nothing. I have negated the material things in front of me and made them immaterial, or conceptual. It's an act of negation because the concept "baseball" does not physically exist in the world—it's an idea that includes within it all of the baseballs in the world. For example, we've all seen a Red Sox game, either at Fenway Park or on TV, and we've all seen just how many baseballs are used during a game. It's a lot. Every single one of those baseballs are material things; if Kevin Youkilis is hit by one during an at-bat (which seems to happen often) it will hurt like hell. But, the *concept* "baseball" can no more hurt Youk as it can you or me. The single concept "baseball" represents all of the material baseballs at Fenway Park, and every other ballpark as well. Conceptualizing is how we understand the world around us—we literally think the world—and by doing so, we reduce material things to immaterial concepts.

The Reduction of the Baseball Player

We also do this when we attempt to understand baseball players. A player's major league career can range from a single game to twenty-plus years. Over that time there is an accumulation of statistics, injuries, public statements, charity work, and memorable events on and off the field. The sum of all these material things represents the ballplayer. Often, however, we don't account for all of the events and material accumulations that make up player's career—there's simply too much information. We must simplify, by way of reduction, to a few basic concepts. For example:

- **.344 BA, 521 HR, 1839 RBIs; Jimmy Fund; refused to tip his cap = Ted Williams**

Often, Red Sox fans can determine a player's conceptual identity through one single material description, or worldly event.

- **Shoving mitt in A-Rod's face = Jason Varitek**
- **Walk-off home run = David Ortiz**
- **Error = Bill Buckner**
- **The Steal = Dave Roberts**

And, of course:

- **Signing with the Yankees = Johnny Damon**

As you can see from this list, some are favorable, and some are not so favorable. One problem with this type of concept formation is that it reduces, or negates, the sum total of a player's career down to a single concept. This ends up leaving out quite a bit of the story of a player's career. A similar type of reduction happens when a fan categorizes the whole game as one error, or the whole season as one devastating loss. Both ways of understanding are oversimplifications. They reduce the sum of events to a concept so singular that it simply cannot adequately account for the complexities of the game of baseball as a whole. This is the case when all of the materials that make up Buckner's entire career are reduced to one single concept—"error." Likewise, associating Johnny Damon with wearing pinstripes negates the many accomplishments he compiled while wearing a Red Sox uniform. Even in the case of a seemingly good concepts, like "The Steal," there's still a reduction of the many material achievements that Roberts accomplished throughout his entire career.

When we as fans make such conceptual reductions we lose the complexity and nuance of a player's career. To reduce the variety of things in the world to one concept is to destroy those things, to negate them in order to create one simplified concept. Baseball isn't the only place where this kind of reduction exists. The dangers inherent in it are explored by Max Horkheimer and Theodor Adorno in their book *Dialectic of Enlightenment* (Stanford University Press, 2002). Horkheimer and Adorno were responding to Enlightenment thinkers who sought as much reduction as possible in order to better understand the world. In the rush to make use of the new way of ideas in the seventeenth and eighteenth centuries, Enlightenment thinkers simplified the complexity of nature into basic categories, hoping to grasp the world through category and number. The older models of understanding, like myth and fantasy, were cast aside as unclear and overly complex systems that led us further away from a proper understanding of the world around us.

According to Horkheimer and Adorno, "Enlightenment's program was the disenchantment of the world. It wanted to dispel myths, to overthrow fantasy with knowledge" (p. 1). The concern with the Enlightenment's approach to understanding is that in its haste to categorize and simplify the way we know the world, much of the complexity and meaning of the world is lost. Though the goal of these Enlightenment thinkers was a wel-intentioned attempt to gain understanding of the world, Horkheimer and Adorno point out that there still remained many things that couldn't be easily reduced, or solved, complex systems of thought that demanded explanations, such as the arts, religion, and ethics. Horkheimer and Adorno sarcastically conclude: "the wholly enlightened earth is radiant with triumphant calamity" (p. 1).

The Emptiness of the Scorecard

This isn't to say Enlightenment thinking has done nothing good for baseball. Take the scorecard. On the surface, scorecards reflect an elegant simplicity, each notation representing a major on-field event. The entire game is captured on a single sheet of paper. Each scorecard, with the scorer's own unique style, reports every twist and turn of the game. But does this provide a sufficient account of the game? When I look back on the play scored 4–3 in the top of the seventh inning on September 1st, 2007, of a game between the Boston Red Sox and Baltimore Orioles, I don't see the amazing diving stab and putout by Dustin Pedroia, which preserved Clay Buchholz's no-hitter. Nor does the notation F4 convey just how amazingly Pedroia can run down a pop fly into short right field. Can 6–4–3 give us enough information regarding just how gracefully Alex Gonzalez turns a double play? The scorecard reduces the events on the ball field to a specific concept or notation. The many plays made by Pedroia, ranging from the spectacular to the routine, are all reduced to one concept: 4–3.

The Material Sin of Wearing Pinstripes

Johnny Damon is the perfect example of a player who has suffered from this type of conceptual reduction. Normally a player's legacy is beyond his control, but Damon's choice to join the Yankees proves an exception to this rule. The simple truth is this: if you play for and contribute significantly to the Boston Red Sox and then go on to play for and contribute significantly to the New York Yankees, you will get booed vigorously upon your return to Fenway Park. This isn't mere opinion; it is absolute fact. Other former Red Sox players who have moved on to other non-Yankees teams are welcomed back with standing ovations, like Nomar Garciaparra, Derek Lowe, Dave Roberts, Kevin Millar, all members of the 2004 World Series team (yes Nomar got a ring!), all members of the team that finally brought a championship back to Boston, and all teammates of Johnny Damon.

Damon also committed the catastrophic act of leaving Boston for more money. Now, as a fan, I don't know Damon's reasons for leaving Boston. All we as fans have to go on is Damon's final decision. It's entirely possible that Johnny Damon grew up a Yankee sfan and really wanted to play for his favorite team. After all, we don't all suppose that every player for the Red Sox grew up in New England and rooted for the home tteam. Maybe there was some specific need for Damon to live in the New York area. Perhaps there were personal family considerations at stake. No matter the reason for Damon's decision, the consequences of that decision are the responsibility of the player. I know that Johnny Damon was the poster boy for the "Idiots" of 2004, but even he should've been smart enough to realize that he was going to damage his legacy as a Red Sox player by choosing to go to the Yankees. In fact, in his attempt to build up his legacy he failed to account for the particularly damning material certainties of his choices. Through both his physically wearing pinstripes and his material monetary gain, Johnny Damon has immortalized his legacy for Sox fans as a "sell out," "traitor," and whatever else is screamed at him at Fenway.

For Red Sox fans, by reducing Damon's career to the concept of a "traitor," we have negated his entire career in Boston. The deluge of boos when Damon steps to the plate at Fenway Park as a member of the New York Yankees confirms the nullification of his past achievements in a Red Sox uniform. Is this nullification justified? As I mentioned above, such a severe reduction, while a perfectly natural human ability, negates the complexity and material value of a player's career. Surely this is unacceptable, right?

If the negation of Johnny Damon's Red Sox career is unacceptable, what's the alternative? Do we deny our natural tendencies to simplify in order to understand? Do we go back to the older models of understanding like myth and fantasy, mentioned by Horkheimer and Adorno? I don't think a return to myth is the way to go, but there must be a way to account for the complexity of the world—or, in this case, the game of baseball—without destroying them through the reductive act of our understanding.

1 4 6 8 9 14 27 42

There's one event that actually serves to counteract the negative aspects of our reductive power of understanding. This is the act of retiring a player's number. It's true that the act of retiring a player's number is an act of reduction itself; actually, it's the most reductive act there is. Forget about stats, events, or charity work. When a player's number is retired he's reduced to one concept, or more specifically, one number.

When I attend a game at Fenway, look toward the right-field façade, and see the series of numbers hanging there, I'm struck with an immediate urge to understand their meaning. There's too much information missing. I'm not old enough to have seen Joe Cronin play, let alone play, for the Boston Red Sox. I look up to the number 4 and ask: "What's that?" "Who wore number 4?" If I'm lucky, there will be a fan, or an author, or a sportswriter sitting next to me who will tell me all about Joe Cronin's career with the Red Sox.

Throughout the chapter we've seen the possible negative consequences of reducing material into a singular concept. With retired numbers we can now see a positive way that reason works to understand the world by focusing on the immaterial. Ironically, it's the severity of the reduction that gives retired numbers the most force and power. No one else will *ever* wear the number 14 for the Boston Red Sox. Rather than being reduced to the number 14, Jim Rice is the *only* number 14 that matters for the Red Sox and their fans. Jim Rice hasn't been simplified; he's been *magnified*. He's been immortalized. His number 14 can never be destroyed. Future generations of Red Sox fans who never had the pleasure of watching Jim Rice play baseball will not be content merely understanding him as the number 14. His retired number—his entire career with the Red Sox—is a story that *demands* to be told.

Retired numbers work to reverse the reductive act of understanding by demanding that the material events that make up a player's career be explained. With retired numbers, one begins with a single concept—a number—and seeks to build his knowledge and appreciation of the player who wore it. Before, when I discussed how fans reduce a player to a particular concept, the fan already has a significant amount of information from which to start his reduction. In the case of retired numbers, the fan begins with little to no information—depending on when the player played—and his understanding is now an expanding, not a reducing, of the player's career. The fan is now *adding* information instead of subtracting, *building up* instead of negating. The series of numbers on the right-field façade at Fenway act as an invitation for players' stories to be told, to be passed on throughout the generations. Retired numbers demand explanation.

Missing Numbers?

Now, am I suggesting that if Johnny Damon had stayed with the Red Sox he would've seen his number retired? No. It would've been very unlikely. However, it still would've been a possibility if Damon had stayed with the Sox for another six years. Whereas now, by joining the Yankees, not only will Damon never qualify to have his number retired, he has also lost any positive legacy he may have had as a member of the Red Sox.

What about Wade Boggs's number 26? Boggs, like Damon, also committed the material sin of donning Yankees pinstripes; his number has yet to be retired by the Boston Red Sox. What about Roger Clemens? His number 21 has also not been retired by the Red Sox. I suspect that neither of their numbers will ever be retired, solely because they went on to play for and contribute significantly to the Yankees organization.[2]

I don't mean to suggest that players should focus all of their attention on having their numbers retired—this is unrealistic. It's hard enough to simply play the game, let alone control how you're perceived while playing it. There are plenty of examples of players whose legacies went beyond what they were striving to accomplish. Bill Buckner and Dave Roberts are perfect examples. Both were playing the game to the best of their ability; one ended up being seen as a goat, the other a hero. Horkheimer and Adorno warned us to be aware of the negative aspects of reduction; but what does this have to do with legacy? While this awareness may not help a player get his number retired, it may help players maintain a legacy that honors all of their material accomplishments throughout their entire career.

---

[2] Both of their contributions were very significant in that they won World Series Championships with the Yankees while the Red Sox were still waiting for their first in eighty-six years. This makes their decisions to join the Yankees even more unforgiveable and the possibility of their numbers being retired very unlikely.

In fact, to play as if your number could be retired seems to me like good advice for all who have seen their fellow players lose control of their legacies. For an example of a player who took control of his own legacy based on a healthy respect for its immaterial nature, think about someone like Curt Schilling. Unlike Boggs, Clemens, and Damon, Schilling vowed on several occasions never to play for the Yankees, despite his reverence for the rich history of their franchise. It's not hard to imagine what Johnny Damon's legacy might have looked like today if he had decided to play anywhere else but New York. But let's be honest, while the disenchantment of Johnny Damon may have been a result of our natural tendencies to makes sense of the world, a re-enchantment of Damon became next to impossible for Red Sox fans the moment he shaved off that beard, cut his hair, and donned a Yankees cap.

19

In Sync with Pink?

STEPHANIE St. MARTIN

> As Commissioner, you're supposed to be objective. It wasn't much of
> a secret, though, that I loved Fenway—especially how it made you a
> participant, not a spectator.
>
> —Baseball Commissioner BOWIE KUHN

The only reason I even went to see the film *Titanic* was because I
wanted to know what travesty would keep the opening of Fenway
Park off the front page of the local papers.

Since its opening on April 20th, 1912, Fenway Park has become
a part of baseball lore. From the Royal Rooters to current day Red
Sox Nation, when you're at Fenway, as Jimmy Fallon put it in *Fever
Pitch*, you're with your "summer family." You got the crazy uncle
who's been sporting the same cap since Williams was on the field,
the aunt who's still in love with Yaz, your grandmother who still
blesses herself when people mention Tony C, and your dad who
loves Dewey. You also know the fans: Denny "Eight and Two-
Thirds" Drinkwater, Lib "The Queen of Fenway" Dooley, The
Howler, the drunks in the bleachers—all of them. Each can rattle
off stats as if your questions aren't even worthy of being asked.
They live and breathe every aspect of the Sox. You're taught to
keep the faith from an early age and curse the Yankees the same
way you curse at all New England weathermen for predicting more
freakin' snow. This is your team, because let's face it, you're blood
is RED for the SOX.

Prior to 2004, even before Pedro and Clemens, being a Sox fan
was clear torture. Most people compared it to watching a movie
where the bad guy always wins and the good guy dies every time,

with each sequel portraying the death as more painful and twisted than its predecessor. Still, the Sox fans stayed loyal to their team. When pitchers and catchers report, the diehards already had their own scouting report printed and bound as if John Henry would send a messenger for it, as if he truly wanted to know their opinion. Of all the sports in the United States it's the Sox fans that reign as the most knowledgeable, and for good reason. Each year the fans find that old jersey, put on their "thinking Sox cap" and try to figure out a way to win the World Series. They looked over stats and past players for a clue that would break the curse the same way a treasure hunter looks over every aspect of history to find a map to Atlantis. Another post-1918 World Series was the Holy Grail, not only for the team, but also for the fans. Fans study the game so it makes sense, so we can piece together the puzzle to solve the problem, which, in this case, was the lack of a World Series title. The issue was, however, that most of the fans never foresaw the villains that would break our "hahts." Bucky "Bleepin" Dent, Aaron "Frickin" Boone, Bill "Glove to the Ground" Buckner, and the Babe—after each incident, hospitals were put on standby in case all of New England had a simultaneous coronary. I remember telling my dad after the Boone incident that it wasn't the Curse of the Bambino but the Curse of the letter "B" (Bucky, Boone, Buckner, Babe) and that anyone on our team with a name beginning with "B" should immediately be traded. After Dave Roberts stole second in the Ninth of Game Four of the 2004 American League Championship against the Yankees and I saw that Bill Mueller was still at the plate, I nearly fainted.

Being loyal to the Sox isn't a new trend—it's been around since 1918—but suddenly there have been some visitors to Fenway Park that haven't exactly been welcomed by the Fenway Faithful. The newest villains of Red Sox Nation are not the Yankees, Orioles, Blue Jays or Rays, they're not the White Sox, Indians or Angels, they are women sporting *pink* Red Sox hats. The pink hat phenomenon is becoming one of the fiercest battles in Boston since Bunker Hill.

The Red Coats Are Coming! The Pink Hatters Are Coming!

If there were a modern-day Paul Revere, he would've hung three lanterns in the Old North Church because apparently Red Sox

Nation's newest enemy is coming from all directions. No one really knows when the Red Sox became the team to root for, but it seems all was supposedly lost for the Nation around 2003. The team itself had done well that season, going 95–67 to clinch the Wild Card in the American League. The team had a new identity, a gritty, scrappy style of play with Trot Nixon being the main "Dirt Dawg." The term exploded all over the media, blogs were created and a new style of hat marketed, and suddenly people were going to Fenway again sparking the longest consecutive sellout streak that began on May 15th, 2003. The popularity of the Red Sox grew even larger. HBO even aired a special entitled *The Curse of the Bambino* on September 16th, 2003 to showcase the pain and heartache of Sox fans. It was suddenly "wicked cool" to support the Sox and, of course, businesses saw this coming from a lot more than ninety feet away.

All of sudden everywhere in New England, everywhere on eBay and Amazon, everywhere in the media—people were selling the Red Sox. Countless books were printed covering every aspect of the team. Memorabilia and apparel were in high demand. One could show their allegiance to the olde towne team while moving with the new fashion trends of more relaxed clothing lines, resulting in the creation of a more relaxed fitted-hat. And, because we live in a society of politically correct people who want to make sure that everyone can be a Red Sox fan, including women—the pink Red Sox hat was created. As good as the intentions were of the creators of the pink Red Sox hat, an urban slur of hatred has become attached to it now. Because the pink hat was "invented" so recently, it's easy to associate those who wear it with someone who is new to the team. It's like being able spot the difference between a novice and an expert, a rookie and a veteran, and the veteran fans aren't too thrilled with their rookie counterparts. Even in the majors, rookie pitchers are made to carry pink backpacks to the bullpen as part of their initiation as a new member of the team. The color is associated with a rookie player and since its creation in 2003 the pink hat has been associated with a rookie fan. Some older fans think there should be a similar initiation for the rookie fan. Only after they wear pink can they attempt an upgrade within Red Sox Nation. Just as a child starts as a white belt in karate, rookie fans should bear the pink until a diehard says they've mastered a level of fandom. Once they prove their skills, they will be awarded a cap in Red Sox colors. Wax on, Wax of, Red Sox-san, and prove your worth to Mr. Diehard-Miyagi.

But does Red Sox Nation have a right to be so mad? Is it fair to put pink hatters in the same group as a person wearing pinstripes at Fenway? Technically, the Yankees are the enemy—the Red Coats—and anyone cheering for the Red Sox is against them. It's as if there's tension amongst the Continental Army and the diehards and the pink hatters are lined up on opposite sides at the Battle for Bunker Hill. After all, we're all supporting the same cause, the same team. Why does it matter what color your hat is if we're all cheering for the Red Sox? I think it's time to get an unbiased opinion from an umpire to see if the rules of spectatorship are in jeopardy before the benches clear.

The Man behind the Plate: Aristotle

Most umpires would agree that the best sound during a baseball game is silence, meaning no one is arguing the call that he just made. If baseball were played in Ancient Greece, the Greek philosopher Aristotle would most certainly disagree. Questions need to be asked about the virtue of what just took place or the virtue of the argument that is being discussed so that the correct answer is discovered. For Aristotle, threatening his life over a bad call really won't faze him (it may phase Socrates if hemlock is considered a Fenway Frank) because, in his eyes, he knows what he is doing—he's being logical. Going up against the "Father of Logic" is like batting against Cy Young or Lefty Grove in their prime—you don't have a chance.

The pink hat argument comes down to a very basic principle found in Book I of Aristotle's *Nicomachean Ethics* known as *virtue*, which is the balance or *mean* of two vices: *excess* and *deficiency*. The argument of the pink hat relies on the contrast between the "love of honor" and the "love of contemplation." Aristotle writes in a way that is just as difficult to understand as Bill "Spaceman" Lee—you know he has a point but, to the untrained eye, he's literally not making any coherent sense and seems as though he is coming out of left field. However, if you can figure out what he's trying to say, it's actually a brilliant thought and not as wacky as we all supposed. If you don't like that metaphor, it's like someone from the deep South trying to understand someone talking in a Boston accent—it's the English language but "wicked hahd" to understand at first.

When it comes to virtue, Aristotle argues that balance is crucial. Virtue is the mean between two extreme ends of a spectrum. For

Aristotle, these two extremes are the vices of excess and deficiency. Baserunning at Fenway could illustrate this best. If Dave Roberts is on first base with two outs and the Sox are down a run in the bottom of the ninth, it's important that he gets into scoring position. Manager Terry Francona needs the virtue of courage to help manage his team to steal the bases wisely. Having a good balance of courage is the mean. Fans would be upset with Francona if he had Roberts stay at first base if Roberts had an opportunity to steal second base and possibly score a run on a single. Francona's decision to keep Roberts at first base is a deficiency of cowardice and wouldn't be considered virtuous; rather it would be a vice. However, if David "Big Papi" Ortiz was at first base with nobody out in the fifth inning and Francona had him attempt to steal second base, fans would be upset because Francona's courage would be considered reckless, or would be in excess—too big and over confident—and this too would be considered a vice. Ortiz could've stayed on first base and possibly scored a run for the team instead of causing a small earthquake by getting thrown out on a foolish stolen base attempt.

Aristotle gives us the secret to finding the mean by stating that when trying to make a decision we need to include rationale based on the right person, the right time, and doing something for the right reason. Trying to balance all three makes this an extremely difficult task and is something that Aristotle calls "praiseworthy and noble." In light of this, Aristotle would argue that it's important that you understand *why* you are stealing second base at that time in the game. You must know how many outs there are, what inning it is, and which player is on first base, because understanding the situation makes all the difference in baseball.

Francona would probably send Ortiz if the game is on the line in the ninth, but only if he was sure that Ortiz could make it, otherwise, the faster runner, Roberts, would pinch-run. And sometimes a gutsy call—like having Roberts steal with *no* outs, in the bottom of the ninth of the 2004 ALCS, with the Yankees ahead three games to none, with all the momentum in the world behind those wearing pinstripes—can change the course of history. Had Roberts not taken off from first and beaten Posada's throw at second, I might still be in the midst of a huge depression and perhaps would've sworn off the Sox entirely.

Based on what we now understand about mean, excess, and deficiency we can now look at the pink hat argument from

Aristotle's point of view. The mean would be "being a knowledge-able Red Sox fan." It would be a good balance of supporting the team and being able to name the starting nine and the Red Sox legends. The deficiency would be what most Red Sox fans call the pink hatter, or someone who knows nothing about the team and has just hopped on the bandwagon. The excess would be the diehard fan who obsesses over the team and has memorized every stat of every player to wear the uniform and makes people feel inferior if they cannot name Dice-K's ERA on July 31st, 2007. There must be a balance to make "Friendly" Fenway friendly. For most fans, you should be able to at least name the players on the field and know that the Green Monster is not a person. Others feel that as long as you cheer when a *touchdown* is scored, it shouldn't matter. Others feel that going to Fenway is similar to getting your license—you should take an exam to see if you are qualified "to root, root, root for the home team." Which argument is correct?

Do You Really Love That Dirty Water?

For the pink hat, or bandwagon fans, the argument is that it doesn't matter what color hat you wear as long as you support the team. This view has given rise to other popular Red Sox hats from camouflage to ones with a bedazzled "B." According to these fans, supporting the Red Sox is honorable in any hat color.

The pink hat has also become the symbol of commitment against a greater force than baseball. Many women who are fighting breast cancer will sport the pink hat in honor of the pink Breast Cancer Awareness ribbon. The color pink symbolizes their fight, or the fight of those they know and love against breast cancer. Those who sport the pink hat while going through chemotherapy often don't hear the ridicule associated with the infamous colored hat. People understand why they purchased the hat instead of the common navy one. It's respected.

Then there are women who are wearing the pink hat as a sign of commitment against another great force—stubborn Red Sox Nation. If they like the Sox and the color pink this is the hat for them. The shocked look of the diehard fan when they can answer the question of "What does the red seat in the Bleachers mean?" is just icing on the cake. Not all pink hatters are ignorant of baseball or the Red Sox. They enjoy the game but don't feel that the Red Sox are a life-and-death matter much to Mike Barnicle's dismay, who once quipped: "Baseball isn't a life-and-death matter, but the Red Sox are." A lot of pink hatters think it's crazy for fans to love a team *that* much and life shouldn't revolve around the AL East standings.

As much as fans that wear the pink hat are trying to reverse their own curse, they need to tread lightly and know when to steal. When wearing this specific form of headgear, you not only need to watch the game, you also need to watch what you say. Right now, the slur of "pink hat" has made its way into the Urban Dictionary as someone who doesn't know what they're talking about. Just like when Terry Francona uses the virtuous mean to wisely call for a stolen-base attempt, the pink hat fans need to display a proper balance of Red Sox knowledge in order to overcome the vice of deficiency.

Being a Red Sox fan is like having family in every city. The Red Sox connect people. As fans travel far and wide, they are often acknowledged on the street by other Sox fans that are proudly showing their support for the team. A head nod, a smile, a "did you catch Lester's no-hitter?"—all occur when two people who share the same passion pass each other in what isn't dubbed a "Red Sox Nation" zone. Aristotle's notion of the "love of honor" in his *Nicomachean Ethics* is similar to this passing on the street—you are a part of something bigger than yourself—you are in the scene and associated with the Red Sox. A lot of people respect you for being a Red Sox fan, and you deserve the recognition for all that you have put your heart through.

But when receiving that recognition, or honor, from your peers is more important than going through the trials and tribulations of the season, when you falsely claim your allegiance just to get noticed, for Aristotle, that isn't virtuous at all. Being a Red Sox fan just to get personal attention takes attention away from the team—this is why Sox fans hate people they see on NESN who are on their cell phones while gawking at themselves on camera. You are there to be a spectator, not to draw attention away from the game. Cheering is one thing but trying to keep the camera on you instead of the batter is another.

The pink hat fan is a culprit of this lack of virtuousness. Although other fans have waved at NESN cameras, the pink hat fan has been seen doing it more often and usually during important parts of the game. The clear fact is that they're not paying attention to what's going on in the field and would rather be on camera. For

Aristotle, this shows the deficiency of the pink hat fan. Their vice lies in taking attention away from the game and putting it on themselves. For some pink hatters, they just want to be *seen* at Fenway rather than *see* a game at Fenway. As a result of this behavior, they have turned everyone against them. If the only people ever shown on television during a Red Sox game at Fenway are wearing pink hats and talking on their cell phones, the group of "pink hats" might create widespread "pink hate."

Tessie and Sweet Caroline Would Not Wear Pink

The main argument that diehard fans have against the pink hatters is "Where the hell have you been?" With the creation of the pink hat, many Sox fans were outraged that people had decided to support the Sox because they were finally winning. People were hopping on the bandwagon, Duck Boats, and the Martha's Vineyard ferry to ship up to Boston and support the Sox. From the backwoods of Maine, to maple syrup farms of Vermont, to the tip of the Cape at Provincetown, a pink hat could be seen.

When a person decides to cheer for a team, you like them, win or lose, you are loyal to the team. With the Red Sox, the line between being loyal and constantly setting yourself up for heartache is insanely close for comfort. It wasn't just the pink hat that made diehard fans "wicked mad," it was the brand new hats that didn't have the stains of shed tears on the fabric. A Sox hat is the ultimate "scar story"—fans can look at each speck of dirt, each stain and tell you exactly what game it's from the same way that people can talk about the pain of a chest scar over their heart from a surgery. These brand new hats in every non-Sox color were just a reminder that these new fans didn't go through the same torture as the rest of the Nation. To make matters worse, it seemed that the women wearing the dreaded pink hat were sitting in the best seats at Fenway—seats that one couldn't even dream of ever sitting in. Even in the battle-cry song *Tessie* the lyrics mention how the Royal Rooters lose their seats to other fans:

> The Rooters showed up at the grounds one day
> They found their seats had all been sold

Even then, diehards felt that one should pay their dues before sitting behind home plate. Let's be honest, any fan that will sit in the most uncomfortable seat in the world (that's only 15" long and dated for a slimmer America) and drink a warm $8 beer, game after game, year after year, has to be a true Red Sox fan and deserves a seat with a cup holder.

What should be made clear, however, is that women have been Red Sox fans for *decades*! Women have been going to Red Sox games long before the appearance of the pink hat, and could probably "outsmaht" most guys with their knowledge. Diamonds are a girl's best friend and in Boston, Fenway's baseball diamond is the most precious. The pink hat isn't about women—it's a bandwagon thing. It's like little kids who grew up in Kansas and picked cheering for the Yankees in the '90s because "they were the best team in baseball." Gross! Well, the same thing is happening to the Sox now. The trend is that cheering for the Red Sox is just as cool as third baseman Mike Lowell is when the bases are loaded—positive things will happen.

We Sac-Flied Our Lives and Minds for the Sox

For Aristotle, the extreme opposite of the deficiencies of pink hatters are the excesses of the diehard Red Sox fan. This is the fan that not only didn't wash, but kept wearing, a shirt with bird poop on it, because he was thinking about the Red Sox when the bird pooped on it and because bird poop is considered lucky. One of my favorite sports writers is the culprit behind this: Bill Simmons. He was thinking about the upcoming 2004 ALCS between the Sox and the Yankees when a bird made the Sox "lucky" on his shirt. Seriously, fans will look to anything, even Old Italian beliefs, to prove that God and now birds care about the Sox.

These crazed diehard Red Sox fans have literally sacrificed their lives for the Red Sox. Weddings are either avoided between April and October or planned around when the team is on the road. Most Bostonians avoid Kenmore Square two hours before first pitch and one hour after the game ends just to miss the traffic. Boston *is* the Red Sox—bagels were dyed red and blue to help the team, the Old Hancock building "blinks red" when the Sox game is postponed,[1] exorcisms took place outside the gates to reverse the curse and the fans even had a Red Sox version of the Lord's Prayer:

---

[1] The Old Hancock Building in Boston is topped with a weather beacon bearing blue and red lights to assist Bostonians in knowing tomorrow's weather. There's

Our Father, who art at Fenway . . .
Baseball be thy game.
Thy Kingdom come,
World Series won,
On Earth, then on to the Cask 'n' Flagon.
Give us this day, oh Pedro Martinez,
And forgive us our losses,
As we forgive those,
Like young Billy Buckner,
And lead us not into depression,
But deliver us from the curse. Amen.

It's not inconceivable to say that the Red Sox are the religion of Boston and that Fenway is the cathedral where all the fans go to worship. In *Bull Durham* (1988), one of the great baseball movies of all time, Susan Sarandon's character echoes this fanatic nature:

I believe in the Church of Baseball. I've tried all the major religions, and most of the minor ones. I've worshipped Buddha, Allah, Brahma, Vishnu, Siva, trees, mushrooms, and Isadora Duncan. I know things. For instance, there are 108 beads in a Catholic rosary and there are 108 stitches in a baseball. When I heard that, I gave Jesus a chance.

Red Sox Nation understands this, but what would Aristotle say? Just like the "love of honor" is found in the woman wearing the pink hat, the "love of contemplation" is found in the diehard fan. As I said before, even before pitchers and catchers report, Red Sox Nation puts on their "Sox thinking caps" to try and figure out how to have a successful season and avoid a mass jumping off the Tobin Bridge. The diehards love contemplation, or intellectual knowledge, about the team—they want to know everything about the players so they might understand their victories (and shortcomings) better. More than gaining accolades and praise from friends and family for being a part of Red Sox Nation, intellectual virtue depends on the fans themselves. Taking a test is up to you—you have to study and you have to be prepared for all the material

---

a simple poem taught to school children to help remember what each light combination means: "Solid blue, clear view. / Blinking blue, clouds due. / Solid red, rain ahead. / Blinking red, snow instead." Except during baseball season, blinking red means the Boston Red Sox game has been called off on account of weather. Another reason why Boston *is* the Red Sox.

assigned—your grade is from your own efforts. When you ace a test, you naturally make phone calls to gloat about your wonderful achievement. You worked hard and it paid off so you want to tell the world. Within all of us is a desire to make our families and friends proud of us. So yes, we do want respect from our family and especially our peers when it comes to our achievements and our knowledge, but embarrassing someone who might not know the material as well as you do isn't really something to gloat about.

The diehard Red Sox fan of excess needs to carefully consider his actions when at Fenway and must stop living in fantasy and live in reality. Case in point—there's no test one takes to become a member of Red Sox Nation. In fact, you just put your credit card in and select which benefits you want and how much you want to spend for the membership. (I am a proud member of Red Sox Nation since 2004.) As much as I don't want to admit that knowing Dice-K's ERA on July 31st, 2007 is useless to me; it is. Yes, knowing his ERA can determine whether he is considered a good pitcher and if the Red Sox may win the game (by comparing the opposing pitcher's ERA), but it's not a certainty. On paper the Red Sox should have lost to the Yankees in the 2004 ALCS, especially after Game Three, but no one—not even the experts—saw the momentum change coming. Upsets happen all the time in sports and it's the coaches' job, *not* the fans, to try to play the game in their favor. Some diehard fans think that knowing all of the Red Sox players' stats makes them a more admirable and honorable fan, however, if they're seeking the honor for themselves, then they aren't a true fan in the first place. And, they are not unlike the pink hatters waving at the camera talking on their cell phone, seeking to make the game all about themselves.

Tie Goes to the Runner

Fenway fans are knowledgeable—there's no denying that—but the line between overzealous and dedicated is just as skewed as dedicated and ambivalent—depending on who you are talking to you, you could be called for a strike. However, most fans *and* players do expect some form of dedication to the team. At Fenway, the Jumbotron doesn't tell fans to start cheering "Let's Go Red Sox!" or to get behind a pitcher when the count is 0–2; it's understood that Sox fans anticipate the game. Knowing the lineup, the starting pitcher, and the opposing team the Sox are playing will aid you in

your quest to becoming a Sox fan. Nobody wants to talk to a
"know-it-all" nor do they want to talk to "clueless" fans that have
never heard of Teddy Ballgame. Warren Bennis may have said it
best when talking about knowledge:

> We have more information now than we can use, and less knowledge
> and understanding than we need. Indeed, we seem to collect infor-
> mation because we have the ability to do so, but we are so busy col-
> lecting it that we haven't devised a means of using it. The true measure
> of any society is not what it knows but what it does with what it
> knows.

Let me repeat that last line: "The true measure of any society is not
what it knows but what it does with what it knows." What you
know is important but how you display it is what counts. Back to
the original example of stealing in baseball, if you make an effort
and wisely know when to attempt a steal of second base, no one
can really be angry with you. The catcher may throw you out but
if you get a good jump on the ball and you are skilled enough to
run, it's worth a shot. Same goes with supporting the Sox: if you
can hold your own and understand some of the game and the main
players on the team, no one should be angry if you've never heard
of a minor player that was with the Sox for only a season.

Before 2004, being a Red Sox fan was like dating a guy who's
bad for you, emotionally abusive, and putting you through
unthinkable heartache year in and year out, but you keep going
back to him because you truly believe that tomorrow will be different. He'll change. Someone once said that misery loves company. The fact is that we all suffered through the tragedies of the
Red Sox: the (other) Boston Massacre, B.F. Dent, Buckner, Boone—
they were like fraternity initiations with Dent's bat as the paddle:
Welcome to the Brotherhood of Red Sox Nation. But when you
finally meet Mr. Right, he's that much more incredible because you
went through all that crap with Mr. Wrong. You appreciate him
more. Maybe that's what made 2004 so unbelievably awesome. Red
Sox Nation had endured so much "hahtache" that it made the victory that much sweeter.

Prior to writing this, I hated the pink hats for the same reason
most people do. But there's something about Boston and its connection to that team that calls Fenway home. We live and breathe
the Sox and hate winter not because of the frickin' snow but

because we want another season in the sun with our boys. Baseball is so symbolic of life—there are ups and downs, good times and times when you want to denounce your faith, but you keep living. Of course we are all jealous of someone who has had an easier journey than our own but we're all a part of humanity. Well, we're all Bostonians, we're all honking our horn in traffic, we're all missing a letter in the alphabet, we're all rooting for the Red Sox, and we *should* all acknowledge one another as Red Sox fans when we pass each other on the street in *any* color hat. I wasn't around before 1985, but I was accepted by those who actually went through '78 just as those who survived '67 accepted them. Shouldn't we reach out our hands to each fan and smile because we're all connected in some way to this infinite faith in a team? I think Aristotle would agree that if we do that, we are truly being virtuous and maybe, at Fenway, good times *could finally seem* "so good, so good, so good!"

20

Bill James and the Science of Red Sox Religion

JONAH P.B. GOLDWATER

Boston Red Sox history is often told as a religious narrative in the language of faith, hope, and redemption. Yet the current incarnation of Red Sox management, led by owner and futures trader John Henry and Executive Vice President and General Manager Theo Epstein, operates using the most advanced quantitative and scientific tools. For this ownership group, the future of the Red Sox is written in the scientific language of mathematics.

The Red Sox hired pre-eminent baseball scientist Bill James as Senior Advisor of Baseball Operations in 2003. He has two World Series rings. But James's legend was established long before, having instigated a scientific revolution in the baseball world. James's annual *Bill James' Baseball Abstract*, first published in 1977, was a mix of daring hypotheses, meticulously collected data, and acerbic wit. The *Abstract* became popular with an increasingly large subculture of baseball scientists throughout the 1980s. But until the mid to late '90s, James's work had little impact on the owners and operators of Major League Baseball franchises. Since then, however, James's scientific revolution has changed not only how fans understand baseball, but even how owners own and players play.

But all revolutions provoke reactionaries; many of whom perceive baseball science as undermining the presumed sacred truths of baseball. For example, the hitter with the highest batting average at the end of the year is traditionally referred to as the "batting champion." But one Jamesean discovery was that batting average is far less indicative of a player's contribution to victory than traditionally supposed, and that as a result, having the highest batting average does not entail being the best or most valuable offensive player. Far from being a batting champion, a high batting average may in fact mask a truly mediocre offensive season. Some argue that this new attitude towards batting average denigrates tradition. Red Sox fans all know .406, and that Ted Williams was the last man to bat .400, but what does hitting .400 mean in a world where batting average is no longer a reliable indicator of performance?

The RBI statistic has met a similar fate. And though all Sox fans know Carl Yastrzemski was the last player to win the Triple Crown in 1967, if the ability to drive in runs is more accurately seen as a function of context rather than an intrinsic ability possessed by the hitter—as has been demonstrated—then the meaning of Yaz's historical feat is diminished. Many fans are understandably averse to seeing the meaning stripped from the numbers they've memorized since childhood. Worse, the new statistics developed by James and his ilk to replace the traditional statistics are exceedingly abstract and so have alienated the "common fan," including many loyal citizens of Red Sox Nation.

Despite the obvious benefits of having better means of figuring out which players are truly the most valuable—signing the right free agents at the right price, for example—the threat to traditional and conventional wisdom that the Jamesean revolution often represents, and the number of cultural, religious, and philosophical beliefs it speaks to may divide an otherwise unified Sox fan base. But it need not. The numbers are in the service of understanding baseball, and with Bill James on our side; they're in the service of bringing winning baseball to Boston. (Matt Clement's, Julio Lugo's, and John Smoltz's contributions notwithstanding.) Furthermore, James's science rests on a philosophy that might help close the cultural divide. I will examine these ideas, helped by the philosophy of longtime Harvard professor, and, for the purposes of this essay, hardcore Red Sox fan, W.V. Quine, whose philosophy of language and science underlies many of James's central insights.

Quine and Quintana Improve the Box Score

Baseball statistics start with the box score, the quasi-pictorial mixture of symbols and numbers that record each event on the baseball field. Fans traditionally buy a scorecard and track the action, keeping their own box scores. Sox fans can even purchase copies of Jerry Remy's scorecard (though of course he would never hock them during a game). The numbers and records that appear in the box score—runs, hits, and errors—are intuitive and commonsensical, the obvious transpiring of a baseball game. If one is tempted to see science as fundamentally opposed to other points of view, or as alienating, it's important to note that science has its humble beginnings in the observations of common sense. As Quine puts it simply, "Science is a continuation of common sense." A box score is the common-sense observation of a baseball game and science might be considered the box score of the world.

Bill James is quoted as saying, in an article written by Dan Okrent:

> A baseball field is so covered with statistics that nothing can happen there without leaving its tracks in the records. There may well be no other facet of American life, the activities of laboratory rats excepted, which is so extensively categorized, counted and recorded. (Sports Illustrated, May 25th, 1981)

James refers to baseball events as being "categorized," which brings up an important philosophical—and scientific—point. Many philosophers have argued that no sensation or perception comes uncategorized. For example, one doesn't sense only a roundish white patch with two red lines crossing it; instead, one perceives a baseball with seams. And one doesn't see that roundish white patch crossing the edge of a pentagonal white figure, but instead one sees a beautiful pitch painting the outside corner of home plate. Instead, philosophers describe this as "seeing as," or perceiving not just colors and shapes but seeing these colors and shapes *as* baseballs painting outside corners on an 0–2 count. More generally, in watching a baseball game, every event is seen as being of a particular category—as a hit or strike or RBI. The box scores reflect this. As do the records; at the end of the year, the players with the most hits or RBIs are considered (among) the best. But are these traditional categories that we use the best categories? Why would we think the player with the most hits—or highest batting average—is the best hitter?

Given how much is going on at any given moment on a baseball field, and just how *raw* raw data is, most everything on a baseball field can be categorized in countless ways. But some of those ways are better than others. A popular way of ridiculing baseball's fondness for numbers is to suggest a particularly trivial category as representative of baseball statistics. For example, which Red Sox player with a last name beginning with Q has the most career RBIs? Let's say, oh, Carlos Quintana. But what makes this category trivial, as opposed to other less trivial categories such as best on-base percentage? First, the Q category is highly restricted; anyone not on the Sox with a name that starts with Q is excluded, and presumably that's quite a few decent ballplayers. But, perhaps more importantly, the category "Sox players with last name Q" is not predictive. One can't predict results on the basis of having a name that starts with "Q" as one might on the basis of, say, having a 95 mph fastball with 15 mph of separation from the changeup, or as one might based on the ability to work the count and get on base—as a high OBP indicates.

Though of course no one would take this Q category seriously, the contrast between the trivial and important gives us an insight into what an improving science of baseball tries to do. Often, good science is just discovering the most useful ways of categorizing information, and scientific categories are typically most useful when they are most predictive. If whether a ball falls in for a hit or not is largely a function of luck rather than skill, then the hit category isn't especially predictive of a player's future performance, therefore the hit category may not be particularly meaningful. Figuring out which categories are most predictive isn't easy. If the hitter about to step to the plate against Manny Delcarmen plays for the Yankees, and if we know that Yankees hitters hit .262 off Manny Delcarmen in day games, then classifying this single event—this at-bat—as of this kind (a Yankee vs. Delcarmen), allows one to say there's a 26.2 percent chance of a hit in this at-bat. Classifying in this way is the basis of prediction. But how relevant to the odds of what's about to happen is it that this hitter is categorized as a Yankee? Is the classification as "Yankee" the most predictive? What if the hitter had just been traded to the Yankees, such that the .262 does not include this particular hitter's statistics? Does this affect the odds of a hit?

For Quine and James, science improves by making our classifications more precise, and more relevant, so that predictions can be more accurate. Though we—and common sense—start by noticing obvious categories like "being a Yankee" (the smell is a giveaway), we must move beyond the obvious to get to the bottom of things. In *Ontological Relativity and Other Essays* (Columbia University Press, 1969) Quine says, the "notion of similarity or of kind changes as science progresses" (p. 121). And as science matures, standards of similarity evolve. For Quine, science

> is a development away from the immediate, subjective, animal sense of similarity to the remoter objectivity of a similarity determined by scientific hypotheses and posits and constructs. Things are similar in the later or theoretical sense to the degree that they are interchangeable parts of the cosmic machine revealed by science. (p. 133)

I'll explain that bit about "interchangeable parts of the cosmic machine" in a moment. In the meantime, in a more mature baseball science, the statistical category of "being a Yankee"—the immediate, subjective, animal sense of similarity based on the visual perception of pinstripes (and smugness)—which naturally triggers our animal aggression is replaced by more advanced kinds and classifications, like thirty-two-year-old slugging left handed hitters with slight uppercut swings. In fact, James invented "similarity scores," as a way of finding counterparts of a given player—in terms of age, or size, or skill set—and then predicting the given player's career on the basis of how similar players progressed in the past. James and others have invented hundreds of new stats in order to predict everything more precisely, which means creating new categories and ways of classifying. And though these ways are often complicated beyond the common sense categories found in the box score, these tools aren't invented just for the sake of being complex. James writes:

> I love numbers, but not for themselves. I don't care for them as conclusions. I start with the game, with the things I see there or the things people say are there. And I ask, 'Is it true? Can you validate it? Can you measure it?' For instance, why do people argue about which shortstop has the best range or which catcher has the best arm? Why not figure it out? You can get a pretty good idea by abstracting information from the available data. (*Sports Illustrated*, May 25th, 1981)

Atom Hyzdu, Atom Laroche, and Atom Stern Are Their Own Universes

If science is a continuation of common sense, as Quine thinks, then science is continuous with common sense, and not so fundamentally different. However, a continuous evolution can, over time, end up quite far away from where it started. "Abstracting information," as James puts it, can be pretty abstract. And the amount of "available data" is staggering. Fans have always been amateur baseball scientists, needing only a pencil and a scorecard to keep track of the stats of their favorite players, which required little beyond basic arithmetic. But the new statistics—those devised to answer the sorts of questions that James asks—require a far more sophisticated method. The Society for American Baseball Research (SABR), for whom "sabermetrics"—the new science of baseball statistics inspired by James—is named, is as professional and sophisticated as any academic institution. For that reason, though one need have no credentials to discover the truths of baseball, a background in statistics or mathematics are almost necessities.

So despite the continuity between common sense and science, and between traditional and Sabermetric statistics, there has emerged what looks like a fundamental divide. Traditional statistics such as BA and RBI, unlike Sabermetric stats such as Value Over Replacement Player (VORP), or Win Shares (a James creation), can be counted by anyone, entirely from one's own box score. At the end of a game, the fan can count up the hits and errors and know, from that one box score of that one game, just what went on that day. That fan need not know anything else that happened across the league. "Box score stats" such BA and RBI have meaning all by themselves, in isolation from everything else. The box score, with its neatly segmented and separate boxes, encourages the thought that each play—each discrete square—is a little universe unto itself. That is, each square seems a self-sufficient atom, something separate and distinct from every other, able to exist without them. A whole baseball game, then, is an aggregate of such atoms, combined and arranged in a pattern that is the box score. And baseball statistics are simply aggregates or tallies of such numbers, each acquired independently, one at a time.

By contrast, Sabermetric stats, even for the players in the game being played right in front of your eyes, do not rely only on your own box score. Many Sabermetric stats include not just the countable actions right in front of you, but also what every other player did that day, and on every other day, and in what ballpark they did it in. Such stats are adjusted or normalized for league-average performances and ballpark effects. In the view of a sabermetrician, a Bill Mueller single in Fenway (a hitter's park) in 2004 is worth something entirely different than a Bill Mueller single in Dodger

Stadium (a pitcher's park) in 2006—different time, different league, different ballpark—despite the similarity of the two events when viewed in a box score.

The Sabermetric single, all by itself, though a distinct square in the box score, is not a self-sufficient atom. That is, it's not an event (or thing) that exists unto itself, and by itself, with meaning by itself. Instead, it's just a bit of data, which only acquires meaning when related to the larger universe of data. Whereas traditional stats are *atomistic*, Sabermetric stats are *holistic*. As a result, it's impossible— by definition—for a fan to be able to track Sabermetric stats just from his own box score, sitting in Fenway in 2004. A scorecard, a pencil, and a pair of eyes, however keen, are insufficient.

Carlton Fisk, Dave Roberts, and the Science of Miracles

Though it's now a cliché to refer to the so-called "butterfly effect," according to which the flapping of a butterfly's wings in Africa, say, through an ever-increasing cascade of tiny events, may result in a hurricane in America; I will refer to it nonetheless. If this sort of process is happening all the time, such that any nearby or local event is shaped and perhaps even brought about by innumerable events from afar, then it would be misleading to think a box score of your local hurricane told the whole story, and it would be misleading to think one could predict the weather very accurately on the basis of that local box score. And if one could only know the movements of every butterfly, so to speak, one could predict the weather better than by just watching the local weather report. Luckily, every event on every baseball field can be recorded. The Jamesean and Sabermetric emphasis on including league averages and ballpark effects derived from inexhaustible attention to every event is their way of tracking butterflies in Africa. The Jamesean School thinks its global statistics are better at predicting the future than local or box score statistics such as ERA and RBI. This sort of holism—in science and in baseball—sees everything as interrelated. Events are global, not just local; holistic, not atomistic.

Because the Jamesean and Sabermetric approach records and charts everything, it can classify everything. Putting events into types or categories allows comparison and establishes uniformity; if two events are of the same type—both singles or home runs, say—they are similar, and given how many events have occurred in the history of baseball, any new event you please can be found to be just like a million others. This allows patterns to be discovered—as when certain types of plays are followed by others, which in turn allows for predictions based on these patterns.

I've suggested that science views all events as interrelated, and so as interdependent, in some or many ways, and also that all events can be categorized and so treated as similar to one another. What is so threatening about this? Why should there be an anti-Jamesean movement? Well, this scientific way of looking at things contradicts two important ideas that many people hold. First, that the event we see before us is localized and distinct from all others, and second, and more importantly, that the event we see before us is *unique*. I already mentioned that Boston Red Sox history is often told as a religious narrative in the language of faith, hope, and redemption. And religions believe in miracles. A miracle is a unique event, something entirely unlike, and independent of, all others. Miracles don't rely on something like a "butterfly effect" to happen, and miracles, in being unique, cannot be classified. Miracles are in a class by themselves—unique. The reason science doesn't accept the religious notion of miracles is that science doesn't accept the notion of unique events at all.

In watching baseball, we yearn for the unique, and hope for the joy and thrill of the miracle. Carlton Fisk in '75 and Dave Roberts in '04 were unique events and felt like miracles. The Fenway organist even played the "Hallelujah Chorus" as Fisk rounded the bases! Now, neither of those players are the greatest players of all time. But who cares? Isn't it an insult to ask whether given 100 such pitches, how many more times could Fisk or Roberts have duplicated their results, as opposed to a "better" player? Using advanced statistical tools, we can know the precise odds of the Sox winning Game Four once Roberts stole the base. But why would we need such information—they did in fact win. It happened. We saw it. And it was great. The meaning of such events isn't how *frequently* similar things *could* happen, but that they *did* happen, *once*, end of story. It's their uniqueness that makes them special, and the idea of reducing them to others of a type or dragging in what appear to be outside factors to explain them seems to ruin what's most special for many people about such moments in the great game of baseball.

Earlier I quoted Quine as saying "Things are similar in the later or theoretical sense [in the mature or advanced scientific sense] to the degree that they are interchangeable parts of the cosmic machine revealed by science." A miracle, in being unique, is utterly unlike every other event. Miracles aren't interchangeable, replaceable, events. Science progresses by perceiving any given event as similar to others; the cosmic machine revealed by science operates on patterns and predictability. But baseball moments are irreplaceable, not substitutable for another similar event. History only happens once; nothing can stand in for Fisk or Roberts. The new science of Sabermetrics threatens to eliminate the unique, the magical.

But can one make any predictions based only on singular events such as how Fisk or Roberts will perform the following year? Sadly, but obviously, not. In 1976, Fisk hit .255 with 17 homers and 58 RBIs. These stats are respectable, but certainly nothing heroic. Roberts, traded to the San Diego Padres in the '04–'05 offseason, batted .275 with a .356 OBP, and stole 23 bases in 2005, down from the 38 he stole in the '04 regular season (between the Los Angeles Dodgers and the Red Sox). And so, whether or not there really are such things as miracles, they don't do an owner or General Manager any good. A GM's job is to fill the roster with players most likely to perform over the 162-game season, because miracles are useless for the purposes of making predictions, and one can't predict when a miracle will happen. (Though it doesn't hurt to acquire someone at the trading deadline that might be used to pinch run in the ninth inning of a Game Four of the ALCS.)

A baseball miracle is a single square in a single box score for a single time and place. And although such box scores or miracles may have *meaning* for other times and places, as memories of history always do, they don't have statistical or scientific *relevance* on their own. The Sabermetric or Jamesean statistics aren't statistics meant for the fans, if by "fan" one means someone who enjoys the game most when unexpected and seemingly miraculous events occur. The Jamesean stats are really for general managers, (or fantasy general managers), who need to watch the waiver wire, know how much a player is really worth over the long haul, and who have a stake in a predictable future, rather than a volatile but hopeful one. John Henry and Executive Vice President and General Manager Theo Epstein hired Bill James for a reason. Not to pray.

Scientists Drink Beer Too, You Know

In a May 2006 article, *Boston Globe* sportswriter Bob Ryan complained that the Jamesean sabermetrician would be no fun to watch a game with. Ryan didn't publish the data on which this assessment was based, but I'm sure he found a sufficiently large sample size of sabermetricians, watched games with each them, and made sure he was in a good mood when he did so that he could know the lack of fun wasn't his fault. But taking Ryan's stereotype seriously for a moment, one might concede insofar as he takes the GM's and not the fan's approach, that one might not want to watch a game with a Jamesean sabermetrician. But it's funny. People often vote for their President on the basis of whether he's the kind of guy they'd like to have a beer with, even though they probably never will have that beer, and more importantly, even though being the kind of guy they'd want to have a beer with isn't the Presidents' job. And, likewise, being the kind of guy someone would want to watch the game with isn't the GM's job. His job is to try to predict the future of each player and use that as a basis to decide whether that player should or shouldn't be on the team. So even if your GM or your President is the kind of guy who prefers the unique to the pattern, or who prefers the miracle to the law, or who prefers the religious to the scientific, to do his job he should use every resource and trust every fact available to him, even if that means losing the meaning of the present moment for the sake of a winning future.

Evidence Rewarded

There need not be incompatibility between the new science of Sabermetrics and the religious emotions and the language of faith, hope, and redemption. If there's anywhere that's a safe place for religious emotions in a scientific world it's on the baseball diamond. Caring need not be jettisoned along with less reliable statistics. Without caring, passion and excitement for the game the numbers are meaningless.

With Bill James, the passion is fundamental. James, quoted by Michael Lewis in *Moneyball* (2003), wrote:

> Both of my parents died of cancer, and I fully expect that it's going to get me too, in time. It would be very easy for me to say that cancer research is more important to me than baseball—but I must admit that I don't do anything which would be consistent with such a belief. I think about cancer research a few times a month; I think about baseball virtually every waking hour of my life. (p. 65)

Despite his single-minded pursuit of baseball and baseball knowledge, and his faith in the value of baseball over even what could save his own physical life, James also exhibits the humility characteristic of scientists and philosophers, and the detachment from ego that's essential in the search for truth. James wrote: "It's not important to me that people agree with what I have to say, just as long as they understand why I've said it" (*Sports Illustrated*, May 25th, 1981).

21

What Really Offends Fans about Red Sox Ticket Resellers

STEPHEN MATHIS

Bob decides to surprise his wife, Kathy, a rabid Red Sox fan, with tickets to a game for the family on the weekend. Bob teaches in a public high school and makes a decent living, but he can't afford to spend too much on tickets, especially given that he will need to buy four of them if he wants to bring the kids along. So Bob begins by looking at grandstand seats, but abandons that idea when he finds that online resellers are asking at least $125 apiece for tickets that have a face value of $50 apiece. But then he finds that the $26 bleacher seats are going for a minimum of $57 apiece, and that's before the site adds on $17 for shipping and $15.96 (7 percent) for "handling."

And that's just to get through the gates. Once Bob factors in food, beverages, and maybe a foam finger for the kids, the sticker shock has him contemplating a weeknight game with just Kathy, because six hours of babysitting is substantially less than he'd pay for tickets for the kids. But bleachers aren't very romantic—or at least not to Bob, anyway—so he goes back to looking at grandstand seats, but at well over $250 for a pair, he begins to think that this is the kind of thing he'll have to save up for, or maybe do as part of Kathy's birthday—all because some guy, or some guy's company, has decided over one hundred percent is the right markup for reselling Red Sox tickets.

Taking One for the Team: The High Price of Being a Red Sox Fan

Unfortunately, Bob's story is all too common and predictable these days. If you're a Red Sox fan living in the northeast, chances are that at some point you've been more than a little frustrated trying to find reasonably priced tickets to a home game. Of course, there are a number of factors that contribute to the scarcity of tickets: Fenway seats fewer people than most major league parks, the Boston Red Sox are a storied franchise with a large and devoted fan base, and the team has been very good for many years now, just to name a few. The result is a situation in which there are many more people who want tickets than there are tickets available.

This situation leads directly to another that only adds to fans' frustration: because of the high demand, resellers have more incentive to buy up tickets at face value in hopes of selling them for a profit. In this way, resellers further reduce ticket availability, and this helps drive prices higher on the secondary market. At first, it may seem that this behavior (and its consequences) explains why Red Sox fans tend to view ticket resellers, especially professional ones, with contempt.

But what professional resellers (that is, those who resell tickets as a business) do to reduce the number of tickets available at face value is nothing special and has only a marginal effect. In recent years, the Red Sox have limited to eight the number of tickets individuals can purchase at one time, thereby undercutting resellers' ability to purchase large numbers of tickets easily. As a result, professional resellers play only slightly more of a role than other individuals play in the face-value side of the Red Sox ticket market. And given the demand for tickets, it's safe to say that if professionals weren't out there trying to buy up tickets to resell, then non-professionals (or at least more than already do) would step in to take advantage of the money-making opportunity.

For these reasons, it seems that professional resellers don't skew the market for tickets as much as fans may think they do. So what's the real source of the offense Red Sox fans take at ticket reselling and at professional resellers in particular?

That "Idiot" Stuff Went Out with Johnny Damon: The Real Offense in Reselling Tickets

Perhaps it's simply the markup in the price above face value. After all, what resellers do is a lot like buying a $15 Dustin Pedroia t-shirt at a sporting goods store and then trying to sell it for $30 on the street just outside of that store—without removing the original price tag. If you were to see someone trying this, it'd be perfectly natural to respond, "Why in the world should I pay $30 for this $15 t-shirt? What do you think I am, an idiot?" In other words, it'd be perfectly natural to take offense at this behavior.

Now contrast the Pedroia t-shirt example to a situation a member of my family witnessed in New Orleans: in the heart of the French Quarter, an area known for its drunken revelry, a downpour caused a flash flood that made an intersection suddenly impassable. Almost no sooner than the people at the intersection had turned off their cars to wait for the waters to recede, a boy appeared with a twelve-pack of cheap beer and proceeded to offer cans to each car for $5 a piece.

Though that story is peculiar to New Orleans's culture and climate (only in a city with drive-thru daiquiri stands and bayou heat and humidity), I offer it as an example here because it's a better analogy to reselling Red Sox tickets than the Pedroia t-shirt example is. The key difference is availability: a lot of what makes the Pedroia t-shirt example offensive is the fact that you could easily walk down the street and buy the same t-shirt for half the price. But unless I had just stopped at a drive-thru daiquiri place, I would have no access to alcohol in the beer example, especially in light of the fact that I'd be stuck at a flooded intersection. Setting aside concerns about drinking and driving (let's say I'm the passenger in the car), the premium I'd pay for the beer would be worth it to me if I wanted some alcohol to get me through the wait because there'd be such limited availability in that situation. We use much the same sort of reasoning to justify paying exorbitant prices for snacks at convenience stores.

The beer example, like paying high prices at convenience stores, makes sense in terms of the basic market forces of supply and demand. I think Red Sox ticket reselling makes sense in exactly the same terms. The fact is that resellers would not do what they do if there were not so much demand for tickets, and resellers can only charge what the market will bear.

My first game at Fenway was in 1992. A buddy and I were taking a road trip through the northeast and stopped that night in Boston—and two hours before game time, we bought tickets in the grandstands behind home plate for little over face value. Oh, and the visiting team that night was the Yankees. As difficult as that story may be to believe (I find myself straining to believe that I'm remembering it correctly and not just making it up), keep in mind that the 1992 Red Sox were terrible (73–89 record) and averaged just over 30,000 in attendance for each home game. Meanwhile, the Red Sox average home game attendance has topped 36,000 each year since 2006, and the team has averaged 92 wins and 70 losses in that same time frame (2006–2008). Even though my buddy and I may have gotten lucky with our ticket purchase that night in 1992, it seems that if we did get lucky, we didn't get *that* lucky: the Red Sox were terrible back then and attendance (and, with it, demand) were way down at that point.

In this way, ticket resellers (of all sorts) and buyers come together to create something of a free market for Red Sox tickets. But considering all of the other forces at play in the market for Red Sox tickets, face value and otherwise, I think we can say something even stronger: resellers help create as much of a free market as we find anywhere else in the overall Red Sox ticket market (and by "Red Sox ticket market" here I mean all ways that Red Sox tickets are bought and sold, whether by resellers or by direct sales from the Red Sox to fans—or to resellers). This is because every other force in the Red Sox ticket market runs counter, in one way or another, to the free-market tendency to set prices according to the laws of supply and demand. This is true of the procedures the Red Sox use for direct ticket sales and for season ticket sales, of Major League Baseball's anti-trust exemption, and even of Massachusetts anti-scalping laws.

Patriot's Day: Toward a More "Democratic" Approach to Ticket Sales

If I'm right that resellers create as much of a free market for tickets as anyone else in the overall market for Red Sox tickets, then what offends fans about Red Sox ticket resellers cannot be that resellers are "ripping off" fans—even if sometimes that's the way it feels—because, again, resellers can only charge what the market will bear. The key to understanding what really offends fans about ticket resellers lies in the fact that the other forces at play in the market for Red Sox tickets tend to undermine, rather than create, a true free market, often in order to promote a more democratic, or egalitarian, scheme of access to tickets. To illustrate my point here, let's take a closer look at the other main forces in the overall market for Red Sox tickets:

Red Sox Direct Sales

In recent years, the Red Sox have set up an online "waiting room" that opens to the public on pre-announced dates. This web purchasing system selects individuals at random from the virtual waiting room, without giving priority to those who have been waiting the longest. Once one passes from the waiting room to the ticket-purchasing page, one can buy a maximum of eight tickets, and that limit applies to each individual (most likely determined by credit card number) for that entire buying period. Part of the point seems to be to keep access to tickets available to the public, and part of it is to keep large numbers of tickets out of the hands of resellers, as much as that is possible. The result is a small-scale nightmare for fans. I have waited for the better part of eight hours in the "waiting room," with my status refreshing every thirty seconds on each of my two computers. Not only did I end up wasting an entire Saturday watching my computer screen, but I also hated the Red Sox over and over again for using a random selection system that was allowing others out of the waiting room before me, even though I'd been waiting longer than they had (I had logged in a minute or two ahead of the designated time, in fact).

This purportedly fairer but also terribly frustrating system for direct ticket sales is far from a free market for tickets. It diverges from a free market in at least two distinct ways: first, it limits availability of tickets to those who manage to get out of the waiting room and into the ticket-purchasing page and does not allow all of those who would like to buy tickets to buy them. Second, it limits the number of tickets buyers can purchase at one time, so that some individuals cannot participate in the market for tickets to the degree they'd prefer.

Add in the fact the Red Sox sell these tickets to the public at a face value that is far below what those tickets will fetch on the secondary market, and the system looks even less like a free market. But the Red Sox likely price the face value of tickets in this way on purpose, as part of a larger marketing strategy that involves losing money on tickets at Fenway in order to make more elsewhere. After all, if the Red Sox wanted to maximize ticket revenue, they could simply auction off each seat for each game. This approach would actually be counterproductive, however, since it would alienate a huge number of fans from the middle- to lower-income brackets who attend only a few games a year. The Red Sox don't want to alienate these fans because many of them watch the Red Sox on NESN, the majority owner (eighty percent) of which is the Boston Red Sox. (Kagan Research LLC, in Monterey, California estimated that the Red Sox made over $100 million from NESN alone in 2004.) Also, these same fans buy a lot of Red Sox merchandise and memorabilia, which adds substantially to the organization's bottom line. Basically, the Red Sox organization is willing to make less on tickets if that means it'll make more on cable revenue, merchandise, and fans' long-term commitment to the team. The result is a direct ticket sales system that is far from a free market.

Red Sox Season Tickets

This one is more about cultivating a long-term commitment to the team amongst a select group of fans. And it's probably also about creating a level of envy and pent-up demand for when these very expensive ticket packages do become available. Even though I live more than an hour away from Fenway and probably do not have the level of income most season ticket holders have, I would be more than willing to fork over the cash necessary to become a season ticket holder. Part of that willingness comes from the fact that I appreciate how rare of a commodity Red Sox season tickets are: On several occasions I've emailed the Red Sox about the availability of season tickets, and I have never received a response. That fact and the fact that the waiting list for even partial season ticket packages is at least five years long together only reinforce the mythic status of Red Sox season tickets, especially among devoted fans. They represent the Holy Grail, and I have no shot—and that makes me want them all the more. And it doesn't help to realize that the vast majority of tickets I've purchased from resellers over the years come from season ticket holders.

Baseball's Anti-Trust Exemption

Of all the aspects of the market for Red Sox tickets that might undermine, rather than promote, the free market, this one is perhaps the most obvious. Federal anti-trust laws exist (under Title 15 of the US Code) to prevent monopolies and other practices that unreasonably restrain competition within the free market. Major League Baseball is exempt from these laws and operates essentially as a monopoly.

There is nothing in legislation that exempts Major League Baseball from these laws. The exemption comes as a result of a Supreme Court ruling in 1922, and the Court has reaffirmed it in decisions in 1954 and 1972. In that last decision, the Supreme Court noted that it was maintaining the exemption in part because Congress had never done anything to repeal it. More recently, Congress has held hearings on baseball's anti-trust exemption, and legislators have argued against repealing it on the grounds (among others) that baseball deserves special status because it is America's "national pastime."

Despite its odd history, the anti-trust exemption allows Major League Baseball to control whether or not new teams or major leagues come into existence and how existing teams and leagues conduct themselves. This means that if Boston baseball fans want to see a major league game, it has to be a Red Sox game. This also means that no other Major League Baseball team can help drive prices down or provide an alternative product in the Boston area. As a result, the Red Sox organization's monopoly on Major League Baseball entertainment offerings limits the total number of Major League Baseball tickets available on the free market, thereby maintaining a shortage of tickets and pent-up demand, inevitably skewing the market.

Massachusetts Anti-Scalping Laws

Calling Massachusetts's law against scalping out of date would be to understate things quite a bit. Passed in 1924, it prohibits any markup over $2 above the face value of the ticket, and of course it says nothing about online resellers. While it allows resellers to add service charges when they resell tickets, those service charges can be only for business expenses other than having to pay over face value to get the tickets in the first place. So if a reseller has to pay over face value to obtain tickets before reselling them, she can't pass that cost (above face value) on to her buyers.

However, Massachusetts officials—and especially Boston Police—have rarely arrested scalpers or investigated the reselling companies they license (Bruce Mohl, "Scalping Law? What Scalping Law," *Boston Globe*, October 15th, 2006).

While anti-scalping laws were intended primarily to protect the public against extortion and exorbitant prices, they also serve to constrain the secondary market for tickets so that pricing is no longer simply a matter of supply and demand. Even though Red Sox fans—those buying the tickets, anyway—appreciate the state's imposing an upper limit on ticket prices in the secondary market, such limits (when enforced) are at odds with free market principles.

But from the start, the aim of the law was not just to protect the public against high prices for public performances and entertainment: Legislators made it clear that another reason for the law was that public performances and entertainment have some broader public value that the state has an interest in protecting or promoting. In 1924, the Justices of the Supreme Judicial Court of Massachusetts ruled that it would be constitutional for the legislature to pass a law regulating the sale and pricing of tickets to theatres and other public entertainment spots if the legislature thought that these were "matters affected with a public interest, and that legislation is necessary for the purposes of safeguarding the public against fraud, extortion, and exorbitant rates and like abuses in relation thereto" (247 Mass. 589, 1924). The Massachusetts Senate responded with an order that argued, among other things, that theaters and other kinds of public entertainment contribute to public morality (though they note that not all do) and inspire philanthropy, patriotism, and good will (247 Mass. 594, 1924).

Rawls in the Cheap Seats: Access to Red Sox Tickets as a Public Good

These forces in the market for Red Sox tickets all run counter to the free market in a way that suggests that many people—and not just fans—view access to Red Sox tickets as what John Rawls called a "public good." Public goods are things of value that we want to protect to some degree from the free market. It's important to note that while public goods so defined tend to contribute to the Public Good or the Common Good, what Rawls meant by a "good" in terms like "public goods" is basically just something we value— much closer to "goods and services" than "the Good" in any larger, universal or moral sense. Rawls saw the distinction in this way in large part because he saw free markets as contributing significantly to the Public or Common Good. John Rawls, in *A Theory of Justice*, argued for what he calls a "liberal democratic" approach (not to be confused with either the political leaning or the political party), which involves, among other things, guaranteeing individual liberties and providing for social welfare. Rawls thought that liberal democracies would use both private and public means of providing for social welfare, with the state or communities providing public goods and the free market providing private ones.

The most obvious examples of public goods are things that all of us share as a resource or perhaps even own together (via the state), like parks, roads, and state universities. Parks seem especially appropriate as an example here. Parks are open to everyone, owned and maintained in common, and offer something individuals in a community can enjoy that they might not be able to have or maintain on their own.

The most obvious examples of private goods are things individuals buy and own for themselves and enjoy individually, like bicycles, hats, and iPods. So if I want to fill up my iPod with old blues music or set it on fire and destroy it, either of these is perfectly acceptable, because I paid for the iPod and it's mine. However, I can't say the same thing about the park down the street.

Rawls thought that there are many goods that do not fall so neatly in one category or the other. But for his purposes (which included trying to structure society so as to make it as fair and as just as possible), Rawls argued that society should treat as public only those goods that are difficult to divide up and that individuals use or benefit from in a shared or collective way. His classic example here is a country's national defense. With respect to things like national defense that cannot be divided at all and that satisfy needs we all share, Rawls argues that the state must step in and take such goods out of the market completely by providing them itself. To see the power of this argument, all you have to do is consider how cumbersome and ineffective it would be to have individuals provide for national defense—if it would be possible at all—via the free market. In the end, though, Rawls did not say just how difficult to divide up or just how shared (or public) a good has to be for us to consider it a public good. However, in part because Rawls liked free-market capitalism (with some constraints), he seemed to think public goods should be fairly indivisible and much more shared than not.

Using these admittedly vague criteria, should we consider access to Red Sox tickets a public good? Obviously, tickets themselves are easily divisible—up to a point, of course—and not easily shared, since it's one individual per ticket. For these reasons, it doesn't make much sense to talk about tickets themselves as anything but private goods. However, *access* to tickets seems to be a different matter. For one thing, when you divide up access to tickets (among people), you're dividing up *chances at* something rather than amounts of something. For another, access to tickets—under the current online system, anyway—does not necessarily have any particular monetary value: you might get through early and get more expensive tickets or you might get through late and get less expensive tickets, but you might also get through and not want to buy any more than two tickets in total. In other words, depending on how things work out, your slice of access to tickets could translate into very different monetary values for you. The same is not true of most private goods, with the exceptions being things like lottery and raffle tickets.

And though each individual can make something like a private choice of how to use her access to tickets (she can use it to buy one ticket or five or eight—or none), a peculiar thing happens if one doesn't use it at all: she loses it. Unlike with most private goods, if one chooses not to use her access at all, she does not retain control over it; instead, everyone else gets that much more access. This means that unlike most private goods (think of commodities like oil, corn, and gold), access to tickets is not something an individual can hoard, let spoil, or destroy.

When you consider how easily shared a good like access to tickets might be, it's also important to consider the fact that the availability of any reasonable level of access to tickets arguably carries with it a broader, more public benefit: it contributes indirectly to a sense of community. For example, I am more comfortable being a member of Red Sox Nation knowing that tickets are generally accessible to regular folks. And this would be true even if I didn't want to buy any more tickets than the two that came with my Red Sox Nation membership. And if such access were not widely available (again, even if I didn't want to use it), I would be reluctant to join Red Sox Nation or might avoid joining it altogether. Under this argument, though, the extent to which some people are already put off by the cost of going to a ballgame at Fenway serves as a reason to question just how positive a public benefit this is. In general, however, such a sense of community is a public benefit insofar as it contributes positively to the culture and the shared life of people living in the northeast (and of those unfortunate transplants who still count themselves part of the Nation).

As I noted above, the Red Sox organization wants to promote that same sense of community because that sense of community serves its corporate interests, and its direct ticket sales and its season ticket sales also tend to promote that same sense of community, albeit in slightly different ways. But the Massachusetts anti-scalping laws promote it as well (symbolically, if nothing else) and presumably were not designed to serve corporate interests, but rather to reflect the public's interest in promoting that sense of community. And in a less direct way, Major League Baseball's antitrust exemption does the same thing: it sets aside the Red Sox as a unique feature of the greater Boston area, and that contributes to its cultural and community status.

Of course, not everyone in the northeast appreciates the Red Sox as an integral and positive part of the broader community, and many of those who do never even try to buy tickets. With that in mind, how can we say that access to Red Sox tickets should have the status of a public good? Why should we devote state resources to protecting that access in the same ways we protect other public goods?

Any Way You Cut It, Fenway Is a Shrine

Before taking on that second, more difficult question above, note that the fact that some—or even many—individuals in a given society never use a particular good does not by itself keep that good from being a public good. There are plenty of public goods that some individuals fail to take advantage of, but which nonetheless provide some broader, indirect benefit, even to those who do not avail themselves of them. Some individuals may never set foot on the grounds of a public park, but having public green spaces helps foster community pride and keeps communities from overbuilding in certain areas. Those who do not drive still benefit from roads, because having ways to get places enhances economic activity in all sorts of ways. And even if one dropped out of high school and never took advantage of the education system, having young people get more education helps those individuals get jobs, which helps the economy, lowers crime, and so on. It's not necessary that each and every person in a society actually use a particular good— or that every person actually be able to use it—in order for it to be a public good (and to be useful as one). Many of us will never have need of disaster relief, for example, and if we all needed it, there wouldn't be enough for everyone to get it, but disaster relief remains very plausible as a public good nonetheless.

But we're talking about access to Red Sox tickets here, not parks or roads or even disaster relief, and access to Red Sox tickets is hardly a typical example of a public good. As I noted above, the tickets themselves are nearly paradigm examples of private goods. And however many of us may feel about it, baseball is not essential to human life and is basically a form of discretionary entertainment: as Robert B. Parker once wrote, "Baseball is the most important thing that doesn't matter." As a result, one can question how legitimate an interest our society has in treating Red Sox baseball, and the public's access to Red Sox tickets in particular, as a public good, especially when our society, at times, seems to turn a blind eye toward other, more serious needs.

When we use state power (or refrain from using it, as is the case with Major League Baseball's anti-trust exemption) to protect a good from market forces, we express our values as a society. Since different societies often value things differently, different societies will tend to treat different things as public goods. This is why Rawls thought there was no clear dividing line between public and private goods. But it seems safe to say that Rawls would have thought that some societies' values (as evidenced by their public goods) were better than others, and societies that promoted superfluous goods at the expense of those essential to healthy and productive lives would be among the worst.

While some argue that our society's values are currently too skewed toward entertainment, perhaps even at the expense of more important things, like health care, it's not clear that treating access to Red Sox tickets as a public good demonstrates that we live under a degraded value system. For one thing, the state devotes very little in the way of resources toward protecting access to Red Sox tickets as a public good: the Massachusetts police almost never have enforced the state's anti-scalping laws, and, as I mentioned previously, the federal government simply refrains from enforcing anti-trust laws against Major League Baseball (so no resources used there, either). As a result, the state's involvement in promoting access to Red Sox tickets as a public good is mostly symbolic in nature. And the public derives value from ticket access having the status of a public good.

In the end, though, it doesn't really matter if we *should* treat access to Red Sox tickets as a public good or not. The fact is that we *do* treat access to Red Sox tickets as a public good, and the Red Sox organization and our state and federal governments go to some lengths to make sure that access operates in that way and has that status in our society. And the fact that we treat such access as a public good explains why fans object to ticket reselling and ticket resellers.

Tearing Down Fenway: Now That Would Be Offensive

It's difficult to object to ticket resellers on the grounds that they overcharge or rip off fans, since resellers can charge only as much as the market will bear. Given this fact and the fact that we treat access to Red Sox tickets as a public good, it seems that what really offends fans (and others) about Red Sox ticket resellers is that they use the free market to exploit a good that we take a public interest in protecting to some degree from market forces. Part of the reason the people of the northeast value the Red Sox is that they contribute something positive to the community—and something they can't contribute in quite the same way if fans don't have some reasonable access to tickets. If that's true, then it's easy to see how resellers threaten, if not directly undermine, that positive contribution. Ultimately, the problem is not that ticket resellers make too much money or cost fans too much money. Rather, the problem— and the thing that really offends us—is that ticket resellers trade on and thereby diminish a good we treat as shared or public, and thus they wrong all of us.

But somehow I don't think that will keep me from calling one the next time I need tickets to Fenway.

22

The Sacred Geometry of Fenway Park

RANDALL E. AUXIER

***Last day of October, Halloween, 2009. 6:30 Central Daylight
Time. Rain delay in Philadelphia.***

First I want to say that A. Bartlett Giamatti is the greatest man who
ever lived, bar none. He is greater than Jesus singing an Elvis song
in a John Wayne movie, greater than everything but the Game
itself. I didn't know him of course, and I know that some of you
did, very well, but I'm talking about the myth not the man, the
Giamatti of my mind, who wrote the words that said what I wasn't
even smart enough to *feel*, until he said it for me. In what follows,
Giamatti will be referred to simply as "the Philosopher," a moniker
we philosophers usually reserve for Aristotle. But Aristotle might as
well have played for the Yankees as far as I'm concerned. Giamatti
is the Philosopher.

Fleecing an Argonaut

Gino Castignoli is his name. You could think of him as a latter day
Argonaut, one of the hearty souls who accompanied Jason (the
original Jason, *not* Jason Giambi) through the Hellespont to distant
Georgia on a quest for the Golden Fleece. But the Giambi refer-
ence isn't wholly gratuitous. The very last hit recorded in the old
Yankee stadium, which is to say the *real* Yankee Stadium, was
Giambi's, and then he wisely set off for home, in the Golden State.
At least he fleeced Steinbrenner and his Mini-me son and took his
booty back to Cali. But Castignoli is the fellow, a native of the
Bronx no less (but obviously a citizen of Red Sox Nation), who

buried a replica of David Ortiz's jersey beneath the visitors' dugout in the *new* Yankee Stadium. Someone blabbed and he got caught, unfortunately, but the story alone was worth the effort. After all there was an Argonaut named Castor. Perhaps an ancestor of Castignoli—Castor in the Latin, Castignoli in the vernacular? Okay, I know I'm reaching.

In any case, Gino now says he hid a 2004 ALCS Program/ Scorecard somewhere else in the new Yankee Stadium, but obviously he doesn't want to say where. Some people say he made it up. But that's what they said about the Ortiz jersey, too, and it was definitely there when they excavated. *I* believe Gino, even though I have a hard time understanding how a native of the Bronx can possibly understand the cosmos so clearly. But the cosmos is a little hazy even to the saints and philosophers of the game right now.

In the pit of my stomach I fear that the Baseball Gods are *not* going to punish the Yankees for tearing down the House that Ruth Built. I mean maybe they can't? Maybe the Yankees are so transcendently evil that they challenge the authority of the BGs? I was certain in 2008, as the Evil Ones were excluded even from the playoffs, that the Baseball Gods were good and just, and I thought, "now, *now* the shoe is on the other foot! The Yankees will suffer *now*! And for the rest of my life they will lose, *lose*, *LOSE*! Muaahahaha!" Yet, as I write these words, only the Phillies, in whom I have no confidence, stand between the Yankees and yet another World Series title. Damn Yankees. They're doing it again. Just *buying* whatever they want, and they never get punished. They've fleeced us all, and even the gods. But maybe not— not in the green fields of the mind. There, in the righteous place, the Elysian fields of Hoboken, the Yankees always lose, and so does the horse they rode in on. There is a little of Gino in all of us, and we know ways to help the Baseball Gods do their righteous work.

Confessions

So you would think, after that little diatribe, that your devoted writer must surely be one of the faithful, as true to the Red Sox as the Philosopher himself. But that isn't quite the truth, so let's have out with it. I'm an interloper here, a member of the St. Louis Cardinals Cult (I grew up in that cult, had a good long fling with the Atlanta Braves due to a stint in that fair city, and then returned to my native religion some years back, when I was able to move back to the Mississippi valley, my ancestral home). Origins matter. The Philosopher was what he was, in part, because of South Hadley. I didn't grow up there, but rather along the banks of the rolling river that cuts the land in half. The Cardinals, as you know, are a pious team in a pious baseball city, and as the 2004 Series showed, they are no threat to you when it really counts, and indeed even the Braves once belonged to your city, so I can be trusted. You'll see.

I'll bet I hate the Yankees as much as you do, maybe more. Not as much as I hate the Cubs of course, but there is a special region of hell reserved for the Cubs (except for Ernie Banks, who should have been a Cardinal and has been given an exemption from hell). Even a Red Sox fan can't quite understand the contempt a true baseball lover must feel for a rival like the Cubs that is *proud* of losing. They wear shirts to the game that say, proudly, "World Champions 1908." WTF? I mean, at least the Yankees want to *win*. What do you do when, having kicked the ever-loving Cub-assess over and over, they just ignore the result and go on drinking strawberry daiquiris? The Philosopher says:

> A "win" is the actual realization of what is centrally an imaginative surge. . . . The spectator, seeing something he had only imagined, or, more astonishingly, had not yet or would never have imagined possible, because the precise random moments had never before come together in this form to challenge the players, is privy to the realized image and assents, is mastered, and in that instant bettered. "Winning" for player or spectator is not simply outscoring; it is a way of talking about betterment, about making oneself, one's fellows, one's city, one's adherents, more noble because of a temporary engagement of a higher human plane. (*Take Time for Paradise*, p. 39)

I don't owe anything to spectators who are smug enough to believe they need no improvement, who are too content to imagine winning. No, that is twisted. I pity the players who perform athletic feats of daring and grace like so many amusing circus tricks for the unworthy dogs, yes, dogs of Chicago's north side. Well, look, you already know the story. The question is, what is Cardinal Boy doing here, with you now, telling you what's so special about your team, and especially your stadium (which, after all, is what I'll be rambling on about shortly)? It's a combination of things really.

Original Sin

First, it's about 1967, when I was six. All of you were six once (I'm assuming). Think back. Marcel Proust said that what is present to us in youth, *truly* present, is the measure of presence itself. To me, baseball *began* in 1967 and effectively ended when they put in the designated-hitter rule (a betrayal so profound I will never get over it; the helpless fall from innocence, when you know life isn't fair, like seeing some older guy hit your big sister, and you're too small to stick up for her—that's how *that* felt, that godforsaken DH rule). Everything in between '67 and the death of real baseball, was *true* baseball. The rest is repetition because the Year One is like first love: you vaguely know that all this has happened to other people before, but you don't care since no one can really ever understand how utterly unique and permanent is every win and every loss in the Year One. And so there was Yastrzemski, in his Fenway, his *lair*, the greatest hitter in baseball, ever, as far as *I* was concerned, and then there was Bob Gibson, the greatest pitcher who ever took the mound, as far as *I* was concerned. And this was the first World Series ever. You know? I think you know.

The Red Sox became real for me, not as losers with a silly curse, but as the threat powerful enough to break my heart—and as the Philosopher said, it is *designed* to break your heart. The Red Sox had to be winners, because if they *weren't*, then my Cardinals would be less noble, less worthy victors, and my personal achievement in cheering them on would be diminished. (All six-year-olds are narcissists.) I believed in the curse, later, of course, but only *as needed*, for the purposes of hope. For example, I knew, I *knew* that in 2004, the curse had been broken, but I believed in it intensely because the Cardinals had won 108 games that year, were the best team in baseball, and *deserved* the world championship, on the piety of the great Pujols alone. But alas, it is designed to break your heart. Sometimes, at least.

But here is one thing you have forgotten, because you hate the Yankees and all they stand for, but you don't happen to love the Cardinals. You remember that the Sox came from nowhere in '67 on the Triple Crown of Yaz and the arm of Lonborg—the impossible dream. But you forgot that Gibson missed July and August with a broken leg. Yes, a *broken leg*. They shoot horses when that happens, you know. Somehow, all injuries just seemed more severe back then, didn't they? You also forgot, and here's the nub, that the hitter who carried the Cardinals to victory was Roger Maris, run out of New York by an evil press in an evil city where it had been his misfortune to play for an evil team and lead them to evil victories (but not over the Cardinals—ha! Put 1964 in your pipe and smoke it, Yankees!—and be aware that only the Cardinals have beaten the Yankees more times in the World Series than they have lost). Anyway, the people of St. Louis loved Roger Maris, an unadorned, plain-speaking mid-westerner, and we hated the Yankees for mistreating a good, pious ballplayer. And 1967 was "the first World Series ever," you know, so the sins of the Yankees were Original Sin. Well, anyway, that's how the world looks when you're six.

The Green Fields of the Mind

There is an image in my mind, of Yaz at Fenway, forced out at second in the bottom of the ninth when Ken Harrelson hit into double play, and Yaz had done all he could do. He hustles into the dugout with his head up, no physical sign of defeat, because he is Yaz, and he knows it's over, but he'll never show it. Gibson would throw a complete-game victory, a shutout, in the seventh game. Maris drove in the winning runs in Gibson's first two Series victories, but on this day, Gibson throws a shutout and hits a home run, winning by his own efforts, and sanctifies Fenway Park for me, in this year, the Year One. Somehow, impossibly, the Philosopher is wrong and my heart isn't broken—until 1968, but that was the Year Two, and by then it was too late: I had become an optimist. The same thing would have happened to you, so don't scoff. George Will famously remarked in Ken Burns's *Baseball* that he had the misfortune to grow up in central Illinois where all the other kids were naturally Cardinals fans and grew up happy and liberal, while he was condemned to be a Cubs fan, conservative and miserable. Many people can confirm what Will says. But I tell you this story about 1967 to help you understand something that, because you are a Red Sox fan, you really never can grasp, which is what it's like to see the world in some way other than Giamatti saw it. Imagine, in your wildest, most impossible dreams, that in the Year One, your team triumphed over the highest of opponents—not the evil Yankees, but the noble Red Sox. What if it *isn't* designed to break your heart?

No, nevermind. You can't do it. That's alright, I understand. Hence, a second story. I was living in Atlanta, 1988, playing softball in a church league (as any wannabe in his late twenties would), and in center field we have this guy named John, from Boston, and he loves the Red Sox, and he's a philosopher of the baseball variety. I detect an odd and unfamiliar fatality in his graceful peregrinations across the green fields of the suburbs (yes, it is possible to track and catch fly balls with a distinct fatality in your gait). Conversations followed. "Did you take it hard in '86?" I venture, adding then, "I thought the curse would be broken." John: "I knew they would lose." So I scoff: "You mean that when it's the bottom of the 10th, Game Six, the Sox have a two-run lead, nobody on, two out, and Schiraldi is one strike, *one strike*, from the World Series championship, you thought they were going to lose?" John says, "You don't understand. I *knew* they were gonna lose." I say, "no way you didn't allow yourself just some little moment of hope." John shakes his head, "you'll never understand." But I want to serve notice to every John reading this book. There is now a town full of Bostonians who were six or seven in 2004, and they won't "get it" either, because they are more like me than like you. For them, the Year One didn't end with a ball dribbling between Buckner's legs.

> **Almost 8 o'clock Central Daylight Time, but finally
> we're underway. Hamels just mowed down the
> evil Yankees, in order. Phillies showing signs of life
> in the bottom of the first. Pettitte is not God.
> (Orel Hersheiser is God, or at least He once was.)**

Got Your Number

The Philosopher wants me to tell you some things about the sacred numbers. He said that, "unless we place whatever we think about America and her games in the context of Greek thinking on leisure" we won't know the difference between our holy days and our working days. There was a crisis in ancient Greece. Actually, there were lots of crises, but this one could have affected your tenth-grade curriculum. Geometry was hip back then, so bitchin' that Plato had posted above the entrance to his Academy "Let None without Geometry Enter." Why? Well it's a long story, and you aren't that interested, but it's sort of like, what if that light-up arrow behind Fenway that says "Bleacher Bar" says instead, "Lemme See Your Report Card." You *know* the brews and the views are inside, and that's where you'd like to chill, but you were chasing girls or powdering your hypotenuse when you shoulda been doin' your homework, so you're, like, not invited? Close enough? Geometry was cool, okay?

Like baseball itself, the origins of geometry are shrouded in the mists of time. The almost mythical figure Pythagoras, like Abner Doubleday, either did or didn't start something that would have made him a lot of money if he hadn't died before the bottom of the ninth. All we know is that in the sixth century B.C. there was a wandering sort of religious dude who liked messing around with numbers and ideas. He seems to have hung his hat in just about every kingdom at some time or another, showed the locals some tricks he learned on the road, and left a few believers in every port. It was, apparently, quite the righteous spiel he gave. He never wrote anything down because, well, let's just say that Pythagoras isn't the kind of guy who would go to the game and keep a detailed scorecard. He could remember what he needed to know.

It's good to be aware that Pythagoras didn't have the Hindu-Arabic numerals we now use, and he didn't even have Roman numerals. He had these symbols you wouldn't recognize, and there were no zeros, and the marks he did use really looked like magic symbols. But it was a practical magic. It was useful, but the question was "why did it work?" The answer was "because everything in the world is made of Number." Now, the word we translate as "number" will look familiar to you: "*arithmos.*" But it's one thing to say that we can count and measure whatever we choose and quite another to say that everything is *made of* Number. This isn't as superstitious as it sounds. The problem is that *these days* we are in such a habit of counting and measuring things that we forget what it would be like to have first discovered all the ways that things can be counted. We might wonder, back in those days, why would any self-respecting *thing* yield its hidden essence to a person who wanted to count or measure it?

Let's say you're a baseball. How many stitches do you have? How much do you weigh? And, most importantly, how big around are you? Now, we all know that a baseball has 108 stitches, but the rest isn't easy to say. A major-league baseball can weigh as little as five ounces and as much as five and a quarter ounces, and it can have a circumference as small as nine inches and as large as nine and a quarter. There's no single number that yields a "Baseball." I'll bet that there have been baseballs used in games that had 107 and

109 stitches, balls that exceeded or fell short of the parameters specified. Add in that there can be up to a mile of yarn in a baseball, and that the density of the cork in the center can vary, and I'll even be willing to bet that of the billions of baseballs used in the major leagues, no two were ever identical in every single measure. *Home run, Jayson Werth, bottom of the second, Phillies 1, Yankees 0.* And yet, if I have a baseball in my hand, there is a definite number that can be associated with all those weights and measures. And— here is the important part—when I consider the relations *among* all those weights and measures, I get a total weight in relation to a complete set of measures that IS this ball, its hidden essence, and I could associate that peculiar relation with an imaginary number, give that number a name, say "Ted," and the name of the number "Ted" just IS this ball in my hand. No other combination of numbers adds up to Ted, so Ted is the essence of this ball. And when I know that this ball is Ted, that Ted is the unique number of this and only this ball, I truly *know* this ball. And to know this ball is to be able to strike out anyone, even Jeter, with it.

　　You don't get it yet? Okay, let's try another one. So you and me are taking a leak at one of the old urinals at Fenway—you know the ones I'm talking about, the double trough where you're looking right at a guy peeing in your direction, so you and me are getting to know each other a little better than we had planned. We get done at the same time, and since we ain't barbarians, we head for the sinks to wash our hands. I'm washing mine in the sink on the left and you're washing yours in the sink on the right. And because I'm not such a normal guy, I say to you, "hey, you see the water going down the drain?" You look at me like I'm from another planet and say, "I got eyes, don't I?" And I say, "Clockwise or counter-clockwise?" And you say, "Clockwise, Einstein." And I say, "you know, in South America it goes counter-clockwise." And you say, "Mind your own business or I'll knock you into Paraguay." And I say, "Wait a minute Mac, I'm just thinkin' here, how do you know that *my* clockwise drain can't just suddenly start swirling the other way?" You look puzzled for just a minute and I have you: "And I mean, if my sink was just a little steeper and maybe had a slightly bigger hole than yours, then the water would drain faster right?" "Yeah, so what?" And I say, "Well, how fast does water drain anyway? Does the altitude make a difference? The amount of minerals in the water? The time of year? The position of the Moon? I mean, I'm feeling like I don't know very much here. For all I know, this varies with Pedroia's batting average." And now you get it, and you say, "Look, this ain't my problem, but I'm tellin' you there's a definite rate for this water going down the drain right now." And I say, "I wonder what the ratio is between that definite rate and the speed and distance I will cover on my way back to the beer line?" You leave.

But now you are getting the picture. *Jeter lines out to right field.* Everything that exists has a whole bunch of relationships to its parts and to all other things, and even when the kinds of measuring we do are different from each other (like length and weight) they all have in common that they are numbers, and we can express the unique essence of a thing by learning its essential (irreplaceable) ratios. Is it possible that there is a number—not like 2 or 3 or 4, but a number that doesn't have a name—that expresses the unique combination of relations that is *you*? Even if you don't believe that, it gives you a sense of what Pythagoras meant when he said that "everything is Number." He didn't mean "numbers," he meant that everything will yield its singular essence to the right insight into its numerical relations, and that the true name of everything resides in its unnamed number.

Pythagoras had said a lot of other things, but among them is that "Number" is the *arche*. This word probably rings a bell, since you've seen it at the start of words like "archaeology" and "architecture." It means "the originary principle" of the universe, and like I been tellin' you, Pythagoras said that was "Number." But what should we be doing about this? Measuring and counting everything from the stars to our turds, seeking the perfect arrangement? Maybe, maybe not. There's always at least two views—by the way, Pythagoras said that "two" is not a number, and neither is "one." You don't have numerical relationships until three appears on the scene, because two is only company, but three is like a crowd. That is another reason your rivalry with the Yankees is clearer to me than it is to you. Duality is just conflict. Balance first enters when there is a runner on third. And I will tell you, since you wouldn't have suspected it, a member of the Cardinals Cult is exactly what you need. Did you know that the Cardinals have the second most World Series titles? But they never got the big head because they only win one every ten years or so. The BGs giveth and they taketh away, mostly the latter. But the Cardinals are also the only team to have beaten the Yankees in the Series more times than they lost. We get it, okay? We're like you, only we didn't sell the Babe.

Trouble in Paradise

So that was some of what Pythagoras was saying. But within a hundred years or so there was Trouble in Paradise. Nobody could quite remember what the Master said. The spiritual and practical meanings of "Number" were coming apart, and the followers of Pythagoras had formed two rival leagues, or rather, one church and one guild, called the Akousmatikoi and the Mathematekoi. These guys were at each other like cats and dogs (or Red Sox and Yankees). The Akousmatikoi named themselves after the word "akousmata" or "things heard" (our word "acoustic" comes from it), because Pythagoras didn't write anything down. They believed in the spiritual teachings of the Master. The Mathematikoi were a secular guild of cruel teachers who would hit your hands with a ruler if you did your sums wrong. They dressed like nuns except they were dudes. Both bunches claimed to be carrying on the work of the Master. I'm not even trying to be neutral here. I'm too much under the influence of the Philosopher, and he didn't like the Mathematikoi: "because of secularism, [numerical] equality, bureaucratization, specialization, rationalization, quantification, and the obsession with records, there is no link to the sacred or transcendent. The Record has replaced the ritual" (*Take Time for Paradise*, p. 24). You never want to underestimate the barbarity and ruthlessness of the Mathematikoi. They'll not only take all your money and repossess your house, they'll defile everything holy in the process just to show you they *can*.

The Akousmatikoi were purists, monks with their vows, deniers of the flesh with their minds on higher things. They believed that "Number" was sacred, was not the key to *knowledge* of the universe but to spiritual *enlightenment*, to Truth in the sense of "ye shall know the truth and it shall make ye free." In short, these guys were the true believers. You've seen them in the stands. They can't afford the best seats (remember Giamatti always sat with the crowd, when he had a choice). They bring their gloves (an act of religious faith if ever there was one), they never leave before the last out, they wait out every rain delay, and they never boo the visiting team, let alone the home team (which is to say, they're not from Philly—and this is why I have no confidence in Philly; they're just mean spirited and those players deserve better fans). Most importantly, the Akousmatikoi never keep score. They don't want to remember the alleged "facts" of the game, they want the *meaning* of the game, as one enactment of something perfect and eternal. Giamatti was an *akusmaton*. There are a lot of people like this in Boston.

Over on the ugly island of the Mathematikoi, they believed in the pursuit of worldly *knowledge*, that getting the measure of the world was the key to unlocking its mysteries and gaining over it the power they believed they had rightly earned, as the chosen and favored of men (and screw the gods, if there are any gods, and the Mathematikoi doubt that). They believed you can count your way to glory, or at least to victory on earth. You've seen them in the stands. They are not only keeping score, they are criticizing the manager when he does anything not supported by the numbers. In their hands, numbers become self-justifying weapons of math destruction. George Steinbrenner is a *mathematikon*. So was that sonofabitch McNamara who suggested that the way to win the Vietnam War was to achieve a certain body count. At least *one* of them recanted. *Victorino sacrifices to left and Ruiz scores, slow though he is. Things are looking up. Phillies 3 to 0 after two.* It wasn't Steinbrenner of course. There are a lot of good people in New York City, a lot of *akusmata*, but they don't call the shots and they really never have, from the days of Alexander Hamilton 'til now. And there have been plenty of *mathemata* stinking up Beantown over the years, like Harry Frazee, who not only sold the Babe, but even mortgaged Fenway to finance entertainment for New Yorkers. (By the way, if you want to call someone an asshole in Ancient Greek, the word is "proctos." They wouldn't understand your meaning, but I would.)

As you can well imagine, as time unfolded, the bean counters got the upper hand on the true believers, in ancient Greece and on the eastern seaboard. It almost always works that way. You can buy a pennant, but you can't buy righteousness in the eyes of the gods. The gods favor whom they will. *A-Rod hits a double off the wall in right—no wait, it's ruled a home run, off a television camera. 3-2 Phillies. Shit.*

Just the Facts, Ma'am

You know the park and you already know the Philosopher's writings. But even we, the faithful, cannot deny that there is mystery in the actual measure of things. So, here is the short sheet. I'm going to use the tense I like to call the "sportscaster's tense," an odd way of using the present tense to recount things that are already over, like you're describing a replay. It's 1912. Woodrow Wilson campaigns his way through the baseball season, against Taft and Roosevelt both. (Taft was a Reds fan, loved baseball more than being President; Roosevelt, a New Yorker, regarded himself as above such a "mollycoddle game.")

During the same stretch, Smoky Joe Wood wins thirty-four games. Back in April, the first game in Fenway, the Yankees (that is, the Highlanders) go down to ignominious defeat. By October, the Red Sox beat the Giants in an eight-game World Series (Game Two ends in a tie, called after eleven innings on account of darkness). The Yankees (that is, the Highlanders) are just awful—last place in the AL, only 50 wins, 102 losses. Fenway hosts five World Series games. The Baseball Gods love the place, so they settle in for the long haul. It is a quirky place, unsuitable for baseball if you think about it abstractly. But in practice the results are beautiful and the BGs bless their new altar, and hover above a series of stupendous and pious left fielders. You love baseball, so you already know that left field is reserved for the weakest fielder on the team —no speed, no arm, big bat. But not so in Boston. The Sox left fielder will always have to be a real defensive player, from Duffy Lewis through Williams and Yaz and Rice and Ramirez, even if sometimes the Sox can't find the right guy. The Baseball Gods love this quixotic search for a left fielder good enough to play right field. *Pettitte hits a dying quail to center, scoring Swisher in a tumble. Tie game.*

Sacred Ground

The BGs love Fenway. They always have. They closed off a space, made the city-bound Garden of the Possible—that's how the Philosopher saw it. He said:

> The Old Poet [Edmund Spenser] said, "Nothing is sure that grows on earthly ground." . . . He had never loved the Red Sox. While he knew of Eden and its loss, he knew nothing of the fall in Fenway. It is not enough to think, as he did, that only once were we to go east, out into the land of Nod. Such a passage occurs without end. It happens every summer, with a poignancy that knows no bounds, in that angular, intimate, ageless green space in Boston. (*A Great and Glorious Game*, pp. 29–30)

There are *some* certainties even in the river of change that is time, and the Philosopher says that the return of the young men to the Garden is one of them. But no one shed a tear when they tore down Tiger Stadium. It was old too. Good riddance. We all knew it. It sucked and the BGs did *not* love it. And they do not love Detroit or Pittsburgh or Houston or Milwaukee or Dallas and a lot of other places for reasons only they can fathom. No one objected when they imploded the Kingdome or Fulton County Stadium or Busch Stadium (which actually wasn't too bad) or County Stadium or even Comiskey Park. A lot of great baseball happened in those parks. Pennants and championships were won, Hall of Fame careers unfolded, but for all that history, the places were not sanctified.

The sanctification of a city-bound piece of ground by the Baseball Gods is not a matter of what has happened in the park. *Damon doubles, Pettitte and Jeter score. 5-3, advantage to the evil ones.* When you think about it, you'll realize the truth in that. It is something else entirely. The BGs have never sanctified a park in St. Louis or Cincinnati, but they sanctified two in New York (Ebbets Field and the original Yankee Stadium), and (I hate to admit this) one in Chicago, I won't say its name, and one in Boston. That's about it. Chavez Ravine may be sanctified, I'm not sure, and I can't quite tell whether the BGs live in Jacobs Field or Camden Yards—perhaps. But there is something you can feel that cannot be quantified, that can't even be described, when you're in such a place.

The two most important confrontations between the Akousmatikoi and the Mathematikoi in modern history occurred in Boston and New York in the late 1990s and the first decade of this century. Both cities faced economic pressure (that is greed driven by Mathematikoi) to destroy a shrine that the Baseball Gods had sanctified, and to destroy it for the sake of material gain and creature comfort. It was an even split, as you know. But the outcome didn't surprise me at all. I have seen enough Middle Atlantic greed in my life to know what to expect from these people. The last time I watched a New York team play a Philadelphia team in the World Series, the Baseball Gods almost, almost opened the earth to swallow up both teams as a punishment for their greed. (I speak here of the 1989 World Series between the New York Giants and the Philadelphia Athletics—you can call them by their greed names if you like.) The New Yorkers tore down Ebbets Field. You had to know what they would do. And here was the argument: they would put in the same dimensions (after all, it's just numbers) for the new Yankee Stadium as the old, keep the name, and move the monuments and a few other totemic items. Do you know that they broke ground for the new profanation on the fifty-eighth anniversary of the Bambino's DEATH? His DEATH, not his birth. Nice touch, George. If you're going to tell someone to fuck off, you might as well do it right.

Now, do you want to know how the Curse of the Bambino was really broken? It happened when the decision was made, and irreversible, to tear down Yankee Stadium, when the Mathematikoi got their way. In effect, they sent the Babe back to Boston, didn't they? At that moment, the Baseball Gods devised the 2004 season and said to one another, "We will show them who calls the balls and strikes around here." But you see, it was very important that the Red Sox destroy the last ounce of Yankees hubris in the real Yankee Stadium, so that is how they did it. In my own department, here in Illinois, a Yankees fan bet a Red Sox fan, in the heat of that gigantomachy that the loser would wear the winner's team hat every day until the next opening day. I did enjoy seeing that Red Sox hat the whole winter. It's not an accident that the lowly Indians embarrassed the Yankees in the first game at the new stadium (a stadium they had the conceit to call by the same name, *as though nothing had happened*). Not all losses come as a result of the play on the field. Some are ordained by the gods.

On the other hand, there was the long struggle in Boston, which has always had troubles with its own cheerless and greedy Mathematikoi. Having held their wrecking balls at bay again and again, the Akousmatikoi of the old city finally won their battle for good in 2004, by destroying the Yankees. *10:20 Central Daylight Time; Swisher hits a solo shot, Yankees extend the distance between their own black hearts and the Happ-less Phillies.*

You see, the reason the Akousmatikoi in Boston have won is not because the Red Sox won the World Series, it's because the Yankees tore down their own temple. That is the reason why, now, Boston never will tear down its sacred shrine. I'll prove it to you. Can you move Fenway, and keep the dimensions? It was suggested, even promised by the Mathematikoi of Boston, wasn't it? But you knew the answer. No. That's the answer. Why not? Fenway isn't just a collection of numbers, it's a real *place*. But what is the difference between the geometry of real *places* and a geometry of mere *spaces*?

Things Your Math Teacher Never Taught You

I didn't have good math teachers. You may have been luckier, but I doubt it. The math teachers are trained by the Mathematikoi almost everywhere. I was taught that the square of the hypotenuse is equal to the sum of the squares of the other two sides. But I wasn't taught why it mattered. So let me tell you a couple of things very quickly that might change your whole view of geometry.

Did you know that a line is really just a *moving* point? That is why a line (it doesn't have to be straight, as Gauss demonstrated) just *is* the shortest distance between two points—the points aren't "two," they are really the *same* point at either end of a *journey*.

Did you know that a plane is just a line, moving as a whole? Did you know that a solid is really just a moving plane? Geometry never was about measuring spaces, it is a set of instructions for getting to the land of one dimension, where the gods reside, and home again. But I have not given you quite the full set of directions, for the one constant is that everything has to be able to move, and that means that *time* elapses. Now, time is pretty mysterious. I cannot tell you what it is, but I can tell you that if you are an Akousmatikon, like the Philosopher (and me), you believe time is a circle, that what begins always bends back upon itself, and that everything that leaves home to circle the bases comes home again somehow, some way. After all, the Babe finished his career in Boston, didn't he? The circle of time is the fourth dimension, the dimension of action, of perfection, of completion, of balance. The Philosopher once used the term "radical equilibrium." That sounds about right. Circular time is radical equilibrium. With it, even a solid baseball park can *move*. If you think Fenway is sitting still, I have news for you. Like every geometrical solid that is more than merely abstract, Fenway moves—in a cicrcle, with the seasons and the planets and the cosmos..

Your instructions for the full journey are these: 1. Go to a game at Fenway; 2. Take the time you spend there and fold it into the timeless solidity of your love for the Game; 3. Bless that solid feeling so that it will remain still, and be calm yourself until that feeling shows you its edge; 4. Ask sincerely that the blessed edge cease its restless, linear oscillations between hope and despair, and the edge will come round to face you. Now you may enjoy the unity that is immanent in every real thing. This is called "bliss." In that place is neither time nor the absence of it, for nothing changes, but all is accomplished. It's the best seat in the park. You can have it any time, for to have it once is to have it always.

Your math teacher made you take square roots, but never told you why. She probably didn't know or didn't think it important. But that square root is a set of instructions for taking any number (well almost any) and finding the square, the diamond, that *is* that number. Give me a number in some unit of measure. I don't know, how about 60 feet 6 inches? Did you know that there is some number out there, which may or may not have a name, that, multiplied by itself *in feet and inches*, just *is* the square that answers to the length of the line from the pitching rubber to the plate? I haven't done the math, but I'll bet there is some relationship between that number and the size of the strike zone, as adjusted to the size of the hitter.

You see, everything is Number. *Werth hits his second bases-empty home run of the night. Rollins is never on base when you need him. Ryan Howard, on the other hand, is never on base at all. But 6–4 is better than 6–3.* If you take any number and a set of instructions, like *x* times itself equals *n* (square root), or since *pi* times the radius of a circle squared equals an area *x*, *x* as a number just *is* that circle, and so on, you begin to realize that every number is a square, every number is a circle, every number is a triangle, and all of those regular forms and infinitely many irregular forms all exist within the point that *is* that number.

If this is true, and it is, then there is some number that expresses the unity that is Fenway Park, some way that if we fold the circle of the seasons into the solid of the stadium and remain still enough to see only the edges of the forms and bless those thin travelers unaware, and bid them to seek their homes, we have the best seat in the house, and from here, the Red Sox always win, because it is the Year One, the origin of all hope and every individual despair. I call that number "Giamatti." Ever notice how "Giamatti" sounds just like "geometry" if you can say it in a Southey accent? *Almost the witching hour, and Posada magically lands a lame little flare that my (dead) grandmother could have hit, but it scores Damon.*

November

Now things really have achieved temporal weirdness. In the eastern time zone, it has reached midnight, so the eastern Akousmatikoi have started setting their clocks back, earlier than the law requires, to get an extra hour of Halloween, a little more

October, a little less November. I can relate. I don't do November. In the central time zone, it isn't midnight yet, so the Akousmatikoi of the Middle haven't yet had the urge to start setting our clocks back, and try not to think about this too much, but since you're one of us, your clock reads 11:11 P.M. and it's also 11:11 on my clock in Illinois, and Matsui (curse his hide), just put the ball over the wall.

And so it is still October in Philadelphia when Rivera closes the deal, but it's a false October. Clearly the Baseball Gods take off for the Bahamas on November 1st. I don't think anything about this World Series counts from here on out. For me, this season ends with the Phillies behind 3 games to 1, down but not out. There can be no baseball in November. I am calling off the rest of the World Series on account of darkness.

VI

So Good! So Good! So Good!

The greatest hitter who ever lived, Ted Williams (1918–2002).
Courtesy of the Boston Red Sox. Photographer unknown.

23

The Dao of Ted Williams

JUNG H. LEE

A sportswriter remembers taking a blind man to meet Williams one day, years after Williams's career was finished. Williams nodded, shook hands, went through the celebrity motions, until the blind man mentioned he played softball. Williams perked up at that.

"How do you hit?" Williams asked.

The blind man explained that a special ball was used, a ball that beeped in sequence so the players could hear it approach. Wait for the beeps to draw close. Swing. Williams asked to see the man's batting stance. The blind man obliged, swinging a couple of times. Williams stood and made various adjustments to the stance. The blind man swung a few more times. Better.

"Now, here's what you gotta do," Williams said, holding the man in the new stance.

"Yes?" the blind man said.

"You gotta stand there," Williams said. "Don't swing early. Wait. You gotta wait until you hear that last fucken beep!"

—LEIGH MONTVILLE, *Ted Williams: The Biography of an American Hero*, pp. 47–48

As absurd as this scene might seem, this is what it must have felt like for Ted Williams to impart his wisdom on hitting to those not endowed with his native reflexes, 20–10 vision, and astonishing skills. Although Williams called it a *science* of hitting, he realized that it was something more akin to a form of art, that there was a certain skill, a certain knack beyond the mere fundamentals of hitting. We can illuminate what this something more was by looking back to early Daoist notions of skill, spontaneity, and the Way,

287

understanding Williams's experience of hitting as a kind of optimal experience where the agent moves spontaneously according to the situation with the unclouded clarity of a mirror. What Williams presents in his "science of hitting," from a Daoist perspective, represents a way to educate this knack through focused attention, total absorption in the object, heightened coordination of one's body and mind, and the discipline of guided practice.

The Way of Daoism

The beginnings of early Daoism can be traced to the Warring States Period (479–221 B.C.) of ancient Chinese history. Early Daoists were animated by a belief in something called the Way (*Dao* 道), a cosmic power that flows throughout the universe to create all phenomena and to serve as the guiding force within the lives of all living beings. While all things in the cosmos move spontaneously on the course proper to them, human beings tend to harm their spontaneity, their natural affinity for the Way, by being led astray by emotions, an inability to unify one's attention, and a mind prone to rationalization.

Although the Way can't be seen or heard or known conceptually, early Daoists maintain that it can be directly experienced through techniques of inner cultivation, essentially a kind of breathing meditation where one would cultivate one's breath in a stable, sitting position. By cultivating their minds and making themselves tranquil, early Daoists believed that they could become one with the Way and embody a kind of cosmic harmony in their everyday lives. The ability of human beings to attain the Way is indicated by the presence of a kind of "inner power" (*de* 德) which represents the concrete manifestation of the Way within the lives of human beings.

Early Daoist literature, particularly the text known as the *Zhuangzi* (around the fourth century B.C.), presents a series of examples from the everyday lives of individuals—sages—who embody the Way in their many mundane activities. In these "skill stories" individuals can seemingly empty their minds, unify their attention, and forget themselves in the activity at hand—all in such a way that it appears effortless, spontaneous, and in some ways preternatural.

First we have an example of a Daoist wheelwright describing his craft:

If I chip at a wheel too slowly, the chisel slides and does not grip; if too fast, it jams and catches in the wood. Not too slow, not too fast; I feel it in the hand and respond from the heart, the mouth cannot put it into words, there is a knack in it somewhere which I cannot convey to my son and which my son cannot learn from me. This is how through my seventy years I have grown old chipping at wheels. (*Chuang-tzu: The Inner Chapters*, translated by A.C. Graham, 2001, p. 140)

In another tale, the same Daoist text tells the story of a Daoist cicada-catcher:

I have the Way . . . I settle my body like a rooted tree stump, I hold my arm like the branch of a withered tree; out of all the vastness of heaven and earth, the multitude of the myriad things, it is only of the wings of a cicada that I am aware. I don't let my gaze wander or waver, I would not take all the myriad things in exchange for the wings of a cicada. How could I help but succeed? (p. 138)

And in probably the most famous example of all, we have the case of Cook Ding, a cook who is so proficient at carving oxen that he "does not look with the eye" and only carves through the use of the Way. He has become such an expert at butchering that he has only used one chopper in his nineteen years as a cook because he only goes by "what is inherently so," never touching the bone (pp. 64–65).

In these examples we can see just how these sages embody the Way in their everyday activities—their actions seem natural, intuitive, effortless. However, it should be noted that the art of Daoist action doesn't spring from a mindless ecstasy or rapturous trance but from a kind of practical wisdom educated by the unity of attention, complete absorption in the activity at hand, and a supreme sense of responsiveness born from disciplined practice. Much the same way that Ted Williams approached the art of hitting.

These skill stories illustrate how the various sages engage in their activities with a focus of attention that crowds out any and all distractions, including self-consciousness. In a tale about a particularly adroit swimmer, a man is asked how he manages to stay afloat in rough waters. He responds, "I enter with the inflow, and emerge with the outflow, follow the Way of the water and do not impose my selfishness upon it. This is how I stay afloat in it"(p. 136). The swimmer suggests that he can mirror the movements of the water by staying attuned to his environment and not allowing his ego to dictate the terms of his path. The swimmer is responsive precisely because he isn't plagued by distractions and can focus completely on the opportunities for action in his environment.

We can observe the same dynamic in the descriptions of catching cicadas. As the cicada-catcher explains, "out of all the vastness of heaven and earth, the multitude of the myriad things, it is only the wings of a cicada that I am aware." The cicada-catcher's psychic energy or attention is so fully invested in the goal of catching a cicada that everything else seems to recede into the background. In a more dramatic way, Cook Ding declares that his focus and absorption in the object is so keen that his powers of attention seem in some ways extra-sensual, or beyond the normal range of the senses. As he suggests, when he carves an oxen, he doesn't look with the eye because of the intimacy that he feels with his object—he can essentially let himself go, being guided by "Heaven's structuring" and "what is inherently so."

These skills also illustrate just how refined the sense of responsiveness has become in the wake of disciplined practice. The wheelwright who says he has "grown old chipping at wheels" embodies this kind of responsiveness in the way that he crafts his wheels. The wheelwright's sense of touch and dexterity have been honed through years and years of dedicated practice, and he can essentially make adjustments on the fly and anticipate whatever circumstances may come his way. In his actions and anticipations, the wheelwright embodies the virtue of spontaneity that is a hallmark of the Way itself.

Everybody Knows How to Hit—But Very Few Really Do

In *The Science of Hitting*, Ted Williams presents his philosophy of hitting as grounded in the following foundations: 1. focus and concentration, 2. what he called "proper thinking," and finally, 3. practice and proper technique. In general, Williams felt as if most of what he had to say about hitting could be reduced to "self-education—thinking it out, learning situations, knowing your opponent, and most important, knowing yourself" (p. 14). Williams felt increasingly that such self-knowledge was becoming a lost art in the contemporary world due to the many distractions that plagued baseball players. As he reminisces, "We didn't have television, we didn't have a lot of money to play around with. A complete base-ball atmosphere" (p. 15). In other words, baseball was supposed to be a way of life—not just a game.

We can see this dedication to the craft even when Williams was just breaking into the big leagues. It was at training camp in 1938 where Williams was first introduced to Rogers Hornsby:

> To hear Hornsby say all the things he himself had been thinking was comforting to the kid. He spent hours in the batting cage with the mid-dle-aged teacher, working on his swing before and after exhibition games, talking and talking, engaging in hitting contests with one of the greatest hitters who ever lived. . . . This pattern would continue for the rest of Williams's life. He would seek out the greats of the game, ask questions, challenge the answers. (*Ted Williams*, pp. 46–47)

Although Williams didn't believe that all ballplayers had to possess such devotion, he nevertheless thought that hitting required a cer-tain degree of focus and concentration.

Get a Good Ball to Hit

It was Rogers Hornsby who first told Williams to "get a good ball to hit," and it soon became one of the foundations of his hitting philosophy. Although it sounds simple enough, Williams believed that most ballplayers lacked enough discipline to command mas-tery of the strike zone and to force the pitcher into the most dis-advantageous situations.

Of course, Williams was blessed with 20–10 vision, but it was-n't just his vision that led to his success but also his plate discipline: he had the capacity to wait for pitches in what he called the "happy zone" (the areas of the strike zone where he consistently hit the ball hard for high averages) and avoid pitches outside of that area. Williams received a fair share of criticism throughout his career for taking too many pitches, but as he points out, "I have said that a good hitter can hit a pitch that is over the plate three times better than a great hitter with a questionable ball in a tough spot. Pitchers still make enough mistakes to give you some in your happy zone. But the greatest hitter living can't hit bad balls good" (*The Science of Hitting*, p. 25).

Like the Daoist cicada-catcher who can focus utterly on the wings of the cicada, Williams's focus of attention directs him to only those balls in the happy zone where he can fully take advantage of the pitcher's mistakes. And like Cook Ding who doesn't need to rely on his eye to carve his oxen, Williams also suggests that it's almost by feel that he can "see" the ball: "I couldn't 'see' the bat hit the ball . . . but I knew by the feel of it. A good carpenter doesn't have to see the head of the hammer strike the nail but he still hits it square every time" (p. 25).

Proper Thinking

In order to "get a good ball to hit," Williams preached the vital importance of what he called "proper thinking," essentially a kind of practical wisdom in regard to the art of hitting. He asked of the hitter: Have you done your homework? What's the pitcher's best pitch? What are his tendencies when he gets into trouble? What did he get you out on the last time? As Williams writes,

> It's not really so complicated. It's a matter of being observant, of learning through trial and error, of picking up things. You watch a pitcher warm up, and you see everything's high, or his breaking ball is in the dirt. If he isn't getting the breaking ball over you can think about waiting for the fastball. Or if he's *making* you hit the breaking ball, you can lay for it. (p. 22)

Williams embraced the kind of statistical analysis that has become the stock in trade of most major league players today. He would scout the opposing pitchers—examine their strengths, weaknesses, trends, and prior experiences, and take a full accounting of his own tendencies as a batter: "A hitter learns in time where his happy zones are. There isn't a hitter living who can hit a high ball as well as he can a low, or vice-versa, or outside as well as inside. All hitters have areas they like to hit in. But you can't beat the fact that you've *got* to get a good ball to hit" (p. 27).

Much of this proper thinking consisted in the scouting that happened before the game, but the essence of Williams's hitting philosophy was how responsive a hitter could be at the plate: "The reason hitting a baseball is so tough is that even the best can't hit all the balls just right. To do so is a matter of corrections every minute, in practice as well as in the game"(p. 66). So, if the batter is grounding out repeatedly, he's probably swinging too early. Popping up—he's probably swinging too late. These are the kind of adjustments that we noticed with the wheelwright as he modulated the speed of the wheel to apply the correct pressure.

Now, this notion that a batter must engage in proper thinking may seem counterintuitive in the context of Daoism, but the kind of thinking that Williams embraced follows what early Daoists recommended in terms of skillful action. That is, while Daoists did reject the kind of disputation (*bian* 辯) or theoretical thinking that was often found in philosophical circles, they did commend a kind of thinking that was akin to "sorting" (*lun* 論) or "grading": "It would cover all common sense thinking about objective facts in order to arrive at a coherent picture of the conditions before responding"(*Chuang-tzu*, p. 12).

We can observe this "sorting" at play in the example of Cook Ding when he comes to an intricate part of the oxen: "Whenever I come to something intricate, I see where it will be hard to handle and cautiously prepare myself, my gaze settles on it, action slows down for it, you scarcely see the flick of the chopper—and at one stroke the tangle has been unraveled, as a clod crumbles to the ground" (p. 65). Like Cook Ding, Williams can properly assess the situation, recognize what the pitcher is attempting to do, and look for a pitch in his happy zone.

Be Natural

Although Ted Williams had specific advice in regard to mechanics, he thought that mechanics should be tailored to the individual, that you should "hit according to your style." This was advice that Williams first heard from Lefty O'Doul when he was in the Pacific Coast League, and those words stayed with Williams throughout his career. As he reasons,

> Now, there are all kinds of hitting styles. The style must fit the player, not the other way around. It is not a Williams or a DiMaggio or a Ruth method. It is a matter of applying certain truths of hitting to a player's natural makeup. If you've got a natural talent to work with, you sure don't try to take anything away from him. You add to what he already has, or you suggest a little adjustment. (*The Science of Hitting*, p. 20)

The trick then was to apply "certain truths of hitting" to a player's natural style. But what were these "certain truths"? Some truths were universally accepted by most batters: weight evenly distributed to both feet, the knees bent and flexible, standing slightly forward on the balls of your feet, the head stays still, the shoulders level at the beginning of the swing. Beyond these universally accepted conventions for hitting, much of Williams's wisdom on the art of hitting can be reduced to ways of making the bat quicker in the hands of the hitter. For example, he taught that a batter should keep his hands closer to his body to increase his speed and to maintain greater control of the bat. Likewise, Williams recommended a more upright bat position to decrease the resistance, making the bat feel lighter.

In regard to hip action, Williams suggested that the batting motion could be interpreted as a pendulum action—a move and countermove. Williams vested so much importance in hip-cocking because he believed that "the way you bring your hips into the swing is directly proportionate to the power you generate" (p. 45). As the batter gets ready for a pitch, he should ideally have his hips and hands cocked, head staying back in place, with the entire body in a coil ready to pivot. When the hips come around, the hands should follow, then the bat.

The swing itself should be a slight upswing (from level to ten degrees). According to Williams, this allowed the hitter the best opportunity to hit consistently with authority. He reasoned:

> Say the average pitcher is 6 foot 2. He's standing on a mound 10 inches high. He's pitching overhand, or three-quarter arm. He releases the ball right about ear level. Your strike zone is, roughly, from 22 inches to 4 feet 8. Most pitchers will come in below the waist, because the low pitch is tougher to hit. The flight of the ball is *down*, about 5 degrees. A slight upswing—again, led by the hips coming around and up—puts the bat flush in line with the path of the ball for a longer period in that 12- to 18-inch impact zone. (pp. 62–63)

Williams believed that following these steps would increasingly lead to greater bat speed, power, and control.

A Guy Who Practiced Until the Blisters Bled

Beyond the focused attention, responsiveness, and training in the fundamentals of hitting, Williams believed that the knack of hitting had to be educated through guided practice. It was only through practice that a player could perfect his skills to the point where his actions would become automatic. Williams understood from an early age that nothing but practice could bring out the natural ability in ballplayers.

Even as a veteran, Williams never lost sight of the fact that his skills needed to be honed in practice, that he needed the repetition to educate his knack. We see this in the following anecdote from 1953 when Williams had just returned from service in the Korean War:

> Vinnie Orlando would talk about the special workouts held at night, after the ballgame had been played, everyone gone from Fenway. Ted was getting his swing back. . . . Gone almost two years. Needed the work. Wanted the work. The lights would stay lit, the ground crew kids would drag out the batting cage, Vinnie would go to right field with a glove, and Pete Cerrone—the guy from Filene's Basement—would pitch from behind the old door on the mound.
>
> Pete would take the baseballs from a basket next to him. One pitch would follow another, each sent back on a line. Pete would pitch and pitch and Ted would swing and swing. The middle of the night. Vinnie would run down the line-drive results in the outfield. No one around. Ted would hit the ball and hit the ball and scream at the top of his well-developed lungs.
> *Whack.*
> "Ted Williams! The greatest fucken hitter that ever lived!"
> *Whack.*
> "Ted Williams! The greatest fucken hitter that ever lived!"
> *Whack.* (*Ted Williams*, pp. 481–82)

Here was Ted Williams, arguably the greatest hitter who ever lived, the last man to hit .400, taking extra BP—*at night*—so that he could get his swing back. Williams regaled admirers with his legendary tales of bloody calluses, but those calluses were only emblems of what he was actually accomplishing through practice—namely, the education of his knack in the art of hitting.

Early Daoists also understood the productive value of training. The wheelwright has perfected his skills to such a degree his actions seem automatic and spontaneous; but he can only possess such powers because of the many years of disciplined practice that he has dedicated to his craft. Likewise, Cook Ding claims that he has carved several thousand oxen in the course of nineteen years. Although the skill can't be reduced to sheer muscle memory, when such practice is combined with the kind of attention and concentration mentioned earlier, we have the perfection of skills that may seem so automatic as to seem supernatural. It's this spontaneity and knack that we can discern in Ted Williams's experience of hitting; and it's in his "science of hitting" that we see a master present a way to educate this knack.

Teddy Baseball

In the Daoist scripture, the *Zhuangzi*, there's a discussion between an aspirant of the Way and a wise, old woman named Chu on the difficulties of teaching the Way:

> "You are old in years, how is it that you look as fresh as a child?"
> "I have heard the Way."
> "Can the Way be learned?"
> "Mercy me, it can't be done, you're not the man for it! That Bu-liang Yi had the stuff of a sage but not the Way of a sage. I have the Way of a sage but not the stuff of a sage. I wanted to teach it to him; could it be that he would really become a sage? In any case it's not so hard to tell the Way of a sage to someone with the stuff of a sage." (*Chuang-tzu*, p. 87)

In a nutshell, the old woman is suggesting that even if a person is introduced to the correct teaching, he may not be able to internalize those teachings if he doesn't have the native talents.

We can see a little of this story in the later career of Ted Williams in his capacities as coach and manager. Although he had the Way of a sage, his students didn't always possess the stuff of sages. Here is an example from his first job as manager of the Washington Senators:

> The players, one by one, seemed to realize that they were not going to be the next Ted Williams. No matter how much he talked, they never were going to have his talent. The bar was too high. They never could get there. The ball-strike count would reach the proper numbers, 2–0, 3–1, and they would look toward the dugout and see Williams gesture and hear him say, "Fastball, right down the middle." The pitch would come—indeed, a fastball right down the middle—and they would swing and foul it back. They would look in the dugout. Williams would be pounding the wall, muttering bad words. (*Ted Williams*, p. 294)

It must have frustrated Williams to remember the enjoyment that he received from the pursuit of excellence and not see the same kind of devotion in his players. "I feel in my heart that nobody in this game ever devoted more concentration in the batter's box than Theodore Samuel Williams," he once said, referring to himself in the third person. "A guy who practiced until the blisters bled, loved batting anyway, and always delighted in examining the art of hitting the ball" (*The Science of Hitting*, p. 12). In this, Ted Williams was singular in his pursuit of the Way.

24

Breaking the Mold: From Ruth to Ramirez

WEAVER SANTANIELLO

> You take a team with twenty-five assholes and I'll show you a pennant. I'll show you the New York Yankees.
>
> —BILL "SPACEMAN" LEE

At the trading deadline on July 31st, 2008, the Boston Red Sox paid Manny Ramirez seven million dollars to leave town. The front office was so eager to dispose of him, they picked up the remainder of his contract and sent him packing to the West coast, where he would resume his act in Hollywood with the Los Angeles Dodgers and their new manager Joe Torre.

Manny had been with the Red Sox for seven and a half years, and was a fan favorite in Boston due to his crazy antics and boyish persona. Not to mention his hitting prowess and his flair for the dramatic. Manny, however, certainly wasn't the first member of the Red Sox to defy convention and the expectations of the baseball world. In fact, many Red Sox greats and Hall of Famers went against the grain of corporate baseball, both on and off the field.

Babe Ruth was known for his reckless lifestyle. As a married man he chased women, drank heavily, drove recklessly, disregarded rules and authority figures, and had a quick temper on the field, especially toward umpires. Likewise, for over twenty years, Ted Williams was a target of the Boston media who scrutinized both his professional and personal life. Constantly at war with the Boston press and sometimes the fans, he was outspoken, stubborn, and has been described as high-strung and aloof. According to Lawrence Baldassaro, in his book *Reflections on a Splendid Life*

(Boston, 2003), Williams was "never a slave to convention or fashion," he lived life his own way and had the "courage to face the
consequences." Likewise, Hall of Famer Jim Rice had an antago-
nistic relationship with the media that most likely delayed his
induction into the Hall for many years. And Bill "Spaceman" Lee, a
counter-culture figure who practiced yoga and admittedly smoked
marijuana, often criticized the Red Sox front office and the manager. He was likely released because of his often-contentious
demeanor. Lee was redeemed by history, however, when in 2008,
he was inducted into the Red Sox Hall of Fame.

These five players represent a unique fit within the context and
tradition of various ethical theories, ethics in general, and the philosophy of existentialism. Within these general categories, the complex natures and legendary stories of these baseball greats can be
told within the context of their times and the expectations they
faced.

Babe Ruth

> I fully appreciate the stand the people made to stop this sale, and
> while it's true I have been sold, I regret having to leave Boston. When
> I come back to Boston in a New York uniform, it will be like coming
> home.
>
> —BABE RUTH, *Boston American*, January 9th, 1920

Aristotle thought that that the best way to live life was to stay balanced. The good life consisted of moderation in accordance with
virtue. Babe Ruth would have none of that! Ruth lived a life of
abundant excess on and off the field. During his six years in Boston
(1914–1919), there was a saying among the Red Sox that "he did
everything right on the ball field and everything wrong off it" (*The
Babe in Red Stockings*, 1997, p. 142). Off the field he had a raven-
ous appetite, and often ate raw meat (approximately two and a half
pounds at a sitting); he was notorious for his love of wine, women,
and cigars. Ruth was also known as a "boy with a big heart," who
often invited orphans to his "Home Plate Farm" for the day, feed-
ing them hot dogs, and giving them bats, balls, gloves, and other
souvenirs when they left.

In 1917, at age twenty-three, he was already regarded as the
gigantic and Herculean Babe Ruth, one of the most picturesque
players in the game. His pitching was spectacular, and he hit titanic

home runs. Overall, he was 89–46 with the Sox, with an ERA of 2.19. A natural hitter, he began transitioning from the mound to that of an everyday position player. By 1919, he was the biggest drawing card in baseball. Ruth had a meteoric rise with the Sox; by the time he was sold, the owner worried that he had become bigger than the team, bigger than baseball itself.

An attempt to shed light on the sale of Babe Ruth can be understood within the context and philosophy of Immanuel Kant. According to Kant, there are two types of imperatives: the hypothetical and the categorical. The hypothetical imperative is based on desires or wants. So, for example, if you *want* to be a good fan, you *ought* to support the Sox even when they're not contending. The categorical imperative, on the other hand, is based on *reason*, not desires.

The first part of the categorical imperative states: "Act only upon that maxim at which you can at the same time will that it should become a universal law." In other words, before telling a lie, you must ask yourself: Do I will that lying should become universal, and that lying should occur in all places and at all times? Kant believed any reasonable person would say no. Reason tells us that if people lied all the time, society would self-destruct. Thus, one should *never* lie under *any* circumstances. If Big Papi asked, "Do I look heavy in this uniform?" many people might say "no" to spare his feelings. That would be violating the Kantian imperative to always tell the truth. The Kantian response would be akin to the advice Terry Francona gave to Papi after the 2008 season: "David, drop a few pounds and come to spring training toned up."

For Kant the same applied to keeping one's promise. One should ask themselves: Do I will that breaking a promise should become a universal law? If the answer is no, then you shouldn't break a promise under *any* circumstances. That's where the philosophical relevance to Ruth's sale comes in. The underlying reason for the transaction consisted of a broken promise between Ruth and then Red Sox owner, Harry Frazee.

A rift between them occurred in 1918, when Ruth left the team in anger and tried to sign with another club. Later, at the outset of 1919, the Boston press reported that Ruth's contract negotiations weren't going smoothly: "Babe Ruth says: $15,000 or Bust; and Harry Frazee says 'bust.'" As the Sox headed for spring training in Florida, Ruth remained a holdout. Several days later, in Frazee's office, Ruth and the owner shook hands and agreed to a three-year deal worth $30,000 (*The Babe in Red Stockings*, pp. 226–27).

However, during the offseason, Babe again grew disgruntled with his salary. In September, he tore up his three-year contract and sent it back in an envelope to Frazee without a note or explanation. The *Herald* reported that Ruth did this on the belief that he was doing himself an injustice not "to better himself in any way possible" (p. 262). In October, Babe headed to California to make movies and play exhibition baseball during the winter. He made it clear to the Red Sox that he wanted $20,000 to play in 1920, or he would insist on a trade. In November, he was furious that Ty Cobb called him a "contract violator," stating he might lick Ty Cobb on sight (p. 266). By late December, headlines began to appear in Boston that Babe Ruth was in the market for a trade. On January 5th, 1920, it became public that Babe Ruth had been to the Yankees without being told about it beforehand. He called Frazee's move a dirty trick, and was personally hurt and angered. The Boston fans were staggered and outraged at Ruth's sale for $125,000 (and a $300,000 loan, with Fenway Park used as collateral).

Ruth's acquisition by New York made front-page news in both cities, dominating the sports pages for over a week. Most stories pointed to the sheer stupidity of trading Ruth. But as the initial furor died down, the Boston fans and media sympathized with Frazee *inasmuch* as they thought their beloved slugger was morally wrong for not honoring the three-year contract he had signed. Ruth believed that a "contract isn't binding on a baseball star who chooses to disregard it" and elects to play somewhere else (p. 267). And Frazee stated that he would've been willing to give Ruth a raise and a new contract "if he had come and requested it in a different attitude than the one taken" (p. 277). Once, when management had broken a promise to the team, Babe instructed the players not to take the field until the manager made good on his promise. Evidently, Ruth clearly expected others to keep their word but didn't apply the Kantian standard to himself.

Many people believe Ruth was sold because the narrow-minded Frazee wanted to raise money for his Broadway productions. The point has been debated by baseball scholars for decades and isn't at issue here; many variables went into the trading of Babe Ruth. Regardless, it's certainly the case that Ruth's dishonor of Kant's imperative not to breach a contract was a major reason for his release. During the 1920s, many held Ruth in contempt for his unethical behavior, even while fans directed their intense anger toward Frazee. But with the passing of a hundred years, and Ruth's legend now at mythical proportions, the Babe has all but been absolved of any responsibility whatsoever for the sale of the century.

Ted Williams and Bill Lee: The Existentialists

We tell lies when we are afraid . . . afraid of what we don't know, afraid of what others will think, afraid of what will be found out about us. But every time we tell a lie, the thing that we fear grows stronger.

—TED WILLIAMS

Existentialism is a philosophical movement centered on analyzing existence and the way people find themselves surviving in the world. In broader terms, it's a philosophy concerned with finding the self and the meaning of life through free will, choice, and personal responsibility. Arising out of the twentieth century, existentialist ideas came out of a time in society when there was a deep sense of despair following the Great Depression and World War II, the times Ted Williams lived through.

The Kid

He fought in two wars and lost four and a half years of playing time because of it. Like some existentialists, Williams was deeply hostile toward politicians, the war, and sacrificing his vocation. Yet, politically conservative, he respected his superiors and served his country patriotically, as detailed in his autobiography: *My Turn at Bat* (1969).

Williams didn't have problems with authority; he respected umpires, managers, and military superiors. His predicament in Boston was how to remain *authentic*, a particular term in existentialist thought where one encounters external forces, pressures, and influences which are very different from, and other than, one's own. To be authentic means that one is genuine, reliable, and without pretense. It means that one maintains one's inner self, even though the self is often threatened by fear and doubt. According to philosopher William James: "There is but one cause of human failure. And that is man's lack of faith in his true self." The notion of authenticity was also expressed by Socrates, with his famous statement that the "unexamined life is not worth living."

The source of pressure for Williams primarily came from the fans and the media, the latter whom he despised and regarded as "Knights of the Keyboard." He viewed the Boston press as liars who loved to create conflict through fictitious headlines, and who probed into his personal life when it was "none of their god dammed business." What perturbed him the most was that even after his playing days were over, they continually criticized him for not performing well in the "ten most important games of his life" (*My Turn at Bat*, p. 151). Regarding the fans, he was hypersensitive to their temperamental natures. He couldn't understand how they could jeer him one moment then cheer him the next. After making an error, Williams recalls: "When I heard those boos I was steaming" (p. 146). But when he made a great catch to end the inning, they were cheering: "And that made me madder still because I hate front-runners, people who are with you when you're up and against you when you're down." Williams continues: "Well, if I'd had a knife I probably would have stuck it in somebody." Ted Williams remained true to himself by never tipping his hat to the crowd. Even when he hit a home run his last time at bat, and the crowd went into a frenzy, he was tempted to but couldn't: "It just wouldn't have been me" (p. 240).

Unlike the Babe, Williams didn't like the nightlife, fancy restaurants, or "phony-baloney" cocktail parties. The foul-mouthed slugger hated the smell of smoke, hated getting dressed up, and especially wearing ties that only choke you and "get into your soup" (p. 73). After a game he might have a beer at the park, then he'd watch TV in his hotel room. During his off time, he was a sportsman who loved to fish and hunt. Teddy Ballgame, unlike many baseball stars, was in the game for the love of it, not because of money or anything else. In deep despair after losing the seventh game of the World Series to the St. Louis Cardinals in 1946, he left the park and gave the clubhouse boy his World Series check, because the attendant had always consoled him when he was down. That night, a despondent Williams got on the train: "When I got in there and closed the door I just broke down and started crying, and I looked up there and there was a whole crowd of people watching me through the window" (p. 129). Also, in 1960, when he hadn't performed well the previous year, he asked for, and received, a pay cut: "So, I signed to play my last year, for $90,000, a $35,000 cut, almost 30 percent" (p. 233).

Williams, the John Wayne of baseball, understood that his colorful antics made for some lively headlines in Boston. And he would burn inside without knowing how to fight it:

> gestures at the fans, spitting in all directions, a flying bat that hit the lady on the head, getting shot down in Korea, unloading a few words on the Marine Corps and the damn politicians, a couple of well-publicized divorces, feuds with other players—feuds, for crying out loud, that never happened. (p. 132)

In the end, Ted Williams remained true to his own personality, spirit, and character, despite being embedded in a bubble of fans and media who pressured him to conform. He retained his authenticity, and was not dehumanized or reduced to a mere object.

The Spaceman

> The problem with the world is that everything moves so fast. We should all slow down. I think that's why I love baseball so much. When the ball is popped up, you have enough time to get in a whole thought.
>
> —BILL LEE

Whereas Williams searched for authenticity, Bill Lee sought *freedom*, often through defying authority, especially manager Don Zimmer and the baseball establishment. Lee can rightly be called a student of philosophy, in the sense that he was a University of Southern California graduate who was well versed in literature and the arts. He actually read and talked about the existentialists.

In existential thought it's said that existence precedes essence. This means that there are no predetermined roles; humans are free to be what they choose. Concepts of absolute equality, anti-discrimination, and anti-stereotyping owe a great deal to the existentialists, and Lee certainly took many cues from them. Lee represented the "Me Decade" of the 1970s; he was full of soundbites and toyed with the press about a multitude of issues: overpopulation, saving the whales, pyramid power, politics, decriminalizing marijuana, desegregation of Boston public schools, and so on.

Philosopher Jean-Paul Sartre wrote extensively about freedom. According to Sartre, we are our awareness. We are Being. We are Being-For-Itself. The past and future don't exist, there's only the present. Regarding free will, Sartre believed that humans are either wholly determined by an external consciousness, which ceases to be one's own, or wholly free. For Sartre, existence precedes essence because there is no God, or external consciousness. Sartre's famous phrase that we are "condemned to be free," means that we have the weight of the world on our shoulders; we alone are responsible for the world and ourselves as a way of being in it. Freedom then, is both a gift and a curse.

Lee embodied this Sartrean existentialism, living solely in the moment and rarely giving much thought to the future consequences of his actions. For instance, in Boston, he "retired" from the Red Sox for a day after his buddy, Bernie Carbo, was traded. When he returned, and was fined, he lambasted Zimmer and the front office publicly. In an article written by Curry Kirkpatrick for *Sports Illustrated* (August 7th, 1978), Lee claimed he had returned on behalf of "future ballplayers yet unborn." He said he was looking for compassion, and stated it was time for everyone to "start thinking about the earth." After being traded from the Red Sox to the Montreal Expos, his career ended two years later when he came to the ballpark too drunk to pitch. Protesting the trade of teammate Rodney Scott, an upset Lee went to the tavern and came back smashed. Lee wasn't scheduled to be the starting pitcher, and it was unlikely the Expos would've used him in the game; nevertheless, he was released by Montreal and was blackballed from Major League Baseball.

Philosopher Albert Camus, often spoke about freedom in relation to ending one's life. Spaceman didn't want to totally leave the world, but often sought freedom in alternative ways, through yoga, drugs, and alcohol. The Spaceman was highly intelligent, yet his actions and comments in the world of baseball, often seemed solely designed to annoy the major league establishment. To name a few:

- **At different times Lee wore on the field a gas mask, a Daniel Boone's cap, and a beanie with a propeller.**

- **He said that a baseball represents nothing more than "some Haitian slave's eight-hour day" (*SI*).**

- **He accused Zimmer (who has a metal plate in his head because of two beanings he suffered as a player), of being prejudiced against all pitchers: "If you've been beaned and nearly killed twice, you're going to want to**

make pitchers live in fear. Aww, Don's all right. Long as he keeps taking those happy pills" (*SI*).

Spaceman's quest for freedom—at least in part—has been attained outside the arena of Major League Baseball. Even today, at age sixty-two, he continues to pitch for semi-pro teams in various places, especially Cuba. In the documentary *Spaceman: A Baseball Odyssey* (2006) Lee said that baseball will die at the highest major league level in America, but the kids will keep playing the game around the world, keeping it alive.

Jim Rice

What was I supposed to say? What was I supposed to do? You talk and talk and now you're a troublemaker, somebody with a big mouth. My rule was to be quiet and when you have something to say, say it.

—Jim Rice

In 2008, Jim Rice was finally elected into the Hall of Fame in his fifteenth and final year of eligibility. This is somewhat curious. He was arguably the most feared right-handed hitter of his time. And his more than adequate numbers didn't change over the fifteen years he waited to get in. Some Rice detractors have argued that Rice fell short of his peers in the Hall of Fame. Others say that his chances increased over time because his numbers looked purer when compared to those of the steroid era. And others held that the delay was due to his nastiness toward the media throughout his playing career. As payback, the Baseball Writers Association of America was punishing him for his reputation as an intimidating, difficult, figure.

In Howard Bryant's book *Shut Out: A Story of Race and Baseball in Boston* (New York: Routledge, 2002), Jim Rice's struggles with race in Boston are brought to light. Rice was unconventional by virtue of the fact that he was the first African American baseball superstar to ever play in Boston, a town and franchise historically entangled in the throes of racism, including the 1970s and 1980s when he played. But Rice refused to be defined by race, and that partially caused him strife with the media as well as with other black players throughout the major leagues.

For several years, Rice was the only black player on the Red Sox; racial tensions pervaded and Rice was isolated. He also had the daunting task of following in the footsteps of two Hall of Fame left fielders: Ted Williams and Carl "Yaz" Yastrzemski. But when other embittered African Americans left the team over time, he claimed that the organization had always treated him well. However, he privately told journalist Peter Gammons how difficult it was to play in Boston, and expressed his bitterness about the lack of black players on the team as well as the club's disinterest in them (*Shut Out*, p. 170). His reputation was that of a distant, hard to get to know guy who was always looking out for himself. Yet he was associated with many charitable organizations throughout his career, especially those on behalf of children. Although an obvious Fenway favorite, he still heard the occasional taunts of the home crowd in left field calling him "Uncle Ben"—the black face on the infamous rice box. The slugger never said anything (p. 169).

Rice simply didn't want to get involved with racial politics. He wanted to be left alone. He wanted to do his job and go home. And he more than fulfilled his duties throughout his tenure in Beantown. In 1989, the Red Sox released their future Hall of Famer, and homegrown player, without a proper farewell. And the Boston press kicked him out the door. Rice bitterly left the organization vowing never to return to Fenway Park. Of course, over the years, healing has taken place between Rice and the new Red Sox organization. He became a hitting coach in the minor league system and is now a commentator on NESN.

The ancient Greek philosopher Aristotle made a distinction between a vice of deficiency and a vice of excess. He thought a virtue could be found between these two vices. For instance, courage is the "mean" between the deficient vice of cowardice and the excessive vice of foolhardiness. It would be *cowardice* for Jason Bay to stand on first base when a wild pitch rattled around the backstop for a long period of time. It would be *foolhardiness* for David Ortiz to attempt to steal third base with two outs in the bottom of the ninth. It would be *courageous* for Jacoby Ellsbury to steal home plate. Especially against the New York Yankees!

In relation to issues of race and Aristotle's virtue ethics, it could be said that Rice was deficient in his silence, especially in refusing to acknowledge or to discuss the unjust racial climate on the team or in the city of Boston. Hall of Fame reporter Gammons said that by lacking solidarity with other black players, Rice missed the greatest opportunity in the history of the franchise to advocate change (p. 171).

At the beginning of his profession, Rice was cordial to the press, but things changed when reporter, Clif Keane, told him not to get "too high and mighty" because he had the power to bring him down. Rice retorted that he couldn't do anything to him: "That was it. That was the beginning," said Rice (p. 166). From that point on, Rice had legendary run-ins with the media that at times became physical. Once, in the locker room, Rice directed comments toward the media-pack calling them scum and maggots. Reporter Steve Fainaru, feeling humiliated, told Rice that if he was going to harass and disrespect people, he would likewise be harassed. Rice grabbed the young journalist and ripped his shirt. Teammates had to intervene and escort the reporter out of the clubhouse. Another time, Rice, trying to be a peacemaker on the field, broke up an argument between a player and an umpire; however, he accidentally knocked the umpire down. After the game, Tom Boswell, a respected reporter for the *Washington Post*, asked Rice how it felt for a reigning MVP to knock an umpire to the ground. Rice said something like: "If someone asks me another stupid question like that, I'm going to pick them up and throw them into the garbage" (p. 169). Boswell blew the story way out of proportion: he claimed Rice had threatened his life and that he had never been so frightened.

On the one hand, Rice displayed a vice of deficiency with his silent demeanor, especially concerning racial issues. On the other hand, Rice displayed the vice of excess in his boisterous and sometimes physical encounters with reporters. Early on in the late 1970s, manager Don Zimmer warned Rice that he should be cordial to the press, because some of the "vindictive bastards" would get him back. Rice replied that if he had to kiss their asses to get into the Hall, he didn't want to get in (p. 166). Had Rice adopted Aristotle's golden mean of "courtesy" toward the media, he certainly would have been in Cooperstown many years before. With that said, members of the media who voted against Rice for reasons other than his performance on the field lacked professional ethics. If popularity becomes the standard for induction, baseball is in trouble. Perhaps the Baseball Writers Association has gained too much power as the sole voting apparatus and the process for induction needs to be revisited.

Manny

When you don't feel good and you still get hits, that's how you know
you're a bad man.

> —MANNY RAMIREZ, after a walk-off home run against the Angels in
> Game Two of the 2007 ALDS

When Manny Ramirez left the team in 2008, Red Sox Nation was hor-
ribly conflicted. After all, he was an enigmatic figure adored in
Boston for his hitting power and childlike demeanor. He was simply
loads of fun to watch. Manny often climbed into the left-field scoreboard; no one ever knew what he did in there, but one time, he was-
n't on the field for the first pitch. At Yankee Stadium, Manny reached
into the stands and stole a home run from Miguel Cairo; he let the
proud Yankees infielder round the bases before revealing his catch
to the mortified player and agitated fans. The day after Manny
became an American citizen, he ran to his position in left field accompanied by a small flag and a thundering ovation from the Fenway
crowd. In Baltimore, Manny made a running catch in the outfield,
jumped off the wall, high-fived a fan, and then gunned the ball to
first base for a double play. "Moonshot Manny." 2004 World Series
MVP. One of the greatest right-handed hitters to ever play the game.

However, "Manny being Manny" also had its negative aspects
and ethical implications, and he wasn't exactly a media favorite at
the end of his tenure in Boston. Manny had stopped talking to
them a year or so before, and they increased their scrutiny and criticism of him, pointing to past and present Manny antics: Manny
requested and was allowed to report late to spring training for
"family" reasons, but he was scheduled during his absence to
appear at an Atlantic City auto show. Manny received the most All-
Star votes from fans one year, but mocked the Midsummer Classic
and Commissioner Bud Selig when opting out due to a bad knee.
Manny disrespected the office of the Presidency, by not attending
the traditional White House reception after the 2007 World Series.
And above all, Manny failed to hustle. Time and again the Boston
media screamed that Manny shouldn't get away with his selfish
behavior just because he was an exceptional hitting machine. And
as Manny's time in Boston came to an end, many Red Sox fans
joined the media in calling for Manny's release.

At the outset of 2008, Manny reported to spring training *on time*.
He was in great shape and was studying Rhonda Byrne's popular

self-help book, *The Secret:* "You've got to be a boat knowing where you're going," Manny philosophized. "We've got money. We're famous. But you've got to know what you want" <www.everyjoe .com/articles/manny-ramirez-practices-the-secret-228/>. The looming issue was his contract: would the Red Sox pick up his option for 2009? And most importantly, did Manny want to stay in Boston? The answer to both questions was no.

The growing separation between Manny and the team became evident during the first few months of the season. In the dugout, he scuffled with teammate Kevin Youkilis, slapping him because he was sick of Youk's temper tantrums when he made an out: "Cut that shit out," Ramirez hollered. As a pinch-hitter, Manny faced Mariano Rivera and didn't lift the bat off his shoulder; many believed he was sending the Red Sox a message that he wasn't going to try anymore. He shoved the team's sixty-four-year-old traveling secretary to the ground for not providing him with enough free tickets to a road game: "Just do your job," Manny instructed. The Red Sox fined Manny an undisclosed amount of money. As the trade deadline approached, he complained of a hamstring injury but the MRIs showed nothing. The players and front office simply could not trust the slugger to perform for the rest of the season, fearing he might sabotage the team.

The divorce between Manny and the Red Sox was sanctified by Manny on July 28th, 2008, just three days before his release: "Enough is enough. I'm tired of them; they're tired of me" (Sean McAdam, *Providence Journal*, July 28th, 2008). In the spring Manny claimed he wanted to retire in a Red Sox uniform. Only a few months later, he pushed his way out of Boston. It would be naive to think that money wasn't the driving issue. In the offseason, Manny had hired the tough negotiating agent Scott Boras to represent him. However, if Manny returned to the Red Sox for twenty million dollars a year in 2009 and 2010, Boras wouldn't get a penny. The fees for those option years would've been paid to Manny's prior agents. The only way for Boras to get paid was to negotiate a new contract for Ramirez. It appears that somewhere down the line, Boras convinced "Manny Being Manipulated," that they could do much better financially—in another city <http://sports.espn.go.com/ espn/eticket/story?page=manny>.

Aristotle believed every activity aims to achieve some good towards an end, and that there was one supreme final good that should be pursued as an end in itself. Aristotle called this happiness.

For Aristotle, the good life (happiness) consisted of the activity of the soul in accordance with virtue. Put another way, virtue and excellence should be pursued for their own sake, not because of the desire to achieve money, power, or fame. Regarding Manny, Aristotle would view his pursuit of wealth as an incomplete end, an end pursued because of something else. During his first few days as a Dodger, Manny gushed that he wanted to end his career in Dodger blue. But in the offseason, his infamous statement made it perfectly clear that "green" was going to dictate where he played: "Gas is up and so am I." The offers did not come rolling in: Manny attributed the lack of offers to the economic recession. But the underlying issue was that general managers were reluctant to invest in Ramirez because they feared he might become disgruntled and quit on them too. He ended up signing with the Dodgers, agreeing to a forty-five-million-dollar two-year contract. So, in the end, he made five million more than he would have made if he'd stayed with the Red Sox. And he had to pay Boras a five percent commission!

Ramirez tainted his reputation throughout baseball by giving up on the Red Sox; many remain dubious that he can be trusted to honor his commitments. History will undoubtedly determine Manny's ultimate legacy. He will always be remembered as a character, but the jury is still out as to the content of his character. Meanwhile, Manny is flourishing in Mannywood. But back in the East, some superstitious fans already fear that trading the 2004 World Series MVP might bring about a new curse: "The Curse of the Rambino."

25

What Kant Would Have to Say about Jon Lester's No-Hitter

KEVIN MAGUIRE

I mean, I don't want to say what he would have done, but if Dave Dravecky [a pitcher on the opposing team] had a perfect game going in the eighth inning and [our] catcher tried to bunt for a base hit and was successful, Boch might have chased him down the first base line. It's all very subjective. It depends which side of the fence you're on. [But the bunt was] chicken.

> —BOB BRENLY, Manager of the Arizona Diamondbacks after San Diego's Ben Davis broke up Curt Schilling's perfect game in the eighth inning in 2001

Jon Lester's no-hitter was an inspirational experience. Here was a cancer survivor recently returned from chemotherapy, had pitched the winning game of the World Series the previous year, and was now invigorating the "Fenway Faithful." As of May 19th, 2008, he was a saint in the mind of every Red Sox fan. But what is it that's so compelling and exceptional about a no-hitter and Lester's no-hitter in particular?

Two things come to mind: first, a no-hitter shows a certain degree of perfection, maybe not as much as a perfect game, but still something "superhuman" in a sense. Second, once it becomes apparent that a no-no is possible, baseball players often feel a duty to perform actions that don't challenge its possibility. No-hitters are so rare, so uncommon, that, until recently, baseball announcers had not mentioned it during their broadcasts fearing that they would be responsible for breaking it up. Players and coaches won't even talk to their pitcher if he's throwing a no-hitter for fear of "jinxing" him. Certainly, a no-hitter permits a certain idea of luck,

and the superstition which surrounds that concept. But what about
the commitments opposing hitters face in those late innings, as the
situation looks more and more futile?

Ethics, the study of right and wrong actions, has a special term
for actions that go beyond what's required. These are called
supererogatory acts. They are "beyond the call of duty," like throwing yourself on an exploding bomb to save the lives of a nearby
group of children. It's not wrong *not* to do these acts—you are not
a scoundrel if you don't do them—but to do them brings extra
credit, beyond the credit earned by simply doing what's morally
required. As a simple example, if I have a duty as a batboy not to
supply any corked bats, then a supererogatory commitment might
be to report any such corked bats discovered on my watch. In this
case I would be doing *more* than my duty requires. Are there
supererogatory duties present in the attitudes of Major League
Baseball players towards the no-hitter, particularly the attitudes of
the opposing team?

There have been huge disputes among philosophers over
supererogatory acts. Immanuel Kant is highly suspicious of them.
Kant believes there is an objective moral law, based on reason. The
fact that supererogatory acts are optional—a person may do them
or not do them—implies that they may be based on subjective feelings, not on reason. Kant says that it's unwise for people to consider these actions because they're not good moral models.

We see the importance of Kant's argument when we look at
Lester's no-hitter. In this case the game wasn't close, the Kansas
City Royals were helpless against Lester's natural ability, and were
losing late in the game by seven runs. Normally a hit is a relatively
common event over the course of nine innings. The duty of a
ballplayer is to try and help his team win the game. Getting a hit is
a means to this end. However, to win the baseball game the team
needs runs not just hits. Therefore, if a team is down 7–0 at Fenway
Park, and that team is the Royals (a virtual farm team since Tony
Pena's departure) we know that a single hit is futile in the late
innings. Nevertheless, almost everyone would agree that a major
league player in such a position should try his best to get a hit, as
it's his duty to help his team.

There has been a great and varied history of no-hitters in baseball. Plenty of pitchers have lost their no-hitters late in games and
have even been subjected to last-ditch bunt-hit attempts, such as in
Curt Schilling's near-perfect game in 2001. We can take Kant as our

guide to the ethics of the no-hitter, and then look more closely at Lester's no-hitter.

Duty and Lester's No-No

For Kant, duty should be based on reason and not on feelings. Moral actions do not go beyond what reason requires. Kant suspects that supererogatory motivations are tied to feeling. For example, if a hotel manager were to go above duty to help the Red Sox by arranging a 4:00 A.M. wake-up call for all of the opposing team's players on the day of the game, this wouldn't be considered a rational action, rather it would be based on a *feeling* of loyalty. For Kant, such an action would be morally dubious. In Lester's case, it's hard not to *feel* for him based on his amazing story of recovery. No one would *want* to break up his no-hit bid. But for Kant, feelings cannot be a part of ethical decision-making.

The ethical duty for the Royals then was to fight back against Lester. And, if the game would've been closer, then perhaps the effort by the Royals would've been more pronounced. However, the idea that winning is sometimes impossible, and that losing is something which has to be planned for and accommodated, is certainly nothing new to baseball. We see managers make decisions that cede losing or winning all the time: replacing position players with bench warmers in blowouts, for example. Our duty isn't always to mindlessly pursue winning in sports. But the idea that there may have been an obligation for the Royals to make less of an effort is controversial for a couple of reasons. One I have already mentioned is that winning the game seemed to be out of their reach. The other is unique to Lester.

There are many baseball enthusiasts, Red Sox fans among them, who would argue that in fact there *are* supererogatory motivations that need to be taken into consideration in Lester's no-hitter. It's likely that most of the Royals players knew that Lester was a cancer survivor. Jason Varitek, referring to the unique nature of the no-hitter, said that "the work that Jonny Lester's had to do—to be able to be part of something like that with him is totally different" (*Boston Globe*, May 20th, 2008). If there were room for supererogatory consideration with respect to a no-hitter, then certainly some would say that the Royals players knew of Lester's past cancer struggle, and perhaps this fact acted as an ethical motivation to get the players to not fight back.

Lester Like a God. But How?

Lester fought cancer for many months, and it was possible that he might never play baseball again. However, once Lester recovered and regained his strength, he became more dominant than before he got sick. Comparably, Jim Abbott, another southpaw, who happens to lack a part of his right forearm, threw a no-hitter against Cleveland in 1993. Abbott's life wasn't in danger in any way and although his story, like Lester's, is an inspiration, there's a difference between overcoming a disability and overcoming a potentially fatal illness. Some of the comparative elements of both stories might be insightful, however.

To go above duty, to go "easier" on a person with a disability is, in essence, insulting that person's own individual worth and developed ability. In the case of Lester, however, he had already proven his mettle the previous year by winning the deciding game of the World Series. The no-hitter was an individual achievement that only added to his legacy in a Red Sox uniform. The Abbott example is helpful in this case, though, for the following reason: it works to push supererogation outside of the individual problems or stories of the people engaged in the action. Whether or not to bunt on Lester in the ninth inning really should, from a Kantian perspective, be the same as whether or not to have bunted on Curt Schilling in his near perfect game in 2001, or whether or not to have bunted in any other similar circumstances with similar pitchers. The cancer simply shouldn't be a consideration at all.

Baseball, as Woody Allen has said, isn't like love, instead it "has rules, it has foul-lines." But we see these rules relaxed in all sorts of circumstances. As long as these relaxations are being applied in every case, or are made universal, it's difficult for the Kantian to disagree with them. However, this isn't the case. In fact, the idea of making exceptions in certain instances for sentimental reasons happens all the time, and Kant says this is what creates problems. He says: "I do wish that educators would spare their pupils examples of so-called *noble* [supererogatory] actions, with which our sentimental writings so abound, and would expose them all only to duty."

Kantians see nobility in baseball because there are so many exceptions to rules. However, I would argue that not all exceptions are made out of sentimentality. Instead, many arise out of the convenience of custom and are devoid of feeling altogether. For example, hit batsmen are rarely called out for leaning over the plate and failing to move out of the way, and this has nothing to do with sentimentality, but instead is done for practical reasons. Julio Lugo and Dustin Pedroia routinely fail to touch second base in the "neighborhood play" and yet the players sliding into their "neighborhood" are still called out.

Rules are codified in baseball, but there are conventions, which often supersede those rules. And this is what the dispute between Bob Brenly and Bruce Bochy was about in respect to Curt Schilling's attempted perfect game. And, something like this must have been in the minds of the Royals players during Lester's no-hit bid. Because it's in the nature of conventions not to be codified, many are confused by their limitations.

The analogy here between a rule and a convention is similar to Kant's distinction between a "perfect" duty and an "imperfect" duty. We're all bound by perfect duties and if we don't obey those duties, then we're at fault, we're blameworthy. Perfect duties are based on reason and must be followed. Imperfect duties concern things we wish would happen. These duties are still morally binding, but are more personal, in that they go beyond what we *must* do and instead move toward a good that we wish to be the case. For this reason, failing to accomplish our imperfect duties doesn't warrant blame because, in a sense, they're a work in progress, and achieving them is worthy of praise.

In Lester's no-hitter, as in most no-hitters that are blowouts, the question concerns the relationship of the perfect duty to the imperfect duty. There may have been an imperfect duty for the Royals not to bunt in the ninth inning. This comes down to a question that was posed earlier: is a hit intrinsic to the duty of a hitter, or is merely producing runs intrinsic to his duty? Once we make this determination, we can ask the question of whether or not the perfect duty to help one's team, generally, as a part of one's profession, is greater or less than the imperfect duty to go above and beyond not breaking up the no-hitter for beneficent reasons.

What *Should* the Royals Have Done?

Perfect and imperfect duties constitute important components of the decision-making capability of the ethical person. Producing a hit seems to be a good example of an imperfect duty, in that it permits exceptions. When Kevin Youkilis hits a sacrifice fly in a close game to get a run in, that's the production of a run without getting a hit. So when he does this, he is acting in a way that benefits the team, and his action is of greater Kantian moral worth than if he were to greedily attempt a hit to improve his own statistics.

In the case of the Royals, however, acting in service of the *opposing* team involves a questionable motive. In Fenway Park, immersed in such a wealth of good will, it's possible that Lester's performance itself was enough to permit the Royals to merely give up their attempts for a hit. But, if they just gave up, then that went against their duty in trying to help their team win. Certainly, different no-hitters have different circumstances, which allow for varying duties. In a close game, it may be harder to achieve a no-hitter because the opposing team is still committed to winning the game. There *might* have been an imperfect duty for the Royals not to bunt, or to attempt to get a hit in the eighth or ninth inning against Lester. But there absolutely *cannot* be a perfect duty to do that.

For there to be a perfect duty not to pursue hits, the Royals would actually be at fault for *fulfilling* their duty to play the game the best they could. This seems implausible for several reasons. Perfect duties with respect to ethics in general are analogous to the rules of baseball in particular. So, if there were a perfect duty for Kevin Youkilis to try to hit a sacrifice fly in a given situation, then there could be no credit awarded to him for having succeeded in his self-sacrifice. This would just be an example of Youk doing his job, part of what Kant sees as intrinsic to his ethical role as a human being. Thus, it could be viewed as a perfect duty of all baseball players that they try their best, but one can't say that there are perfect duties in situations involving no-hitters. As Brenly himself stated, it's a subjective matter. It's not that we can say there's a perfect duty to give up in the later innings of a no-hitter.

What *Would* You Have Done?

We've ruled out the possibility of a perfect duty not to pursue hits in the later innings of a no-hitter in a blowout, either for the reason of Lester's compelling personal story, or for reasons of general baseball conventions. The question remains whether or not there would be an imperfect duty not to get a hit. I've pointed out that such an imperfect duty focused on Lester's compelling story would be rather insulting, as it could conceivably call into doubt the significance of his achievement and disrespect his abilities as pitcher. But could there be an imperfect duty to not break up a no-hitter in later innings, something that would credit a baseball player's individual worth?

In fact, there is an imperfect duty to do this, and hitters who do this are a credit to baseball because they exemplify the unwritten nature of the game's history in the furtherance of something more honorable than simply winning. These actions will not be supererogatory because they will not constitute going above and beyond duty. Instead, they will be the imperfect duties of a player such that they are real obligations, which if not performed, will simply mean that credit won't be awarded, but neither will their lack of action be blameworthy.

It's easy to see some of the Kantian arguments that could be offered to object to the idea of an imperfect duty to avoid getting hits in the late innings of a no-hitter in a close game. There might be an argument that there's a perfect duty to win that is tied to hitting that ultimately no imperfect duty can overrule. After all, imperfect duties and perfect duties are not supposed to conflict in any way in a Kantian framework. If there were a perfect duty to win that overrules any imperfect duties rooted in the conventions of baseball, then it would seem ridiculous to ask the Royals to not attempt a hit in those later innings. But this puts a premium on winning. The Red Sox of all teams, and most of their fans, know that winning isn't everything, not just in some clichéd, childlike way, but also in a bone-aching, multiple generations not seeing a world championship way. And winning at any cost shouldn't have been an issue for the Royals fans either, who are all too familiar with the infamous George Brett pine tar incident against the New York Yankees. The important thing is that for Red Sox fans, unlike Billy Martin, winning without due attention to ethical and sportsmanlike conventions isn't any achievement at all.

From a Kantian perspective, the Yankees present interesting questions with respect to supererogation in their relationship with the Red Sox. Kant would hold that egalitarianism is necessary between opposing teams. No matter how evil the empire of certain teams, to Kant this would just suggest they lack "cultivation" and thus were inferior. Greater rivalries wouldn't produce greater obligations for the Royals rather than the Yankees. Kant holds that if there's an imperfect duty, that imperfect duty holds in all instances. We see even with the Red Sox–Yankees rivalry that there's a sort of commonality of discourse—the runner on first base talks to the first baseman during these rivalries just like any other game. For Dustin Pedroia to react to a no-hit attempt by Andy Pettitte differently than a pitcher from another team would be unfair. And this supports the idea that there *is* an imperfect duty to act in a certain way during a no-hitter, no matter what teams are playing.

Obviously, this doesn't extend directly to the idea that there's an imperfect duty to not pursue a bunt-hit in the bottom of the ninth in a no-hit blowout. But it does suggest the very notion of imperfect duties is present in the conventions of baseball. Now, having said that, one has to have the Kantian dignity to withstand what would be the popular appeal of a Jacoby Ellsbury drag bunt in the bottom of the ninth to break up a Yankees no-hitter. He would no doubt be cheered by hoards of Boston fans who would relish the idea of not falling victim to a no-hitter against Yankees. But such a motivation would be ill-conceived in that it would go against the Kantian idea of respecting everyone's humanity in itself and not using them just as a mere means to an end. Whereas, in this case, the end is the maximizing of personal pride over more all encompassing moral duties.

That's Bush League!

The idea of the "bush league" play or action is simple: it's an action that for whatever reason goes against the conventions and spirit of baseball. Leaving your spikes up when sliding into second; that's bush league. Throwing at someone's head; that's bush league. However sure and clear these instances can be to baseball enthusiasts, actually describing what *makes* a bush league play so contrary to the spirit of baseball is more difficult. But clearly there are two different ideas of the bush league play—one that permits, even requires, the idea of supererogation, and one that denies it.

One could make a claim that the duty of a player is to do anything to win, and as such, going in with your spikes up might help, and might be in accordance with that duty. But, in the case of bush league plays we have to go above and beyond that duty to not do it, and thus, supererogation is required. The other claim would be that the things that the duties themselves include are obligations that run contrary to the aims of winning—this would be the Kantian stance. It isn't that a bush league play is wrong or bad because we fail to do something that, were we to do it, we would be given credit. Instead, a bush league play for Kant would be more about duties contained within playing the sport itself, and in this case, supererogation would *not* be emphasized.

So, is bunting in the bottom of the ninth of a no-hit attempt a bush league play? Something that's bush league is very different from something that's "wrong," in several important senses. I've already mentioned that the nature of the imperfect duty pertaining to not bunting in the no-hitter held true under certain circumstances. To merely say it's bush league is less egregious than to say it's wrong. We say "bush league" offhand to describe an action that simply didn't conform to conventional behavior. But the action isn't morally wrong in any way, specifically because we've already ruled out before that there could be a *perfect* duty to not break up the no-hitter. It seems then, that to a Kantian, when we say "bush league," we mean that they ought to have given themselves the credit that they would accrue from an imperfect duty, not that their action is a perfect duty. So it doesn't mean it's necessarily wrong—it just means that they should've had the dignity to take the action that would've credited them as making the morally correct decision. There can be a duty to do or to not do a particular thing, and it is not wrong if we perform the opposite of the prescribed action. However, it does seem that Brenly is right when he claims that it's bush league, in that it's not "wrong," but it is certainly not dignified.

Lester's Duties and Capabilities

So far I have discussed the duties of Royals players who were facing Lester in the late innings of his no-hitter. I have dismissed the possibility of a duty not to pursue an action to break up the no-hitter out of an inclination or feeling of sympathy for his battle with cancer. I looked at the possibility of an imperfect duty to not break up the no-hitter because there was little chance of winning, which, if it weren't followed, could easily be termed bush league. Now there's the question of Lester's own duties in the no-hitter.

Does a pitcher have a duty to complete a no-hitter regardless of the implications this has for the rest of the team? For example, the pitcher could be physically hurt but be perfect through five, or six innings. Or it could be the end of the regular season, and it would be more advantageous for the team to take him out and rest him for the playoffs. Terry Francona spoke after another no-hit bid Lester had going on September 25th, 2008, about having to take

Lester out due to his pitch-count (*Boston Globe*, September 26th, 2008). The question of supererogation or self-sacrifice comes into play here as well.

The ethical motivation should always be duty to the team and to the individual when those coincide, so self-preservation in the case of an injury, or preservation for possible postseason attempts at greatness, are important considerations that overrule individual achievement. There's no obligation to leave the pitcher in during a no-hitter regardless of pitch-count. The control of this, from a Kantian perspective, is always from the superior who administers the general rule, in this case Francona. And certainly a rule that stipulates an absolute pitch-count limit is in and of itself a very Kantian construction—admitting little to no exception to the rule.

A more challenging question involves issues relating to the financial consideration of the team. Lester isn't in control of when and how he pitches—Francona could have taken him out for any reason. But since complete games have become such a rarity in the modern era, no-hitters aren't necessarily advantageous to the long-term interests of the team, or to the pitcher himself. Should managers pull them for the financial good of the team over the good of the pitchers' career and overall achievement? The Kantian implications here are important, because it puts the goal of the overall success of a team in question—is it to win one game, several games, a whole season, or multiple seasons?

Obviously the long-term success of the team is in the interest of the fans, but short-term competition is important for the nature and integrity of the game. The September 25th no-hitter in the making would have to be sacrificed for the good of the team, but the team's success in terms of competition and their success in terms of finance are two different matters entirely. It seems as if the financial considerations of the no-hitter should be put aside, especially given the depreciation of the complete game in baseball. In fact, the no-hitter doesn't just represent something close to perfection; nowadays the no-hitter has the additional merit of the ability to make it through a two-hour game and a total of nine innings.

For the Kantian in the end, there's no such idea of achieving ethical perfection. For Kant, our desires are never perfected, and thus, no real action can be perfect when measured by its inclination, which is why inclination plays such a small role in his ethical system. We may have all tuned into our TVs that magical night and felt we were watching perfection. We may have felt there was some form of cosmic realignment that allowed us to go into work the next day and to do a stellar job finishing up our duties, or having a great time with one's family that evening and having it all feel "complete." But in a Kantian framework, it's never "perfect" or "God-like."

Even though Lester will return to the mound a hero, it will be fleeting for this Kantian. There's never a chance for perfection, as we see in David Ortiz's former success, which now seems to be fleeting. The reason Kant is suspicious of supererogatory actions is because he sees them as attached to feeling—and as Sox fans, we must admit that our feeling about players is fleeting as well. They come and they go. Lester's achievement will always have a place in his history, and the history of the team, but it wasn't perfection. I've argued here that the Royals had an imperfect duty to lay down their swords in the top of the eighth and the ninth, but it wasn't due to Lester's perfection, or to his cancer—it was for their duty to the game. And that's a legacy that gets to the core of the Sox fan's commitment to the game: faith in the imperfect and adherence to the commands of duty.

26

What We Talk About when We Talk About Lowe

FRED ABLONDI

As most Red Sox fans can tell you, Derek Lowe was the winning pitcher in the deciding game of the 2004 ALCS. But what if he had lost the game? Does it make any sense to even ask the question? In other words, just what are we doing when we consider that he might not have won the game? To be sure, Red Sox fans from the years before 2004 are particularly practiced at the game of asking "What if?" We're all too familiar with expressions of mourning and disappointment, especially regarding the team's many World Series Game Seven losses. We say things like, "If only Johnny Pesky got the ball to the plate quicker, Enos Slaughter wouldn't have scored," or "If Jim Rice hadn't been injured in 1975, the Red Sox would have defeated the Reds." But what exactly do we mean when we speak this way, uttering what philosophers call "counterfactual conditional statements," or just "counterfactuals" for short? Can such statements be true, or false for that matter? How could we ever know? Or might such utterances be meaningless?

Well, here's one way to present the problem. Some philosophers, and many non-philosophers, think of truth in something like the following way: true sentences are true because they accurately describe the way the world in fact is. True sentences are said to "correspond to," or "picture," the world. The statement

"Tim Wakefield is on the mound."

is true if and only if there are two things, Tim Wakefield and a mound, and the former stands to the latter in the relation of "being on." Some philosophers talk of Tim Wakefield's being on the mound as the *truthmaker* of the statement "Tim Wakefield is on the mound." What makes the statement true is that it accurately maps or mirrors the way things stand in the world at the time it is uttered.

Okay, fine, but here's the problem: how does this way of thinking about truth deal with counterfactuals, that is, statements about how things *might* have been had such and such happened, but how things were in fact *not*, because such and such did not happen? At first glance, it may seem that counterfactual statements cannot deal with an idea of truth that mirrors the way things stand in the world. By their very nature, counterfactual claims state how things *do not* stand in the world—they can have no truthmakers. It's precisely because Johnny Pesky held the ball that Enos Slaughter was able to score on Harry Walker's hit to center; it is by it's very nature as a counterfactual statement that the claim

"If only Johnny Pesky got the ball to the plate quicker, Enos Slaughter wouldn't have scored."

has nothing to mirror, nothing that it can accurately picture—after all, if it corresponded to a fact, it wouldn't be a counterfactual! (To be fair to Mr. Pesky, I wasn't alive in 1946, and have only seen the play on which Slaughter scored from first base on archival footage. To my eye, he didn't appear to do anything out of the ordinary on the play. My father, on the other hand, who was eleven at the time and not in attendance at the game, has always insisted that Pesky held the ball for a beat too long before getting the relay to the plate. But even if Pesky did, it shouldn't be forgotten that Slaughter's run came in the bottom of the eighth, and that the Red Sox had two on with no outs in the top of the ninth, yet were unable to score. Pesky surely cannot bear the entirety of the blame for the loss.)

Despite this, we want to say there is *something* true about such counterfactual claims. Surely it's *in some way* true to say:

"If Bob Stanley had struck out Mookie Wilson with the seventh pitch of Wilson's at bat in the 10th inning of Game Six of the 1986 World Series, the Red Sox would've won the series."

For those readers not familiar with the 10th inning of that game, on his seventh pitch to Wilson, Stanley threw a wild pitch on a 2–2 count, allowing Kevin Mitchell to score from third base and tie the game. What happened after that, none of us need reminding. For some philosophers, the way to spell out this "in some way true" is to invoke the notion of possible worlds. Possible worlds are ways that the actual world could've been—they're worlds in which one or more of the counterfactual statements of our world are instead *factual* statements. On this account, to say that had Bob Stanley done such and such is to say that there's a possible world in which Bob Stanley *in fact did do* such and such.

But matters quickly get complicated: What is the status of these worlds—if they're not the real world, just what sort of worlds are they? How are its inhabitants related to us, the inhabitants of the actual world? And why should we care what happens "there"? These are questions that need answers before we can decide if an appeal to possible worlds is the best way to understand the truth of coun-terfactual claims. They certainly do *seem* true, since the painful dis-appointment that they express is so very real—think of the scores of "Oh, if only . . ., then we would'a won" utterances so many of us Red Sox fans have made over the years, particularly in regard to the team's Game Seven World Series losses.

The World Series losses to which I am referring are those of 1946, 1967, 1975, and 1986, each painful in its own way. We could also consider for our purposes the Game Seven loss to the Yankees in the 2003 ALCS, specifically claims about what would've hap-pened had Pedro Martinez not pitched the seventh inning, or at least not pitched so long into the seventh inning, but that wound is a little too fresh. It might be nice, on the other hand, to consider the possible worlds that don't contain Bucky Dent. Finally, I am aware, of course, that the Red Sox have won two World Series in recent years, both in four-game sweeps. That I continue to dwell on their dramatic, traumatic, heart-breaking losses says much about what thirty years as a long-suffering fan has done to my psyche.

A Proposal from New Jersey

To begin with, I'm going to drop a name here, and that name is David Lewis. And before you rack your brain trying to remember what position he played, let me quickly say that Lewis wasn't a major leaguer, but was for many years a philosopher at Princeton, and as far as I know he wasn't a Red Sox fan (his passion was for Australian-rules football). But Lewis is relevant to our concerns because of his work on counterfactuals. Not only does he appeal to possible worlds to explain how they can be true, he believed that these other worlds exist, that they're concrete and no less real than is this, our world. Furthermore, Lewis believed that counterfactual worlds are just like our world in terms of the *kind* of thing they are, namely, each is a world; they differ only in the particular things they contain. Our world contains the things that in fact happened, while possible worlds contain what might have happened.

On this view, which is known as *modal realism* ("modal" referring to concepts such as possibility and necessity, "realism" meaning these things really exist), "actual" becomes a word like "this" or "here" in that it means different things when said by different people in different places. We call our world the actual world, and individuals in a given possible world—possible from our point of view—call their world the actual world (and our world a possible world). So, for example, in a world in which the Red Sox won the 1986 World Series, the inhabitants of that world say, correctly, that the Red Sox actually won the 1986 World Series, while in our world we are, unfortunately, stuck saying that they could've won, but actually lost.

As Lewis himself admitted, his is not a common-sense view. In fact, when it came to people's astonished reactions to his modal realism, he famously responded that he didn't know how to refute an incredulous stare. But he thought that modal realism is the best way to explain a number of philosophical concepts and questions, including how counterfactual statements can be true, and so the cost of this oddness was worth the price. Of course, philosophers being philosophers, not everyone agreed that this was the best way to handle the problem, and over the years a number of objections have been raised against modal realism. Let's take a look at a few of them.

Roger Clemens Could Have Been a Knuckleballer?

Let me clarify something I said above. Strictly speaking, on Lewis's account the modal realist is not saying that there's a possible world in which Bob Stanley struck out Mookie Wilson. Stanley and Wilson, like all individuals, including you and me, can exist in only one world. Nor do worlds overlap such that you could be in two worlds at once. Rather, it's their *counterparts* who exist in this possible world, counterparts who are in many ways very similar to them, the difference being that in that world, Stanley's counterpart struck out Wilson's counterpart. We all have our counterparts existing in some but not all possible worlds—it can be fun to think of what some of yours are doing now! So our question concerns how we should think of the various possible-world counterparts of the Red Sox players of the actual, that is, our, world.

In many instances, this isn't too difficult, and can even be a bit amusing. We can imagine what it's like in a world in which Bobby Doerr played his entire career at shortstop, or a world in which Louis Tiant never sported a moustache, with no trouble. Recall that this appeal to possible worlds is just what Lewis holds makes counterfactual claims like

> **"If Ted Williams hadn't gone into the service,**
> **he would be higher on the list of all-time**
> **home run hitters."**

true. In this example, there's a possible world in which Ted Williams's counterpart doesn't go into the service, and as a result accumulates more home runs. At the cost of accepting the reality of possible worlds, we get what looks to be a tidy explanation of how counterfactual conditionals can be true.

Things can quickly get complicated, however. We can ask: Is there a world in which Curt Shilling's counterpart resembles the Curt Schilling of our world, except that the counterpart is a member of the Green Party? Or how about the world in which Carl Yastrzemski is a lifetime .190 hitter, or the one in which Bill Lee is, well, normal? The counterpart to Carlton Fisk who, as a result of a childhood illness that our Carlton Fisk did not contract, weighs 120 lbs. as an adult, and who happens to be deathly afraid of physical contact is so different from the Carlton Fisk of our world that we're left asking in what way they can be meaningfully called counterparts. And this is important: notice that we still want to hold that the counterfactual conditional statement

> **"If Carlton Fisk were deathly afraid of physical contact,**
> **he wouldn't have been such a great catcher."**

is true. So perhaps the problem is going with modal realism and counterpart theory as the way to explain *how* it can be true.

Another related problem for modal realism can be brought out with the following example. Consider a possible world in which Carlton Fisk's counterpart was not born on December 26th, 1947 as the Carlton Fisk of our world was, but instead on April 29th, 1951. That's not so hard to think of—he's the same guy, just with a different birthday. Then let's add that he's born in Lynwood, California and not Bellows Falls, Vermont. Again, not too big a deal. Now let's also say that instead of growing to be six feet two inches tall and weighing 220 lbs., he is in this world only five feet ten inches tall and weighs no more than 165 lbs. Further, in the possible world under consideration, he's a curly-haired shortstop with the nickname "Rooster" who, after many years with the Red Sox, is traded along with Butch Hobson to the California Angels. Finally, in this world Rick Burleson is just as he is in our world, *except* that he was born on December 26th, 1947 in Bellows Falls, Vermont and not on April 29th, 1951 in Lynwood, California, grows to be six feet two inches tall, 220 lbs. (and not only five feet ten inches tall and 165 lbs.), is a square-jawed catcher affectionately called "Pudge" and who, after many years with the Red Sox, is traded to the Chicago White Sox. Just who hits the game-winning home run in Game Six of the '75 Series? Which one is in the Hall of Fame? Telling who's who from one world to the next can become a very tricky matter indeed!

A Ballclub by Any Other Name

What about the team itself? Like all teams, "the Red Sox" isn't a fixed or static thing, but something that changes its parts—the players, coaches, and so on—while remaining the same team. They're still the Red Sox, regardless of the particular individuals that make up the team. Even if the entire roster were to turn over during the course of the season, such that none of the players on the opening day roster are with the team on Labor Day, the Red Sox are still the Red Sox. For example, in the case of such a complete turnover, it would still be proper to say "I went to the Red Sox game last night" to describe your activity the preceding evening, whether you uttered that statement in April or in September. So in a like manner, we might say that a world with a Red Sox team made up of counterparts of the Red Sox of our world is still the Red Sox.

But again, we soon run into a problem: What do we say about a world with a Red Sox team that does not and has never contained any of the counterparts of the actual Red Sox? If modal realism is true, it would seem that there's a possible world in which counterparts of the entire roster of the '86 Mets play for the Red Sox, and counterparts of the entire roster of the '86 Red Sox play for the Mets. Who am I rooting for when they play each other? Or consider the 2009 Red Sox team that has, say, an A-Rod counterpart at third base, a Mariano Rivera counterpart as closer, a Reggie Jackson counterpart in right field and a George Steinbrenner counterpart as team owner? Are we really still talking about the Red Sox? We want to say that the statement

> ### *"If A-Rod played third for the Red Sox, he wouldn't get booed so loudly at Fenway."*

is true, but to explain how it can be true by invoking such a possible world strikes us as intuitively wrong. However populated, the feeling is that without Ted Williams, Dom DiMaggio, Rico Petrocelli, Bernie Carbo, Dwight Evans, and the like, these are not *our* Red Sox. So just as the modal realist would seem to have the problem of explaining, if she can, how the players like the svelte and speedy George Scott or the power-hitting Oil Can Boyd are in any meaningful way the counterparts of individuals in our world, she also needs to tell us how the counterpart teams to our Red Sox are in any meaningful way the Red Sox.

Yeah, Yeah, but Who Really Cares?

This worry raises what seems to be another significant problem, namely the matter of our not being able to see much—or any—reason why we should *care* about these counterparts, or even why their counterparts in the actual world should care about them. Consider: It's certainly true that, all else remaining the same as it was in our world, if Jim Lonborg had won Game Seven of the 1967 World Series, the Red Sox would've been world champions. To explain its truth, the modal realist appeals to a possible world in which Jim Lonborg's counterpart wins Game Seven for the Red Sox. But why should we care about him or them? "Our" Jim Lonborg, going on two days rest, was no match for Bob Gibson and the Cardinals. Of what possible interest is it to us or to him if there's a Jim Lonborg counterpart who threw a no-hitter in Game Seven?

Think of it this way: according to modal realism, there's a world in which your counterpart owns the Red Sox. Are you excited for him or her? Or is it like reading that someone a lot like you won the lottery? In both instances, a shrug of indifference seems the most we can muster. The objection, then, is this: When people talk or think about what could've been, what they're concerned about is what could've been *for them*, not how things were or are for some individual very much like them. When we say, for example,

"Calvin Schiraldi might have won the sixth game of the 1986 World Series."

we're not, according to Lewis, talking about how things could have been for our, actual Calvin Schiraldi, but for a counterpart of his. But I am certain that Calvin Schiraldi isn't at all concerned with somebody else, someone who is in many ways like him, who in some possible world won what was in that world the deciding game of the 1986 World Series for the Red Sox. Nor, for that matter, am I concerned with my counterpart who enjoyed watching the Red Sox victory parade in October of 1986.

Where in the World(s) Are We?

While we all would agree that

"If Bob Montgomery and Carl Yastrzemski had homered in the bottom of the ninth in Game Seven of the 1975 World Series, the Red Sox would have been world champs."

is true, for the reasons discussed above, I suggest that we not follow the modal realist in explaining the truth of this, or any counterfactual conditional statement by invoking the existence of concrete possible worlds containing counterparts of the individuals of this world. Talk of how things might have been "if only" so-and-so had done such-and-such is a staple for sports fans in general and the members of Red Sox Nation in particular.

Odds are that as I write this there are two guys at the Cask 'n' Flagon arguing about what might have happened in the sixth game of the '86 Series! And yes, I agree that it's nice to think of living in a world in which Ted Williams, Carl Yastrzemski, Dwight Evans,

Freddy Lynn, and Billy Buckner all got to sport World Series rings, or in which Harry Agganis and Tony Conigliaro had long, successful playing careers. But according to counterpart theory, these counterparts are not our Teddy Ballgame, Captain Carl, and so on, nor is it we who get to cheer them on. So I think we ought to look elsewhere for a way to explain how counterfactual statements can be true. In the meantime, I'll take pleasure in considering the actual world, in which these words were actually said by Joe Castiglione at the conclusion of the ninth inning of a game that Derek Lowe actually won:

> Foulke to the set, the 1–0 pitch, here it is. Swing and a ground ball, stabbed by Foulke. He has it. He underhands to first. And the Boston Red Sox are the world champions. For the first time in eighty-six years, the Red Sox have won baseball's world championship. Can you believe it? (WEEI radio, October 27th, 2004)

The Boston Red Sox
All-Philosophers Team

BILL NOWLIN

Catcher: Bill **MOORE**

First Base: **ARISTOTLE** "Harry" Agganis

Second Base: **ARQUIMEDEZ** Pozo

Third Base: Joe **CICERO**

Shortstop: John **GODWIN**

Left Field: **DANTE** Bichette

Center Field: Ernest **NEITZKE** (it's sort of like Nietzsche)

Right Field: Dwight "**DEWEY**" Evans

Starting Pitcher: Josh **BECKETT** (RHP)

Relief Pitchers: Danny **DARWIN** (RHP); **EMERSON**
Dickman (RHP);

Rick **WISE** (RHP) and Jennings **POINDEXTER** (LHP)

Manager: Dick **WILLIAMS**

The Starting Lineup

FRED ABLONDI teaches philosophy at Hendrix College in Arkansas. Until 2004, he spent a good deal of time worrying that he had inflicted upon his first-born son the same curse with which his own father had burdened him, namely, a lifetime of passion for a team that would inevitably break his heart. Though he likes thinking and writing about seventeenth-century philosophers, Fred is happiest when watching his boys play baseball and his girls dance.

RANDALL E. AUXIER likes the Red Sox. But he wants to apologize for Tim McCarver. Like Tim, Randy grew up in Memphis, and like Tim, he learned to love the St. Louis Cardinals. Like Tim, he has no idea why anyone is willing to play for the Phillies. Unlike Tim, Randy did not become a major league catcher or television commentator, but he understands that everyone finds Tim McCarver annoying, and that many must wonder, "Is it Memphis, or the Cardinals, or what is it?" Randy wants to assure anyone who will listen that it's not Memphis or the Cardinals: it's just Tim. His accent is our fault, but his annoyingness is all his own. In light of his essay on baseball stadiums, Randy thinks that many people would smile if they knew that Memphis had renamed its awful, decrepit minor league stadium after Tim McCarver just a couple of years before the thing was mercifully demolished. Apparently no one suggested that the beautiful, new downtown stadium be named for such an annoying person. Randy fears that McCarver will call every World Series from now until one of them dies. Unlike Tim, Randy teaches philosophy at Southern Illinois University in Carbondale, which enables him to take in a Cardinals game when the gods demand it.

DICK BRESCIANI is a Boston Red Sox Vice President and Team Historian. He joined the club in 1972 as assistant public relations director and statistician,

337

and later was in charge of public relations concerning ownership, the team, and the media. He became a Vice President in 1987 and has coordinated Red Sox publications, historical archives, uniformed alumni, booster clubs, the annual national Tony Conigliaro Award selection, and the Red Sox Hall of Fame selection committee. A graduate of the University of Massachusetts with a degree in Journalism, Bresciani has been inducted into four sports Halls of Fame: the Cape Cod Summer Baseball League, the University of Massachusetts, the Boston Red Sox, and the New England Italian-American. In 1997 he received the Robert O. Fishel Award from Major League Baseball for public relations excellence. He grew up in the small central Massachusetts town of Hopedale and made the thirty-mile trek to Fenway Park and Braves Field with his family many times as a youngster.

JOEL W. CADE was the fat kid who played catcher on his little league baseball team. Having discovered his dream of playing for the Red Sox wasn't likely to occur, he turned his attention to scholarship and is currently ABD at Loyola University Chicago. His work focuses upon Philosophy of Religion in the Continental Tradition. Joel's dissertation examines the role of alterity in the constitution of subjectivity beyond onto-theology. Even though Joel is stuck in the land of the Cubs, he continues to be a rabid Red Sox fan.

ERIN E. FLYNN's best pitch is teaching and writing about nineteenth-century German philosophy at Ohio Wesleyan University. He recently punched out "Celebrating the Agony of Life," an essay about Nietzsche and Led Zeppelin in *Led Zeppelin and Philosophy: All Will Be Revealed*. He also throws a little philosophy of action, as well as fielding questions about art, especially movies. He didn't grow up in New England, but has been a Boston fan since he was seven, when his dad happened to mention that Jim Rice was a good hitter. His friends didn't know who Jim Rice was, and as far as he can recall, it was his first experience of being cool.

NOLEN GERTZ is currently pursuing his doctorate in philosophy at the New School for Social Research, and working on a dissertation about the meaning of warfare. Not to name drop, but as a child he once ran into someone at Logan Airport who looked a lot like Clemens. Once, in his teen years, he spent over an hour at a McDonald's in Revere watching someone who looked a lot like Nomar eat fries. More recently, at a diner in Manhattan, he had a very awkward exchange with someone because, well, he looked a lot like Schilling.

MARCUS GIAMATTI is a lifelong Red Sox fan, an actor, musician, and writer. A graduate of Bowdoin College and the Yale School of Drama, Marcus was raised in New Haven, Connecticut where he played baseball through high school. Though he never achieved his dream to one day fill the shoes behind the plate at Fenway Park of his boyhood idol Carlton Fisk, Marcus was a decent defensive catcher with speed but had absolutely no bat. Much to his surprise, Marcus was asked twice to play in the Legends and Celebrity Softball Game, in Pittsburgh and San Francisco—due to his work as Peter Gray on the long-running CBS series *Judging Amy*. In the slow-pitch game Marcus had the honor to catch Hall of Famer Rollie Fingers, and snag a foul popup off the bat of Dave Winfield. Being asked to play long toss by Fred Lynn and Wade Boggs remains the most thrilling moment of Marcus's life. His father, Bart Giamatti, was President of the National League and the Commissioner of Major League Baseball. Marcus currently lives in Los Angeles with his wife and daughter.

JONAH P.B. GOLDWATER is a Ph.D. Candidate in Philosophy at the Graduate Center of the City University of New York, where he's writing his dissertation in Metaphysics and the Philosophy of Science. He teaches at Baruch College in Manhattan, and he writes the "Baseball and Philosophy" column for *The Faster Times*. Jonah attended Rich Gedman Baseball Camp in the late 1980s, and won a Most Improved Player award at Mike Andrews All-American Baseball Camp in July 1989. He has been a Boston Red Sox fan since 1986.

CHELSEA C. HARRY is working on a doctorate in philosophy at Duquesne University. She completed a Masters degree in philosophy at the University of Hawaii at Manoa, where she worked on comparisons between contemporary Western thought and Japanese, Chinese, and Islamic philosophy. Her article, "Ibn Bājja and Heidegger on Retreat from Society," was recently published in the *Journal of Islamic Philosophy*. As a child, she was a fanatic collector of Topps baseball cards, which required many feverish trips to the 7–11 for a chance to get Clemens, Boggs, and a big hunk of Bazooka gum.

RORY E. KRAFT, JR. is an Assistant Professor of Philosophy at York College of Pennsylvania. This means that he's surrounded by Phillies, Orioles, and Pirates fans, all of whom he tolerates better than the occasional fan of that team from New York. When not following the Red Sox, he works in ethical theory, applied ethics, and pre-college philosophy. He is editor of *Questions: Philosophy for Young People*, an annual journal.

PETER KREEFT popped out of his mother's womb in Paterson, New Jersey in 1937 as a certified Yankees hater and Sox Fan(atic). He moved to Boston in 1965, where he's Professor of Philosophy at Boston College. He has published over sixty books, including a forthcoming novel (*An Ocean Full of Angels*, 2010) in which the plot climaxes during the afternoon of

October 2nd, 1978 in right field at Fenway Park, when a wayward angel twice put a ball into the glove of sun-blinded Lou Piniella in the greatest single baseball game ever played.

MATTHEW M. KONIG (ABD, Brown University), the lone Yankees fan to infiltrate *The Red Sox and Philosophy*, did his Masters Degree at Tufts University in Medford, Massachusetts. He's eternally grateful to the baseball gods that his time at Tufts ran from 1998 to 2000 rather than from 2004 to 2006. Matthew has enjoyed consorting with the Red Sox faithful but must now report back to the Evil Empire.

JUNG H. LEE is an Assistant Professor of Religion at Northeastern University. He teaches and publishes in the areas of comparative religious ethics, East Asian Religions, and the philosophy of religion. He likes to combine his love of ancient Chinese culture and the Red Sox by eating take-out and listening to WEEI on random summer nights.

SANDER LEE is Professor of Philosophy at Keene State College. He's the author of the book *Eighteen Woody Allen Films Analyzed: Anguish, God, and Existentialism* (2002). His essay "Rights, Morality, and Faith, in the Light of the Holocaust" appeared in the anthology *Genocide and Human Rights* (2005). He has also written numerous essays on issues in aesthetics, ethics, Holocaust studies, social philosophy, and metaphysics. He was last seen trying to sneak into Fenway disguised as Wally.

KAROLINA LEWESTAM is a PhD student at Boston University. Her area of specialty is ethics. She arrived in Boston from Poland three years ago, thinking that the "Green Monster" was a Sesame Street character. Fortunately, her apartment looked onto Kenmore Square, where she was brutally educated in baseball issues by the crowds heading to and from Fenway. Her real achievements include sailing the world and successfully surviving the first year of parenthood. She has done several other things too, including working in advertising, music TV, serious TV, teaching in a high school, and launching an educational think-tank in Poland with her friends. Her plans include finishing her dissertation, finishing her novel, quitting smoking, and meeting a wolf in its natural environment.

MICHAEL MACOMBER is currently finishing his dissertation on the aesthetic theories of the Third Earl of Shaftesbury at the New School for Social Research in New York City. Michael's first experience with Red Sox baseball was provided to him by his great-Aunt Joyce, who was known for residing in the "Red Sox house." Her house was painted entirely in red and white and her kitchen was adorned with Red Sox decals. When Michael was young, she told him all about Ted Williams and Yaz. She passed away shortly after the Red Sox won the 2004 World Series. This book is a direct result of her passion for the Red Sox.

KEVIN MAGUIRE is a full-time Instructor of Philosophy at Southern University in Baton Rouge, Louisiana. Other than Kant, his interests are in modern philosophy, theoretical and practical ethics, and philosophy of race. Outside of philosophy, he submitted paperwork to the Boston Archdiocese about a possible exorcism of Johnny Damon, but the Cardinal told him the theological experts were unanimous that it would be impossible to fully get out all the evil. He's spearheaded several efforts to implement uniforms in public schools—compulsory Varitek or Pedroia jerseys, doo rags, and bloody socks; he had to fight the school nurses on that last one.

STEPHEN MATHIS is Associate Professor and Chair of the Philosophy Department at Wheaton College, where he teaches courses in legal philosophy, social and political philosophy, and ethics. Professor Mathis first fell in love with the Red Sox during the years when they seemed to meet the Oakland A's in the playoffs every year. At that time, he thought Roger Clemens was the second coming, but later renounced his faith in the Rocket and came to associate him with another R-moniker that many Bostonians later used to refer to him—"Rat Bastahd"! Now he's convinced Dustin Pedroia is in fact the second coming.

After a miserable experience as the right fielder for his little-league team during third grade, **COREY MCCALL** thought his brief love affair with baseball was over. Luckily, he spent time in Boston for graduate school and was able to take in a few games at Fenway. He's been hooked on Red Sox baseball ever since. He now thinks about baseball and ways to avoid having to play baseball or any baseball-related games such as softball or cricket at Elmira College in Elmira, New York.

JOHN MCHUGH is a graduate student at Boston University. He's presently writing two dissertations, one on Adam Smith's philosophy and the other on Carl Everett's. His meticulous analysis of game situations once made him an excellent fielder, while his brute indecisiveness made him a horrendous hitter. The combination of these traits left his childhood manager unsure what to do with him and John himself with no choice but to embark upon a career in philosophy. His hobbies include running the Tony Fossas fan club, serving as an unofficial spokesman for Mike Greenwell's Family Fun Park, and Googling "Wade Boggs stories" as often as possible.

Robbed of exaltation in his youth, **BILL NOWLIN** turned to ruminating about fate and the Red Sox. Armed with graduate degrees from both Tufts and the University of Chicago, he became a professor of political science at the University of Massachusetts at Lowell, but then helped found Rounder Records of Burlington, Massachusetts and has helped oversee the production since 1970 of more than three thousand record albums of roots music and its contemporary offshoots. Later in life, he became a more-frequently published ex-professor who has written or edited more than twenty-five books on the Boston Red Sox, or Sox players such as Ted Williams and Johnny Pesky. Among his most recent books are *Red Sox Threads* and *The Ultimate Red Sox Home Run Guide*. He also works as assistant editor of the Red Sox fan magazine, *Diehard*. He likes to say that he's traveled to more than 125 countries, but his favorite place remains Fenway Park.

BRYAN PILKINGTON studies and teaches philosophy at the University of Notre Dame. He specializes in ethics and is currently writing his dissertation on dignity. Born in Flushing, New York, he comes from a long line of baseball masochists. Though an avid Mets fan, he has great respect for the Red Sox and their fans' (until recently) similar taste for suffering. He attributes this appreciation to his fiancée's diehard Red Sox family, not including one black sheep (in Bronx pinstripes), and is grateful for their acceptance of him despite his Metropolitan associations. Bryan's promising baseball career was cut short in little league due to a poor on-base percentage. He reached base on more hit-by-pitch calls than balls hit by his bat.

JAMES F. PONTUSO is Patterson Professor of Government and Foreign Affairs at Hampden-Sydney College in Virginia. He has authored or edited six books and published more than seventy articles, reviews, and essays. He has lectured or taught in a dozen counties. His most notable achievement occurred in 1951 when his father took him to his first and Joe DiMaggio's last ballgame at Fenway Park. The Red Sox fielded a team that included Dom DiMaggio, Johnny Pesky, Bobby Doerr, and Ted Williams.

ORLA RICHARDSON is a PhD candidate at Boston University. When she's not working on, or thinking about, issues in the Philosophy of Science, she's indulging in her first and only true love: watching, playing, talking, and obsessing about sports. Although originally from Ireland, she currently lives in Central Square, Cambridge.

After a successful career as a New York Mets fan and a high school first baseman, **DAVID ROOCHNIK** attended Trinity College. He received his PhD from the Pennsylvania State University. He has written four books and numerous articles on Greek Philosophy. He was very happy when he moved to Boston University in 1995 because it was so easy for him to retain his distaste for the Yankees by becoming a Red Sox fan.

WEAVER SANTANIELLO is Professor of Philosophy at Penn State, Berks. She's the author of two books on Friedrich Nietzsche, and editor of *Nietzsche and the Gods*, and has written various articles, including an essay in *What Philosophy Can Tell You about Your Dog* (2008). She became a Red Sox fan in 1967, due to the passion of her grandmother, Mi-Mi, who listened to every game on the radio and kept score. Weaver's all-time favorite player is Yaz.

STEPHANIE ST. MARTIN was raised in Raynham, Massachusetts, which is far enough away from Fenway so she isn't tempted to build an apartment inside the Green Monster but close enough that she still bears a wicked Bahston accent. A Masters candidate in Philosophy at Boston College, she spends her time reading Plato between checking the Red Sox, Pats, and BC Eagles scores on her blackberry. Voted "The Automatic Out" by her little league softball team, she's still trying to learn how to hit a twelve-foot arc. She wants to thank her family, especially her sisters for showing no interest in sports thus being forced by her father to learn the Red Sox lineup by heart in second grade.

PATRICK TIERNAN is Chair of Religious Education at Boston College High School where he teaches courses in religion and science, ethics, social justice, and world religions. He's also a doctoral candidate in educational administration at Boston College. He has presented on topics in theology and education at the American Academy of Religion and National Catholic Educational Association in addition to writing and editing for various religious publications. He is also known to sing "Sweet Caroline" to himself, believes Green Monsters are real, and thinks the original translation of John 3:16 read, "For God so loved the world, that he gave us the Red Sox!"

JOSEPH ULATOWSKI, born and raised in Boston, joined Red Sox Nation eighty-two days prior to the legendary Game Six of the 1975 World Series. Most recently in 2009 he was picked up by the UNLV organization after being let go by the University of Wyoming organization. (No hard feelings!) He played minor league ball for the University of Utah organization, where he completed his PhD in 2008, and the University of Mississippi organization. He is happy to report that members of his classes who have dared to wear a Yankees shirt or hat, or openly admitted to their fanaticism for the Yankees, have all received failing grades.

Boston-raised **ANDY WASIF** earned a BS degree at Syracuse University—and has been doing that ever since. A recovering stand-up comedian, he has penned "How to Talk to a Yankee Fan" and "Red Sox University." Check out his regular blogs at sportsfanlive.com or all his humorous works at his homepage thewasif.com. Andy can also be followed on Twitter @thewasif.

Stats